Shaky Apron Strings

SHAKY APRON STRINGS:

A Legacy of Love in Letters

Mary Ann Althaver

Mary Ann Althaver

LELA Publishers

ISBN 978-0-9904846-4-6

Library of Congress Control Number: 2014920871

Printed in the United States of America

First Edition

Front Cover Photo by Joan Ramseyer

10 9 8 7 6 5 4 3 2 1

For my daughters, Emily and Amy, my grandchildren,
Andrew, Lexi, Ellis, and Lauren,
and for future generations

TABLE OF CONTENTS

Cast of Characters

Lovisa Gertrude Ostrander, daughter of Simeon and Charlotte Cole Ostrander

George H. Hansler, husband of Lovisa Ostrander Hansler

Luella "Blanche" Hansler, daughter of George and Lovisa Ostrander Hansler

John Merritt Hill, husband of Blanche Hansler Hill

Dorothy Blanche Hill, daughter of John Merritt and Blanche Hansler Hill

Jean Hansler, stepmother of Blanche, and mother of
Katherine "Kate", Lena "Dee", and Roy Hansler

Nathan and Eliza Merritt Hill, parents of John Merritt Hill

Charlotte "Lottie" Bradley Wellemeyer, cousin of Blanche Hansler Hill

Charlotte Jean Hill, daughter of John and Blanche Hansler Hill

John Merritt "J.M." Hill, Jr, son of John and Blanche Hansler Hill

Hope Wellemeyer, daughter of Dr. and Lottie Wellemeyer, cousin to
Dorothy Hill

Walter Lee Barningham, husband of Dorothy Hill Barningham, father of
Sara Lee and Mary Ann

Introduction

Moving Forward, Looking Back – A Legacy of Letters

It came to me slowly, in middle age, the full awareness of the powerful legacy inherited from my mother and maternal grandmother. Always, I had known the extent of my love for them, and their pervasive influence on me, but had never fully understood what shining and rare people they were.

My dearly loved role models and inspiration are gone, my grandma dead for over fifty years and my mother for more than twenty, but they are with me still, guiding my choices in life, and occasionally reaching out from the other side with hints of their continuing presence. As the most influential people in my growing up years, it is no surprise that they are still shaping my perspective on life, my values, and morals even now.

I lost my grandma, Blanche Hill, when I was only ten years old, a devastating blow, and one which I thought I could not survive. My mother, Dorothy Hill Barningham, succumbed to Alzheimer's disease while I was still in my forties, another overwhelming loss. Fortunately some things remain: their spirits and the certainty of their deep love for me, which transcend death.

It is not just their advice and love residing in my head and my heart, it is their outlook on life, their ability to face adversity and come up smiling and making the best of things. They gave me these precious gifts, which would be enough in themselves, but they also left another exceptional and priceless gift.

As the family archivist, I inherited boxes full of riches—letters of love, of joy, of loss, of hard times, and of hope for the future—all bundled up with worn ribbons and rubber bands grown brittle with age. The envelopes are frayed and age-stained, some bearing artistic doodles, lists of things to do, accounts of money spent or owed, grocery lists, and recipes. The handwriting ranges from elegant copperplate script to hurried scrawls and the addresses change far too often for my grandmother's family, revealing their nomadic life style.

Small leather-bound diaries are full of the everyday details of life, as well as the occasional momentous events. They divulge so many facets of these women, and sometimes are equally revealing for what is left unsaid. Clippings from magazines and newspapers, cartoons, and inspirational verses give insight into what stirred their emotions and caught their interest.

Still grieving, feeling lonely and lost, I immersed myself in their world for comfort, gratefully exploring these precious bits of their lives. My dreams and thoughts of my mother, lying helpless in her bed for so long, robbed of her once brilliant faculties of speech and comprehension, gradually gave way to images of the vibrant young woman she was in her early years and to the loving mother she had been. It was a healing thing for me, working with their letters.

After sifting and sorting through these treasures of the attic, peeking into their lives, learning about them through their communications with others, their scrapbooks, yearbooks, and diaries, I realized that they had left me the means to tell their stories in their own words and those of their friends and family. Grateful for the opportunity to discover Mother and Grandma as they were throughout their lives, as children, as young adults, and even as they aged, I began typing their letters, piecing together the materials they left me. The elements of their life stories were all there, fairly crying out to be told.

Turning it into a book intimidates me at times, since I want to make it the best I possibly can, but I feel confident that in some mysterious way, Mother and Gram are guiding my efforts in this undertaking, just as surely as they are always helping me find my way in life. I want to share their talents, strengths, and enthusiasm for life, as well as give a glimpse into the world in which they lived.

This book, my tribute to Mother and Grandma, is my legacy to my two daughters, my four grandchildren, and generations yet unborn. I hope they will feel the love and strength of these exceptional women and come to value their heritage. Perhaps it will even inspire readers to create and preserve a written legacy of their own lives, a gift for generations to come after they are gone.

Creating Connections:

A Chain of Strength

In only a 500 year span, genealogists claim over a million people contribute to creating any one person. I know all these people and their genetic offerings make me unique, but in my heart, two of them receive special credit for shaping me. How lucky I am to be a part of the human chain that included my mother, Dorothy Hill Barningham and her mother Blanche Hansler Hill.

My maternal grandma forged a strong link in our family chain. Perhaps the loss of her parents so early in life explains her great love for her family and her insistence on maintaining a happy family life. Blanche conformed well to society's expectations, but in her marriage she was the strong one, and might have been the bread winner had it been allowed. Her husband was an insurance salesman who was too kind-hearted to be a good businessman and consequently, there was never enough money to have a secure home.

Blanche wrote in her diaries and letters of ideas she had for making money and working outside the home, but her ideas were unacceptable in an era where women stayed home and raised children. Even so, she helped keep the family afloat when her husband's income kept them moving from home to home, each less expensive than the last.

My grandma always made a place warm and inviting, even if it meant turning a threadbare rug over and painting a design on the opposite side. Stories of her economies and simple touches which cost little or nothing are plentiful in my family. When times were really lean she wasn't above taking in a boarder or selling a few treasured antiques to pay the rent.

With an eye for fashion, she could look in a store display window and go home and create the same look on her sewing machine. In today's world she probably would have started her own business. With her energy and enthusiasm, she would have been very successful.

I think I loved her best for the small homey things she enjoyed because she stayed home and had so little money—her love of plants, books, crafts, and the simple things in life, like having the neighbors over and sharing a simple snack. In her diary she was known to write about the number of blossoms on her prized African violets, the joys of a piece of lemon meringue pie, or the satisfaction of cleaning a room thoroughly, simple things that go unremarked by most. I can only imagine the joy she would have felt had she been able to stay in her own home with a yard full of her favorite plants. But this was not possible, given her husband's lifelong job troubles.

Dorothy grew up in a loving and very supportive family, but with no sense of permanence, due to the family moving far too often. Though she was a bright child, she was held back for a second year in kindergarten because she was so shy. Later she overcame this reticence; in her college years and her adult life she became a talented public speaker, writer and artist.

When it came time for Mother to settle down, she chose security over excitement and married my father, Walter Barningham, a young lawyer just starting his practice in Pontiac. He was a traditionalist and did not want his wife to work once children were born. They built a modest home, which was a marvel to my grandma. She wrote: "Walter and Dorothy have such a lovely home, I hope they'll be able to keep it." In my father's world, people always kept their homes and their jobs permanently. My parents stayed in that house all of their married years and my father dutifully pursued his occupation in spite of the fact that he would have been happier building houses. A stable man did not change jobs and would certainly never throw away seven years of college and law school to be a carpenter.

Walter fulfilled himself by building a cottage with his own hands on the shores of Lake Huron, further amazing my grandma. Here was a family with two homes, and able to keep them! My parents were never wealthy, but they were comfortable. Mother never had to sell her furniture or home to make ends meet. I know security was important to her, but sometimes I think her choice of husband weighed heavily on her. Walter was a man who loved Dorothy dearly, but he lacked the warmth and capacity for joy that characterized Mother's childhood home. He was the strong silent type and certainly a good provider, but did not meet her emotional or intellectual needs very well.

I was born in 1946, in an era when most children still had stay-at-home mothers. Mother seemed content to stay home with us, but she wanted to be a writer. While my sister and I were small, she took correspondence courses and wrote short stories as time allowed. She wrote about "the woman upstairs" who kept challenging her to write something important, to spend her time on things more intellectual than dusting and doing household chores. I understand this feeling and think her "woman upstairs" is now residing in my head!

Mother listened to her creative muse at times, and created stories I love dearly. If she was occasionally preoccupied, it didn't interfere with her being a wonderful mother. My sister Sara and I always felt we were her number one priority and she was always there for us physically and emotionally.

In my first year of college, my father had a stroke and his solo law practice ended. I worked my way through college, much as my parents did before me. I was proud to do so, though this too hurt my father's pride. There was no income after his stroke, so Mother went to work as a social worker, with a nursing home caseload. I am sure she made her clients happy with her cheerful visits and warm personality. My father's pride was badly damaged when she became the breadwinner. He kept track of her earnings, hoping to pay her back one day. His health deteriorated further and he died at age 61.

After Mother retired, she took up oil painting. Her innate artistic talents had been dormant for years and she enjoyed her time with a paint brush in hand. She created several lovely paintings, which, along with her short stories, some about her mother, are precious to me.

Alzheimer's disease hit Mother in her seventies, robbing her gradually of her intellectual abilities and later, even the simplest skills. In a devastating ten year process, she became a shell of her former self and I suffered at close hand the pain of it all. I brought her to live near us and eventually had to place her in a nursing home nearby. As the years passed, I became ever more involved in the nursing home life, making it a daily part of my world. For years I was outraged at the horrors of this tragic disease and so hurt by the loss of the brilliant woman Mother had been, but eventually, I became resigned to it, and by the time of her death, was praying for her release from the sad existence she had to endure.

I was privileged to be at her side when she died and so thankful that in her final moments, her face was transformed and her old self shone through. I was truly convinced she was going on to a new realm, and quite sure Grandma was waiting there.

Her death freed me to remember the richness of her earlier life. My grief brought forth a flood of reminiscing, which made clear the powerful legacy she and her mother left me. I plunged into their letters, diaries and memorabilia, realizing that telling their stories and restoring their voices on paper helped me heal and provided a way for their descendants to know them through their own words.

Mother and Gram were strong, inspiring links in my generational chain, showing me, each in her own way, that you can stay home with your children and still meet your own needs for self-expression. Both were curious and never stopped learning. Each found satisfaction through creative outlets and through writing about their experiences.

Simple pleasures were enjoyed by both. They reached out to people and made them feel cherished and unique. Each endured physical illnesses and hardships with grace. Together they showed me what is important in life; love of family, belief in self, creativity, moral courage, and perseverance. I hope to add a worthwhile link to this chain and pass it on to my own daughters and grandchildren, strong and intact.

The Master Link:
Lovisa: A Bright, Brief Spark

Lovisa has been calling to me from the great beyond. I think of her each time I pass the old walnut cupboard which houses her antique china platter and a lone dinner plate. The china looks nearly new, despite its 1880 vintage, the green and white transfer ware border is crisp and unblemished. Spring like, the design features daffodils and a city by the sea, all in green. They are pieces of the puzzle that is my maternal great-grandmother Lovisa Gertrude Ostrander Hansler. For forty years, these lovely dishes have been decorative focal points in our home, a daily reminder of this link in my maternal ancestry.

Lovisa's photo is fixed in my mind too, revealing a young woman on the cusp of maturity, oddly dignified with her solemn face, regular features, and striking tresses. Her hair is pulled back from her face, but curls are still visible at her ears and on her shoulders. Someone has touched the photo with a sepia tone and a bit of color, her hair is tinted auburn, eyes a penetrating blue.

Sadly, this attractive girl never grew into the mature woman she might have been. She was married at fifteen to George H. Hansler, gave birth on April 5, 1882 to my grandmother Blanche at only sixteen, and was dead at seventeen, soon after giving birth to a premature son.

In my mind's eye, I see a simple home in Brownsville, Ontario, Canada where Lovisa set up

Lovisa Ostrander Hansler

housekeeping with George. The daffodil dishes are spread on the kitchen table, Blanche's high chair stands close by, the remains of a meal are still evident, and Lovisa's long muslin apron has been tossed carelessly on a chair, her meal and her life interrupted by the sudden start of her unexpected labor.

I wonder how different my grandmother's life would have been had she not lost her mother so tragically young. I wish Lovisa had lived long enough to raise her daughter and enjoy her grandchildren, long enough to use up her pretty dishes, to scratch and chip them, long enough to break a few and shed tears over the loss. She only had seventeen spring times in her life, as she was born in January, 1866 and died in early May, 1883.

In the family archives is a sad little note, paper and envelope bordered in mourning black, written in a tidy copperplate script, informing a family member of Lovisa's untimely death, and the grief her parents felt over her loss. I cry every time I read it.

Blanche's grandfather, Simeon Ostrander wrote this letter to his sister:

Dear Brother and Sister,

I suppose before this reaches you, you will have seen the account of our dear Lovisa's death. She was taken with Erysipelas which brought on premature confinement. The child only lived about one hour. We thought she was getting along very well, but she was taken with Inflammation and died very suddenly. Neither me nor her mother got there until after she died.

George said she died very easy, just like going to sleep. She did not even breathe hard. Oh, Mary, it is very hard for us to part with her. She was so very dear to us. Our hearts are broken. It makes us feel so very lonely when we think we can never see her again on earth. I hope we may live so as to meet her in heaven.

Hansler is going to leave the little one with Lot and I. We love her very much. She is a very sweet child. I can't write any more this time. With kindest love, we are yours,
Sim and Lot

I think Lovisa's spirit is trying to tell me about her, wanting someone to know what kind of girl she was, what kind of woman she might have become. She is a vital part of my chain of female ancestors, certainly not the first to succumb to the dangers of childbirth at an early age, but one who tugs persistently at my heart. Surely she loved her curly haired toddler Blanche dearly. I hope she knows what a positive impact her child has had on my life and the lives of all who knew her.

As I gaze at the cupboard, looking at her wedding china, my mind whispers to her: Lovisa, you are important to me and I honor you. I will keep you in my heart and cherish your beautiful daffodil dishes as a reminder to enjoy each spring I am allotted and to treasure the years I am blessed to have with my own dear family.

Blanche
Early history and letters to Blanche

Luella "Blanche" Hansler

Blanche went to live with her grandparents, Simeon and Charlotte Ostrander, in Tilsonburg, Ontario. They provided a kind and loving environment, but Blanche was devastated by losing both of her parents at once and far too young to understand any of it. She enjoyed the security of her grandparents' love, but soon began what was to be a lifelong series of moves. In later life, Blanche created a long list of every place she had lived. Home was always a temporary place for her.

When she was four, her grandparents and Blanche moved to Wingham, Ontario, where Simeon owned a shoe store. This was followed by three more moves in Ontario before they settled in Sanilac County, Michigan. This brought them closer to their surviving daughter, Eusebia.

In addition to the upheaval of all these moves and many school changes, to add to her confusion and insecurity, her father had re-married and started a second family with his new wife, Jean. Blanche must have wondered why he didn't send for her, and if she had been totally replaced in his affections by his new daughters, Kate and Lena, and later, by his son, Roy.

Only two letters from Blanche's father, George Hansler, are found in the family archives. How sad that he did not even spell Blanche's name correctly.

Charlotte and Simeon Ostrander with granddaughter Blanche Hansler

3

Tilsonburg
July 3, 1891

My Dear Blanch,

I received both your letters and must say I am ashamed of myself for not writing you sooner, but I seem to have so much business on hand that I neglect it. I am very much pleased to see that you can write such a good letter and you are learning so fast. Kate has been going to school for some time past. She will soon be able to write you a letter. They talk about you quite often and would like to see you. Well your brother's name is Roy Alexander. He is getting to be quite a big boy—he weighs 15 1/2 lbs. and can laugh like a good fellow. We would like very much to have you all come and make us a good visit and we would have lots of fun.

Well I have 110 young chickens and over 100 old ones. I am going to send you over a dandy pair this fall that you will have for your own so you can raise chickens. We have got a nice black and white pup. He is a spaniel and we call him Frank. I would like very much to see you all. I will have to close for this time.
Love to all from Pa

His last letter to his daughter bears a picture of a chicken and the letterhead:

Burns and Hansler, Breeders and Importers of Fancy Poultry
Tilsonburg, Ontario

Dec. 22, 1891

My dear Blanch,

You will have to forgive me for not sending you any picture this time, but we have been so busy that I could not get time. I send some money to buy you something for Christmas and also an odd piece for you to keep. We all would like to see you and would have liked to have had you here for Christmas, but seeing we can't, we wish you all a Merry, Merry Christmas and Happy New Year.
Yours lovingly,
Pa

P.S. I expect to go to Philadelphia, PA the 4th of Jan. to the Greatest Poultry Show on Earth. I will take about $200.00 along in

4

cash as it costs $1.50 a bird to enter. We took nearly $700.00 in premiums in Sept. in York State at four shows.

The next information on George is his obituary, from August 18, 1892, Tilsonburg, Ontario.

"When it was announced throughout the town last Thursday that the attack of erysipelas with which George H. Hansler was suffering had turned to blood poisoning and that he was not expected to live, the news struck consternation into the hearts of all his friends, for only a few days before he had been down to his place of business, and while many knew that he was ill, no one thought of his indisposition terminating fatally, which it did about midnight on Thursday.

Erysipelas first made its appearance on the left side of his face near the upper lip and spread to the right side. His system not being in a healthy condition, blood poisoning set in, and although all that could be done by medical skill was done to stop the spread of the poison through the system, the efforts were without avail.

George H. Hansler

Deceased was a young man, being within a few days of 33 years, and was widely known throughout this section of county, having been in business in Eden, Brownsville, Aylmer, and Tilsonburg. For some years he was the senior partner in the firm of Hansler and Graves, Mr. J. Walker having purchased Mr. Graves' interest in the dry goods store and the name of the firm changed to Hansler and Co. Deceased was also a great fancier of poultry and bred and dealt extensively in thoroughbred chickens, having at the time of his death a large number of his own rearing at the Buffalo exposition.

Hansler was twice married, his first wife being a daughter of Mr. Simeon Ostrander, of Michigan, formerly of this town, by whom he had one child, who is now living with her grandfather. His second wife was Miss Clarke of Charlotteville, who, with her three children, is left to mourn the loss of a kind husband, and to whom the sympathies of the citizens of the town are extended."

Another harsh blow to Blanche—at age ten, she was truly an orphan. Her stepmother Jean wrote her at this time:

Tilsonburg, Aug. 23, 1892

My Dear Little Girl,

Your sad little letter came late last night. I am so sorry that you were not able to get here. I hardly know how to begin to write you the particulars. I feel so numb, Blanche, so lonely, and oh my dear, this is Papa's birthday and the sun shines, the birds sing, their little hearts full of life and joy just the same as if the greatest sorrow that can come had not touched us. He was taken sick on Friday, but did not go to bed until Tuesday. He had erysipelas, which poisoned his blood. The fearful disease did its work so quickly, taking life from such a strong man, full of life and vigor. On Wednesday he appointed his pallbearers and who he wanted to bury him, so you see my dear, he was not unprepared. I could not believe that the end was so near and thought that it was the medicine, that his mind was wandering, but alas! It was not so.

I cannot collect my thoughts to write you as I would like. I am not at all well, but hope to be able to write you more and better soon. What can I say to you, except that God will comfort you and may he spare you in after years this trouble that I am going through. The girls send love to you all. Tell grandma to think kindly of me if she can and that I loved him as I loved no other living thing. I am afraid it was worship. My dear, good-bye, remember poor mamma in your thoughts and prayers.

Blanche Hansler, 1898

Your loving mother,
Jean

The next letters show a developing relationship between Blanche and her stepfamily. She loved her grandparents dearly and thought of them as parents, but there was an empty space in her life and, in characteristic fashion, she reached out to fill it by drawing closer to what family she had left.

Blanche's half-sister Kate Hansler wrote:

Woodstock, Ontario
Feb. 10, 1898

Dear Blanche,

I was pleased to receive your letter. We will have such times writing to each other. When I received your last letter I was too small to write without mamma spelling each word for me. We live a mile from school as Lena and I are too far advanced to go to the ward schools. Roy has just started and writes the words on mother's back every night till he goes to sleep

What a big girl you must be. I am a pretty fair size myself, although I cannot come up to that. We would like very much to have a visit from our big sister and I tell you I would show you around the town in fine style. We have no photos of ourselves alone, but intend getting some and would be very glad to exchange with you. I guess I will stop right away as it is time to retire.
Your loving sister,
Kate

P.S. With love from all and kind remembrances to your Grandma and Grandpa.

A note below this says:

My daughter,

I hope you will come and see the sisters and brother and assure you that they will be glad to come and visit you as well.
Mother

Blanche was living in Cass City, Michigan, where Simeon had a store and sold furniture and shoes, when she received the following letter from Kate, on pink note paper decorated with a very nice pen and ink sketch of a bunny:

May 31, 1899

Dear Blanche,

I am writing you on some of my Easter paper. It is rather out of season, but I thought perhaps you would like it better than the plain. I am very fond of drawing, both with pen and pencil. Are you? If you do anything that way, send me some please. It will soon be holidays and I don't suppose you are sorry.

We had a contest in elocution and I took first prize. My prize was Shakespeare's works and Longfellow's poems. They were beautifully bound in black leather, one having a padded cover.

We would be so glad if you would come over this summer. Don't you think you possibly could? Consider it well and reply in the affirmative, won't you, Blanche dear?

Roy passed first this month in his room and I passed second in mine and Lena twelfth in hers. But if she is not extra at school, mother says she don't know how she could have managed without her in housecleaning time, but she has not done a bit since. She makes the cutest doll clothes and hats. Mother wants her to be a milliner.

Roy is fair-haired and the very image of our father. People say Roy and I look alike and like papa. Lena looks like mama's sister that is dead. She is pretty plump and slow to get over the ground, which Roy and I are not. Lena is singing a song somewhat like "After the Ball" and mother is reproving her for singing that on Sunday. Roy is just joining in. Oh! I wish you were here, but you will come in the holidays, won't you?
Yours affectionately,
Kate

June 3, 1899

Dear Blanche,

I just this minute received your letter and am so glad, oh so glad you can come. Mama says nothing could ever happen that there would not be a place for you here. We will be all so glad. We are all perfectly wild! Of course we will all be at the station to meet you so

you need not be afraid. It was so nice of your grandpa to let you. I must close now for I am in a hurry to post this.
Kate

Simeon uprooted the family again, moving to Cass City where he had a store, again selling furniture and shoes. In Cass City, Blanche attended high school. She spent one year with her uncle, Alfred Cole and his son, Charles, and daughter, Lucy, in Detroit. While there, she and Lucy went to the Military School on the West Side of Detroit.

In 1900, at age 18, Blanche went to Milwaukee, Wisconsin, to spend the winter with a cousin. There she clerked in the Boston Department Store. She next moved to Detroit, where she worked in the office of the Detroit City Gas Company until April of 1904. In Detroit, she moved often too, from Mrs. Hatton's home to Lucy Cole's, then to the YWCA, followed by a time with the Hobart family where she had a hard lesson in life. She wrote, "Minnie Steed and I came home for lunch one day and caught Mrs. Hobart taking money out of Minnie's purse. It was the first time I had known that someone you know could steal."

Blanche at 19

Blanche made friends quickly and seemed to enjoy those she made while she worked at the gas company. During this time, her grandparents wrote:

February 8, 1904
Dear Blanche,
I feel so anxious about you. Our roads are all snowed up and there are so many fires and all kinds of troubles. I will be so glad when you come home to stay. I'm so homesick to see you. Yesterday I really felt you must come. John has been here quite often since you was home. We are always glad to see him; he is one of the

dearest boys. It will soon be spring and I will be so glad. I have not been to church since Christmas. You are doing well, getting good wages. It will come good. I am so glad. It is dull here, we do not pay expenses. It will be better soon.

February 9, 1904

We just got your letter this morning and are all tickled to death to hear from you. So glad you're alive and well. Do not work so hard. You are getting lots of nice things. Oh my, how glad I am you are coming here to live. We will be so happy I can hardly write. I was so homesick Sunday for your pa and ma, you will make up for them. I think John is just the boy. We all think so much of him. I haven't written much—it is hard work for me. There is so much I want to say, have to wait till you come home.

John Merritt Hill

Good-bye, darling.

Grandma

The next letter bears this return address:

The Up-to-Date Shoe Store,
S. Ostrander, Prop., Cass City, Michigan
April 11, 1904

Dearest Blanche,

Your letter reached us all right and we were glad to hear from you and shall be so glad when you come home so you can rest up. You need not be afraid of our forgetting you as you are too near and dear to us for that. I am glad you have such a good friend in Miss Steed. You can thank her for us for her kindness to you.

Business is rather quiet here yet. The road bridge and also the railroad bridge south of town were carried away by the flood, but the mail and passengers come over on a footbridge. Hoping to see you soon, when we will tell you all the news. I enclose you $30.00 in this letter. Now come soon and may the Lord preserve and keep us all until we meet again.

From Grandpa

Blanche returned to Cass City and was married at the Methodist Church to John Merritt Hill on June 22, 1904. John, born May 4, 1882, was the son of Nathan and Eliza Merritt Hill.

A scrapbook contains this newspaper account of the wedding:

"A quiet church wedding took place last evening in the parlors of the M.E. Church, when Miss Blanche Hansler, granddaughter of Mr. and Mrs. S. Ostrander, with whom she has made her home for a number of years, was united in marriage to John M. Hill, son of Mr. and Mrs. N. Hill. The ceremony was performed by Rev. M.W. Gifford, in the presence of a company of invited guests. The decorations were not elaborate, but very pretty, a canopy being arranged in white and green and the altar rail being trimmed to match. Ferns and palms completed the decorations.

Miss Lottie Bradley supported the bride, and Roy Hill acted as best man. Miss Cecil Fritz presided at the piano, playing softly the strains of "Hearts and Flowers" during the ceremony. At its conclusion the guests departed to the newly furnished residence of Mr. and Mrs. Hill, at the corner of Sanilac and Maple Streets, where a reception was given. The happy couple slipped away unexpectedly on the evening train north, and are spending a few days with relatives near Woodstock, Ontario before settling down in their pretty little home. All wish them much joy."

John and Blanche's first home was a house they bought from John's father in Cass City. They did not stay there long, nor were they to stay anywhere long throughout their married life. In the fall of 1905,

Blanche on her wedding day

John and Blanche moved to North Main Street in Lapeer, MI where John was working for a marble works selling monuments. Blanche's grandparents were also ready for another move, as shown in this letter:

August 2, 1905

Dear John & Blanche,

We are pleased to hear you like it so well in Lapeer. If some of these people want to trade a nice farm for my stock, I am ready to trade with them.

Our sales are quite good—$155 last week. I am talking with Sykes here about buying my business. He will let me know in a few days. Our stock is about $3,000 now.

John is selling goods nicely. I hope your trade will keep up. If you see any farm that is OK let me know and I'll come and see it. I can hardly wait to see you in your new home, but we must be patient as everything comes to them who wait. Lottie and Grandma will write the news. I can't do much at letter writing. I received the money, $5.00, all right. Please write once a week, as it seems so good to get a letter. John, your folks are well.
With love, I remain your loving
Grandpa

John and Blanche's financial difficulties started early and lasted all through their marriage. This letter from Simeon gives a peek into their situation only a year after their wedding.

Sept. 19, 1905

Dear John,

Yours received this morning and I took it to the bank and signed. I thought Mr. Pinney maybe wanted it paid up some by the way he spoke to me. He wanted to know what the matter was with John Hill, if he had gone to the wall. I think if I were you I would try and pay at least a part of it when due in 60 days. You can't afford to pay bank interest longer than is really necessary. Let me know how you are fixed when your note is due and see if we cannot fix part of it.

We are all well now and enjoying ourselves as well as we can. I picked some tomatoes and corn this morning. I guess I'll have the potatoes dug this week.

I haven't sold out yet. I guess I'll pack goods until spring and take a rest through the winter. You must excuse this letter. I can't think nor write either this morning. I hope you are all well and en-

joying yourselves with lots of love and good wishes, I remain your ever-loving,
Grandpa

October 6, 1905

Dear John & Blanche,

I was looking for you up at our fair but don't see you yet, so I guess I'll write some. We are all OK and trying to sell shoes. I hope you are well and happy. There is a big crowd here at the fair—all kinds of folks and a lot of snakes—human and other kinds. Some are in the beer and whiskey, they bite the hardest. Our stock is getting lower all the time. It is about $2300 left—no chance to sell.

How do you think our chance is to do shoe business in Lapeer? I mean permanently. Can you tell me what you have there in the shoe business? I hope you like it very much there yet and are happy and contented. In regard to Pinney's note due in November, I will try and help you out on it if I can and take the note or a part of it at less cost to you. I don't care much for Pinney anyway. He wants the earth and a part of the moon thrown in. I think you are doing well and will soon be all right, so just keep feeling good.

Things don't go just as I want them with me, but I'll make it come all right somehow so I'm quite happy because if I can't farm, I can run the store a while yet.
Grandpa

Blanche and John Welcome a Daughter
Enter: Dorothy

By 1906 Blanche and John had moved again—this time to 100 Monroe Street in Lapeer, where John was in the marble and granite monument business. It was here that Dorothy Blanche Hill was born on Wednesday, February 12, 1908, at 11:30 p.m. John's parents, Nathan and Eliza Hill were surprised by the news.

Cass City, Michigan
February 20, 1908

Dear John M.,

The announcement of Little Dorothy's arrival received and we are glad you are all well, hope Blanche will get along nicely. Yes, you surprised us all right—or me. I was so blind when I was there, and when you did not come for Christmas, I never suspected that was what was keeping you from coming. I am glad you have a little girl. How do you feel—very much aged, I suppose, since you became Papa and Blanche Mama. Mae is waiting to take this to the office, so will leave the remainder until next time, only I want to send congratulations to Mr. and Mrs. Ostrander also as they will be rejoicing I know. Write again and let us know how Blanche is.
Lovingly,
Mother

Blanche's stepmother was also surprised by the birth. She wrote:

Woodstock, Ontario
February 16, 1908

My Dear Children,

You really should not spring such surprises on your unsuspecting relatives without the least preparation. You cannot imagine how delighted we all were.

I am just longing to hold my wee granddaughter in my arms and to kiss her blessed little mother. How pleased your dear father would have been. We are overjoyed because "she is a girl" too and we like the name you have chosen very much.

I am glad you got along so nicely and that baby is well. I know from personal experience what good care you will have—both you and babe. I don't exactly mean John but I hope someone will be good to him too. This is Roy's birthday. He is 17 and is a great tall boy—5'9". I have heard nothing since the news came but Aunt Lena and Uncle Roy. Now I will not tire you with a longer letter this time. Be careful Blanche for an "ounce of prevention is well worth a pound of cure."

Lena and Roy send their love to the trio and Lena says send Miss Dorothy to the post office—there will be some mail for her.

With fondest love to you all I am lovingly, Mother

*Blanche Hill
with baby Dorothy*

One of Blanche's friends wrote from Detroit:

Dear Blanche,

So you are a mother? A woman's highest vocation. Aren't you supremely happy? I suppose John is just as proud as he can be. I am so happy for you, Blanche and do hope all will go well with you and baby. I am so glad your baby was a girl, because I could tell by your letter that your heart was set on one.

Do you know, Blanche, you are the first of my girlfriends to have a baby? I can just see you fussing and playing with her and making all sorts of things for her. It is a good thing you are so handy with your needle. I certainly will have to come and see you both. As soon as I get my bills paid I will come. When you are well and strong write me all about yourself and little Dorothy. Such a pretty name.

Love & best wishes
Hazel

The Early Years:
A Family on the Move

Dorothy, like her mother, was not to remain in one house for long. When she was nine months old, John sold his marble and granite business in Lapeer and bought a laundry in Oxford. The family moved to Main Street in Oxford, where they lived until spring. Then they moved again, this time near the church. Here Dorothy had a yard to play in and one of the

Dorothy and Hope having a tea party

anecdotes in her baby book relates that she loved it so much outdoors they could hardly coax her into the house for meals.

Dorothy Blanche Hill, age 3   *Dorothy at work*   *Dorothy and cousin Hope Wellemeyer, ready for church*

Dorothy's baby book is evidence of how well loved she was. It is crammed full of pictures, first outings, cute sayings, dress scraps, lists of gifts, visitors, cards, holiday memories and Blanche's fond tales of Dorothy's early life.

Simeon wrote:

Well, John, old boy, you are having pretty hard luck these days, but be of good cheer, nobody is dead yet—for that we can be thankful. I am glad you kept well and didn't have scarlet fever so you could continue the business. There may be brighter days in the future in regard to money for me. Don't worry. I'll get along all right—for a while longer. My business is pretty slow. I guess I'll run up someday soon and see how you all look.
Well with lots of love and good wishes I am still your loving,
Grandpa

Blanche received this letter from her stepmother Jean:

Woodstock, Ontario
November 8, 1910

My Dear Child,

I wish so many times your dear father had kept you with him and he was sorry a good many times too, especially so when you went so far from him, but I suppose it was for the best in some way, for if you hadn't gone away then you wouldn't have met John. So you would have missed what I hope is your greatest joy. How is my dear baby? I think the other grandmothers have rather the best of me. They can see her often, while I must content myself with a picture, and they have other grandchildren and I have only her. I can hardly bear to think of it sometimes. I do hope you will be able to come before long. With love to you and John and Dorothy, I am lovingly, your
Mother

In her later years, Dorothy wrote this account of her early life:

My father had a laundry in Oxford. He was well-liked in the community, but as one of his customers said, "John, I can't be a Christian and wear your shirts; the starch is just too much!" Needless to say, he had to do something else for a living, so we moved to Pontiac October 17, 1910, and by that time he was in the insurance business.

I remember the first house in Pontiac, a red shingled house, at 27 S. Johnson Ave., where we moved when I was under five. That Christmas I loved the decorated tree, and the little packages hanging on it. At the very top was a soft woolly scarf, hanging so high I

couldn't touch it. It never occurred to me that it might be for me, though my mother would point it out. But on Christmas morning, I found that the incredibly soft, lovely item was mine. In addition there was a winter coat of brown and a velvet muff and hat. That was a magic holiday, which I never forgot.

Later we moved again to 7 Liberty St., where my little sister, Charlotte Jean, was born May 11, 1913. I remember her well and used to love to hold her in my rocking chair. She had lovely dark auburn curls and was very sweet. My mother said that now she had everything she wanted, with her two girls.

The Hill and Wellemeyer families

Difficult Times:
Hardship and Heartbreak

Blanche's cousin, Charlotte (Lottie) Wellemeyer, wrote from Vassar:

May 21, 1913

My dear Cousin,

I have been pretty slow extending congratulations but they are most sincere even though they come at this date. Am so glad she is a girl baby. She will always be nearer the hearthstone. Of course my boy is the finest ever, but he's mine. I too feel very proud of her name. She and I have the honor of being named for the same relative so we have a closer bond, you see.

The children are well and Hope is crazy about little Charlotte, wondering just how large she is and all. Bradley smiles but doesn't make any remarks. I don't want to tire you, so I'll quit. I am enclosing this little gift for the baby. I thought Charlotte's mother would know better than I just what she would appreciate most.
Lots of love from us all,
Kiss those girls for Aunt Lottie

Blanche, Dorothy and Charlotte Jean

Tragedy struck the Hill family when their 10-month-old baby, Charlotte Jean, died of spinal meningitis March 23, 1914. The funeral was held from their home and she was buried in Lakeview Cemetery in Clarkston.

Blanche's stepmother wrote:

59 Geoffrey St., Toronto

My Dear Child,

What shall I say to you in this, the greatest sorrow of a Mother's life? I am powerless yet I would have you know that all

our love and sympathy are yours. I know how empty your hearts are and how broken. I am so glad and thankful that you have John and Dorothy to live for—to help them bear the burden of this great sorrow will be good for you. I do hope that you are keeping as well as possible, dear child, and I would love to be near you. If a change would be helpful to you, you know you will be welcome any time. Give my love to John and a dozen kisses for dear Dorothy and be assured of all our sympathy. My heart aches for you, dear girl. May you be comforted and may you have faith—a great and consuming faith— is the wish of your sorrowful and loving
Mother

Dorothy continued her story:

Our next move was to 127 W. Huron St., a lovely big white double house with a nice upstairs. Mother promptly rented a room to a nurse, Lillian Campling, who stayed several years with us.

My brother, John Merritt Hill, Jr., was born here on September 30, 1915. People didn't go to hospitals much then, and Mother had a nurse for the birth. Though we were still very sad about the death of Charlotte Jean, it was exciting to have a new baby in the house.

I loved this house, a duplex. There was a connecting door between our half of the house and the neighbors and they had three little girls with whom I loved to play. The only drawback was Mother's gardening ideas. She had the longest rows of nasturtiums I've ever seen; all planted in the hot sun, and it was my job to pick every blossom daily. I found out later that she had what we call a green thumb.

I must describe Marian Keyser's home, which was next door. The house was one of a kind. Her father was the wealthiest druggist in town. The house was large, totally black and shingled, with a huge front porch and immense rooms inside. It was completely carpeted, upstairs and down. The living room was filled with large black leather couches and big chairs. The staircase to the upper floor was massive and curved to a large landing. The bathroom was huge and had a marble lavatory, with ornate gold fixtures. I had never seen such furnishings in a home. The house had the strangest effect on me, dark and mysterious. It had glamour combined with gloom.

On the first day of school Marian's mother took her to school. Her mother wore a full length black taffeta dress, which swept the ground as they walked. It was not strange that the teacher assumed that this was Marian's grandmother, and was red with embarrassment when she was corrected.

The little girl who lived on the other side of our house was Maxine Stoddard. Her family owned the leading department store in Pontiac, and the youngster had been coddled by her mother, who did the buying of dresses for Waite's Department Store and who had been a New Yorker and a model before her marriage to the heir to Waite's. Maxine, who was a little younger than I was, had a wonderful bike and every other luxury that money could buy, but she was a sad little girl, whom I came to know better in high school.

I started school at the Crofoot School kindergarten, which was held in a huge semi-circular room, very awesome. Little chairs went around the perimeter and it was also used as a gym. I loved kindergarten and my teacher, Miss Hartwick, who was young, blonde and beautiful. However, I was very shy, and it was decided that I should stay there awhile before going into the first grade.

When I finally reached first grade I watched everyone arriving on the first day with interest. Suddenly Annabel swished in, wearing a white ruffled dress, and sat down near me. She was overwhelming, the voice of experience, she was repeating first grade. Never have I been so impressed with failure. She knew the ropes! Her glory, however, was short lived and I don't remember her after that.

I loved to read, and I always loved school, except in the fourth grade, where I had a dull, uninspiring teacher, whom nobody liked. The boys thought it sporting to dip my long curls in the inkwell (the built in kind) on the desk behind me. My mother was irate, as ink was very hard to remove from my white middy blouses.

Blanche's grandparents were aging and moved to Croswell to be with their daughter, Eusebia, in their later years.

Dorothy and John Merritt Hill, Jr

Simeon wrote:

Croswell, Michigan.
October 13, 1915

Dear Blanche and family,

I will write you a little and let you know that Ma and I are in Croswell and are quite well for us. I would be very glad if we could come in and see you all, including that newcomer. I hope you are real smart and also the baby. Your Grandma is all right now except some rheumatism or something of that kind. I work a little. I am going fishing soon. I can walk quite good—I go to town and back and it don't seem to hurt me much. I must be careful as I might do too much. It is real nice and comfortable here. The most trouble is to find room enough for our clothing and things. We have a bed, dresser and bureau, red couch, center table, wheelchair, two chairs and a little stove smaller than ours at home.

I notice John is doing pretty well toward winning the prize. I saw two weeks when he stood second. I hope he can win it as it would help pay expenses of that John Merritt Junior. I have not got any fair offer for shoes yet. Thought maybe John would know by this time in regard to that insurance stock.

Well, bye bye
Grandma & Grandpa

Dorothy wrote:

In one of our rare longer stays, we lived in a terrace at 9 Elizabeth Lake Road for seven years, near the gates of the Pontiac State Hospital. I used to roller skate up and down the sloping walks to the hospital, do a few fancy turns on the porch-

Simeon and Charolotte Ostrander

es, which were smooth and marble-like, better than sidewalks, and then coast all the way down the hill to our home.

One of my friends in fifth grade wanted to make up a semester, so both of us recited all day, in two groups and took our books home to study for the next day, so I gained a semester there. Sixth grade was routine, with my worst subject being arithmetic. In the seventh grade, we were no longer in grade school and due to the need for extra classrooms, we were moved into the high school building, but were still separate from the high school students. It was a banner year for me, both scholastically and socially. Miss Selden was a rare combination. She expected excellence and not one of us ever knowingly let her down. We put on plays and had lots of extracurricular subjects tossed at us. It was the best school year.

During this time, Blanche was worried about her grandparents, but limited in her ability to spend much time with them, due to the needs of her family, lack of money, and the distance from Pontiac to Croswell.

Blanche's Aunt Eusebia (Aunt Sib) wrote about Simeon and Charlotte Ostrander's failing health:

> January 7, 1916
> Croswell, Michigan

Dear Blanche,

Your letter received. Grandpa seems a little better, the swelling of the legs has nearly all gone down and that is a good sign. He is very weak, but I am in hopes he will gain strength the same as when at your place. Grandma is about the same.

About the stock, Grandpa says Doctor has a man to look at it. He says he wants John and Doctor to work together and sell it the best they can. He won't be here a great while at the best and it is better sold.

I must close now and remember no news is good news. It is hard to write so much but will let you know if there is any danger or he is worse. Write to them as often as you can, it gives them something to think about. I am glad John thought they were comfortable. I am doing all I have strength or means to do for them. I would do more if I could and I think they are more comfortable than many who have greater means.

Fondly,
Aunt Sib

Blanche's grandmother, Charlotte Ostrander, passed away on January 29, 1916 and Blanche suffered another great loss. Blanche's mother-in-law wrote:

Fresno, California
March 6, 1916

My Dear Daughter,

Your letter received telling us of your great loss, you have our heart-felt sympathy. She was such a dear good woman. We all loved her and feel the loss with you, but not to the extent of course that you do. She was a mother to you as well as grandma and you loved her as such. It is a comfort to you to know that she has gone to be with Jesus whom she loved and served while here. May He bless and comfort you both and give you grace to trust him more, is my prayer.

I am very anxious to see my new grandson and Dorothy. Glad to know she is such a help to you. Children are such a comfort aren't they? Of course they make work and are a care but what is a home without them, precious little things.

Write again soon and perhaps we will both get the habit.
Lots of love to all,
Mother

Simeon followed Charlotte in just a few weeks. They were laid to rest together in the Lakeview Cemetery, where their great-granddaughter Charlotte Jean was also buried.

Blanche felt the loss keenly of these two kind people who had been like parents to her. To lose them both so close together was very difficult, but she had her own family to think of now.

Dorothy and John Merritt kept their mother busy and the years passed quickly, especially with all the moves the family made.

John Merritt "J.M." and Dorothy

Blanche Hill aboard ship   *John Hill aboard ship*   *Dorothy in Vassar, 1921*

Landing in the Land of 10,000 Lakes

Dorothy, always a writer, continued her story:

> *I went through ninth grade in Pontiac High School before moving to Faribault, Minnesota in 1922. My dad had gone ahead to scout out the territory he was to cover for his insurance company. They wanted him to see how well insurance would sell in an area near the twin cities. He rented a house for us, but when we arrived, Mother was horrified. It was an ancient gloomy place, which actually had bats in its belfry and a landlord who lurked around, making her nervous.*

> *We only stayed a month or two there in the summer and then moved to 414 Fourth St. in Northfield, where the famed Jesse James had robbed the bank long before. I remember there was a plaque on the bank, relating the affair. We rented a very nice house across from a park and only a block from the high school. It was a lovely little town and we were all very happy there.*

Dorothy and John Merritt

Father, an excellent salesman, traveled to the twin cities and other nearby places to drum up business for the company.

In Northfield our next door neighbor was Martha Watts, who could have played the part of a New England spinster without changing a hair. Her front porch was as immaculate as her house. On either side of the doorway one could learn interesting facts from the up-to-date clippings displayed there. It was like a room in her house, filled with items on current events, or whatever her keen mind determined to be of special interest. No article ever got stale before it was replaced. She was a frugal soul where small things were concerned, saving berry boxes and cutting them into neat little splinters to light the stove, thus conserving a few matches. Martha held nothing back, including bad news. She told my mother that our house had been contaminated, and she looked so worried that we had visions of packing up immediately. After a great deal of hesitation, she finally confided that the boy who had lived there previously had urinated in the register upstairs. After scouting out the "contaminated" area and discovering no fumes, we relaxed, no longer fearing the bubonic plague.

Around the corner from us lived two school teachers, maiden ladies, one of whom had been a missionary to China. I learned to know both of them well. Lillian, the tiny one, taught chemistry. Her sister was a tall, massive woman, with a no-nonsense hairdo on top of her head, but with the most enchanting sense of humor—one of those straight-faced kind who can crack one up.

Mother found friends in a group of young women, largely faculty wives at Carleton College. Everyone new in town was welcomed, as if the residents hadn't been able to get along before the newcomers arrived. I had never seen so many blondes in my life. Swedes and Norwegians filled the high school.

The churches were interested in us too. We soon learned that it was not a mark of quality to go to the Methodist Church. To have any status, you should be Presbyterian or Lutheran. Methodists were far down the social ladder.

The town was divided geographically. Carleton College was a beautiful grouping of lovely buildings, with an artificial lake on the campus. At the other end of town was St. Olaf College, high on a hill, gray, stark and cold appearing, but it had a choir that was known for excellence, which traveled all over the U.S. giving concerts.

Our house faced a little park and across the street from it was the parish house, which was being used by the Methodist Church for a youth center. It had been a lovely private home at one time, and here I saw the first tapestry wall coverings of my life.

The high school also faced the park, so we lived in a square surrounding the park. It was such a short distance to school that I couldn't believe it, but with the snow piled up four or five feet high on both sides of the sidewalks, I was grateful when going to school in the winter. Hardy Scandinavians living on nearby farms walked much farther to school and I didn't envy their trip.

I loved the Carleton campus, especially its beautiful stone chapel, and I used to go in and climb way up high and look down on the pews cushioned in blue velvet, and listen to the organist practice. Sun slanting through the beautiful stained glass windows brought out the loveliness of the place.

Once we went to Minneapolis and bought a little white bull terrier for my seven-year-old brother, who had never had a dog. All of us enjoyed this pet. John would hitch him up to a little cart and go riding with him.

Mother took in a roomer, a boy who was a freshman at Carleton. He and his friend Paul used to hang around and talk to me, a fourteen year old, and I was very impressed. Paul planned to go around the world on a trip. He and his friend talked about stowing away on a ship and seeing the world.

One day Mother saw a rough looking character walking across our lawn and told me to watch out, he looked like a tramp. Soon she had to eat her words as he turned out to be our landlord and the owner of a huge farm outside of town.

My reception at school was amazing. Everyone knew who I was and where we were from. They asked me to do a reading for them in assembly. I had been learning some Swedish dialect readings and had the nerve to get up and mimic a Swedish character, in their dialect. Such applause I never heard, and it seemed that they really enjoyed the takeoff. Paul Johnson, a big blonde Swede and head of the student body, was one of the best-natured people I ever knew. Some of the Norwegian blondes were almost silver-haired, with beautiful blue eyes.

27

I learned there were two groups of students, those who came from the area around St. Olaf College and who were largely Swedish, and those who lived near Carleton and were Congregationalists, the socially elect. If you went to parties among them, you were first introduced to the mother, with whom you were to chat before the party began. Then next day you were to make a call at the home to express your gratitude.

It was a little much for a humble Methodist, whose social training had not included these flourishes. But the party refreshments were out of this world, including exquisite molded ices in the shape of flowers, pumpkins or any exotic shape imaginable. As I was invited to both parties of the "elite" and the more comfortable commoners, I had to walk carefully and remember which rules applied where. I was invited to be a model in the fashion show which Carleton College put on, as they wanted a few younger girls. Mother found out with horror how little college girls wore under a dress, but it didn't bother me as I was tired of Ferris waists!

My Scotch grandmother was visiting us when the Methodist minister called one day. He had the nerve to tell her a joke ridiculing the Scotch. I doubt if he ever trusted his luck with that story again. The day my grandmother left, my Dad was to take her to the train in the city. But he didn't calculate very well and she missed it. The saving grace of that episode was that the train was wrecked, and she was so grateful to him for missing it that he was forever in her good graces.

Among my new friends was Carolyn Overstrd, a Norwegian girl who became my best friend. We vowed we'd always be

The Hill Family in
Northfield, Minnesota

close, but all too soon my father decided that the area was not good enough for the insurance business and we had to move back to Michigan. I never hated to leave a place so much. It was so hard to say good bye to all my friends, but at least I'd had two wonderful years in Northville and took away a lot of fond memories.

Blanche was bright and curious and very interested in people and new things. Her days in Northfield were typical happy ones, as she always adjusted to her new surroundings very well. She made close friends everywhere, and always joined the Methodist Church.

Among her old letters there are many from people she left behind in her endless moves and they always express how much she was missed. One of her great tal-

Dorothy and yearbook staff in Northfield

ents was to make a cozy home and find friends and good neighbors wherever she lived. Her Pontiac friends wrote often while she was in Minnesota and she kept in touch with many of them over the years. She liked to paint with watercolors at this time. Collecting antiques was one of her passions for many years. Blanche was never without hobbies and interests.

One of her friends wrote a typical letter, stating: "We still miss you and could very well use your talents and energies, but you have no doubt made yourself felt where you are and our loss is their gain. I suppose you have done lots of pretty things since I saw you last. Have you finished all your upholstering, I wonder, and how is your painting coming along?"

Return to Michigan

Dorothy wrote:

May 1924 found us back in Pontiac, Michigan, living across from the high school. The speech teacher, Mr. Viola, was excellent and he directed a school play in which I played the part of Dulcy. I thoroughly enjoyed this experience.

At the same time, Mother took in a roomer, Miss VanArsdale, a teacher at the high school. I recall how many items were on her dresser and how I hated my job of dusting each and returning them to their exact spot. She always let me know if I had left a speck of dust anywhere. She was not my favorite person and said I'd never rate an A in dusting. We moved again after a year, this time to 69 South Shirley Avenue.

Mother and Dad decided to buy this frame house on the East side of town and fix it up. I believe it was the only house they ever owned except perhaps when they were first married. It had a one flue furnace, which would burn either wood or coal, and there was a good place to keep warm, on the large register, which served the whole upstairs, and downstairs. We redecorated everything in this house and improved it a great deal. Here I did my beautiful job of painting baby food jars for spices, and hand lettering each one carefully. Since the rug in the dining room was worn to the core, it was given a paint job and decoration on the back side.

I was busy finishing high school, walking three miles each way. Meanwhile, Mother decided she'd like to sell real estate part time, but she told her Sunday

Home at 25 Shirley Street, Pontiac, Michigan

school teacher about her plans and was told that she mustn't harm her family by working outside the home. She always regretted the decision to take this advice.

I graduated from Pontiac High School in 1925. My cousin Hope, who was afraid to go away to school alone, came to live with us.

During this time, John was suffering health problems. He developed an enormous goiter and eventually went to Ann Arbor to have it removed, strangely enough by a surgeon named Dr. Collar. Blanche was terrified of hospitals and operations. The family was very reluctant, but it seemed there was no choice but to face the surgery. Money was very tight and Blanche's half-sister Kate wrote:

Memphis, Tennessee

May 17, 1926

Dear Blanche,

Mother and I are having a regular "bee" writing to you. Our intentions have been good and you have been so continuously in our thoughts. This morning we made a desperate effort and you note the result.

The news which you wrote us was both good, and bad—good because I am so glad that you have all come to realize the necessity of removing the awful handicap under which poor John has been struggling along. Bad, because I know the great anxiety you will labor under until it is all over. But I know you are all brave and I really think everything will be wonderful in six months or so.

Dorothy is a brick and I am just so proud of her. When the stress and strain are over, and she can be spared, I want you to let her come and visit me. It will do her good to get away and see new things and the child will surely deserve a real nice holiday.

Blanche, my dear sister, I want to impress upon you that you are not alone in this world. Do not worry over the future because you know, and John knows, that whatever happens I will see that all is well, insofar as I am able. If John could just undergo this operation feeling that he need not worry about his little family, I know it would help him to come through it so much better.

You will let me know just as soon as you can how everything turns out, because I too, am anxious. Remember, won't you, that if there is anything I can do, I am more than willing. And I am the proper person to come to. Lots of love to all the family, and tell John to keep a stiff upper lip, but I know he is such a good sport he will anyway, and lots of love to you.

Katherine

Not long after John's successful surgery there was talk of selling the house. Blanche wrote this letter while Dorothy was vacationing at Greenbush with Aunt Lottie's family.

August 2, 1926

Dear Dorothy,

Tis Sunday morning and raining nice drizzles. Daddy hasn't felt very good this week so I let him rest instead of getting up for church. I miss you, especially in the evening. I don't have any little girl to go anywhere with me. I am glad you will soon be home in one way, but in another way, I'm sorry for I wanted to get the painting done while you are gone and I just can't. Too many other things to do I guess.

Mr. Markley saw Daddy yesterday and he said "Well you sure made a good move when you bought your house, the way everything is booming in that section. You surely ought to get $6,500.00." I agree with him, only I think maybe we can get more if we can fix it up in time to sell when everything is booming. People were looking at the place where Taylor's live this week. They are asking $7,600.00, can you beat it?

When do we meet you? We will be glad to see our little girl. I am still hunting for a bed for your room. Have only had one letter.
Lovingly,
Mother

Greenbush—August 2, 1926

Dear Mother,

Had a nice trip to the high Rollaway Sunday. We took a picnic lunch and got back about five. We are still alone up here. I guess the rest will come tomorrow. How are the rest of the Hills? Is Daddy feeling good? Haven't heard much from you, but take it for granted that no news is good news. Have been playing 500 this afternoon with Aunt Lottie. The lake is rough and gray today and it's rained some.

I hope you and Daddy aren't worrying about this fall, for I simply won't have it. I've thought it all out and decided that there are things bigger than a year at college. In the long run it is small in comparison with health and happiness. They can be had without it and please don't feel that it will be a disaster for me to work this year, even with Hope going to school. I know that I'll be happy for there are so many things before me.

These woods make one realize what things are essential and I have had time to figure out values pretty clearly. I'm enjoying every minute of my vacation. What would you suggest that I could do for the Wellemeyers?

With love,
Dorothy

August 6, 1926

Dear Dorothy,

Yes, dear, I've done quite a lot of thinking and planning about this fall. I don't feel quite sure what is best to do, but I know I want you to go to school. It seems as if I can't have it otherwise, but Daddy isn't doing much yet. I feel he will soon have some business, if it were only a salary it would be so much easier. Anyway, I know you are a darling and if I could do as I liked you would have everything you want.

Was talking to Mrs. D. who thinks you are getting along real well with your work. I still have my little job. I charged them $5.00 for the back work I did and there is so little work so far I hadn't the nerve to ask over $3.00 a week. They acted as if that was fine. Uncle George said it was worth a dollar an hour. I don't mind doing it at all; wish I had a couple more little jobs like it.

I guess we will come after you, if not, will telephone. We would have to come home Sunday, so you could get ready for work. Well, dear, I must wind the cat and put out the clock and tuck myself away.

With a heap of love,
Mother

Dorothy—the Working Girl

Dorothy wrote:

Hope and I went to junior college at Pontiac High School. Later I found myself employed at the Wilson Foundry Company, where I was a comptometer operator in the payroll department. Here I met both Josephine Smith and Margaret Echtinaw, who became lifelong friends.

We earned $90.00 a month and had a good time working, even though the smelly foundry was right outside our window, and our sandwiches always tasted like foundry. We had to hand post and write paychecks and balance books without error—long pages of employees' names and salary amounts. Penmanship was very important and, in those days, I wrote well. During the noon hour we ate our lunches and amused ourselves by rolling our chairs all around the room and acting like idiots.

I stayed there nearly two years, leaving in February 1927. During that year I also gave expression lessons in a little studio downtown, charging $1.25 a lesson.

Cousin Hope and I finally went away to college, both enrolling at Ypsilanti, but I did not like it there. After a month, I became quite ill, quit school and returned home. I continued with my correspondence classes in writing through the University of Wisconsin.

Here is an example of Dorothy's writing for these classes. It was written about the chapel she loved on the campus of Carleton College in Northfield, Minnesota. It reflects her maturity as well as illustrates her talent for descriptive writing.

Vesper Hour in the Chapel

Noiselessly we slid up the crooked gray stairway that led into the balcony of the little stone chapel. It was the vesper hour. The whole chapel breathed of peace, soft twilight and prayer. The silent pews, gray and dim as the coming dusk, waited, listening for the message of the day. Then it came, quietly at first, but growing in beauty and intensity as the organ pealed out its answer, reaching to the very arches that upheld the vaulted ceiling. The tones almost

died away in the far distance and there came a haunting whisper—
a half-remembered sadness—a wistfulness that grew and merged
into a longing for the return of the day that was past. The melody
increased in volume until it echoed and re-echoed into the furthest
corners of the chapel, until the air trembled with sadness, reverber-
ated with power.

And still twilight paused, touching the shadowy pews, not
quite certain that the day was over. The slim blue aisles, the vel-
vety platform, showed the dull blue shadows of approaching night,
but high above them raised by some artist's hand was the one
tribute to the dying day. A great stained glass window composed
of slender golden panels with the figures of saints outlined against
the setting sun rose high above the dim grayness of the quiet chapel, bringing to life, if only for a moment, the stately figures, giving a last radiant glimpse of a day that was done. Now the organ
is hushed, the last wistful note is mute. The silence transcends in
beauty all the music that has gone before. It is the perfect answer
of the vesper hour.

The next story shows clearly how Dorothy felt about her
clerical jobs, which she knew she must do as a means to go back to
college. She had set her sights on Albion College and was saving her
money to achieve her goal.

The New Office Girl

The girl entered with mind and heart on tiptoe—eager
to learn all that this great office had to teach her. The efficiency
thrilled; the mechanism appalled her; the difficulties overwhelmed
her. Then with much vigor she set about to fit herself into the
amazing machine. Every effort was concentrated upon becoming a
perfect cog of the machinery. However, with knowledge came the
inevitable sight of flaws; then perfection and awe vanished with
startling suddenness.

The place was stripped and ugly, barren of all its glamour,
it remained merely a crowded and littered room, full of scurrying
beings and rattling machines. It fairly shouted the importance of its
trivial details.

Detail ruled the entire place, forcing every mind to bow to it and acknowledge its immensity and power, until at last the very minds and souls of the people there were bent to worship this idol. The office had become full of warped personalities. In vain had been the struggle against this god, for those individuals who fought hardest against being enveloped in a dull routine had been ensnared, through lack of guidance, by the idol of pleasure, whose demands were never satisfied, but became more and more insistent.

Thus all of the office force had been caught in some snare. To the new office girl came a feeling of revulsion and hate, for here before her was a sample of what waited for her when she shall have settled herself within the walls of the office away from all inspiration, resigned to the worship of detail.

Dorothy started a scrapbook about this time and its first page shows a sweet photo of Dorothy as a small child and one of her at about age 19.

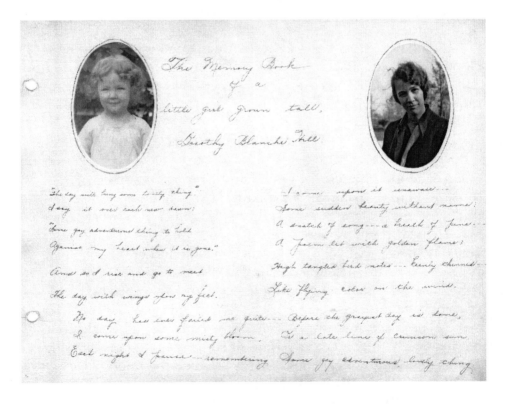

She called it "The Memory Book of a Little Girl Grown Tall—Dorothy Blanche Hill".

This poem by Grace Noll Corwell follows in Dorothy's handwriting and clearly represents Dorothy's love of life:

Each Day Will Bring Some Lovely Thing

The day will bring some lovely thing,
I say it over each new dawn:

Some gay adventurous thing to hold
Against my heart when it is gone.

And so I rise and go to meet
The day with wings upon my feet.

I come upon it unaware —
Some sudden beauty without name;

A snatch of song—a breath of pine —
A poem lit with golden flame;

High tangled bird notes—keenly thinned —
Like flying color on the wind.

No day has ever failed me quite—
Before the grayest day is done,

I come upon some misty bloom,
Or a late line of crimson sun.

Each night I pause—remembering
Some gay adventurous, lovely thing.

Fall 1928
Albion College at Last

The family finances, never very healthy, were even worse at this time, but neither Dorothy nor her family ever gave up on her having the college education she so desperately desired. This finally paid off when she was able to attend Albion College in the fall of 1928.

Dorothy's college years produced a treasure trove of letters showing the love, support, and warmth of the family. Though Dorothy was 5'9" tall and towered over her mother, she was still Blanche's little girl and she missed her very much.

At Albion College, Dorothy was very happy and thrilled with the educational opportunities available. She shared the details of her new life with her family, knowing how interested they would be and how they would miss her. Her mother's letters tell of life at home and of her hopes for her daughter. Dorothy truly made the most of her college years, as shown in the letters following:

Susanna Wesley Hall
Albion College
September 17, 1928

Dear Mother,

Arrived, settled, enthralled! It was a long afternoon and a busy one. Have unpacked and stowed away everything. The room is dusted; the lace doilies are under the glass on the dresser, with another lace doily on the little bookshelf. Some of the Y.W. girls brought a bud vase with a yellow and a white flower in it. The candle sticks are exquisite on the dresser with it.

Later—I was interrupted to go join a game of bridge which didn't materialize, for we all went downstairs for a cozy evening in the recreation room.

I had to pinch myself at dinner to realize that all the surroundings were real! I wore my brown outfit and the dinner was delicious! Everyone is very friendly and anxious to get acquainted. I have seen every type of girl, and of dress. Our rooms are so lovely we hate to leave them.

After dancing and being entertained tonight we roasted marshmallows and sang with only the fire for light. It is all so wonderful it seems like some cameo of exquisite dancing, living figures caught for a second in their joy. Then they sang "Good-Night Ladies" and before we knew what had happened we were climbing the stairs to our rooms. Now it will soon be time for lights out. (I have a whole little book of rules, you know!)

Tomorrow will be a big day with everyone trying to register, but we shall love it all. (Nothing seems hard this year.) I bumped into Margaret Luther shortly after you left and so she and Dorothy King and I have been together. I pressed three dresses, so expect to be able to appear in public after all.

I shall never forget our firelight and singing. The andirons were cut in intricate lacy patterns and glowed in the firelight and all was happiness, radiance and beauty. Albion does truly live up to the highest. I wish you all could have heard the grace we sang at the table. Please forgive the writing—more tomorrow.
With big hugs for my family,
Dorothy

Susannah Wesley Hall, Albion College
Reprinted with permission of Albion College

Women's Self-Government Association
Susanna Wesley Hall
September 1928

House Rules

Excerpts reprinted with permission of Albion College

CLOSING HOURS
The closing hours on Monday, Tuesday, Wednesday and Thursday nights are: ten o'clock for Senior and Junior women, nine o'clock for Sophomore women, and eight o'clock for Freshmen women. All girls leaving the dormitory after eight o'clock must sign out. On Friday and Saturday nights doors will be closed at eleven-thirty. On Sunday nights doors will be closed at ten o'clock. All canoeing shall cease by nine p.m.

QUIET HOURS
Quiet hours are to be observed on Monday to Thursday inclusive from 8:00 p.m. to 12:00 M, and from 1:00 to 4:00 p.m.; on Friday from 9 p.m. to 10:00 a.m.; on Sunday from 3:00 p.m.to 4:30 p.m.; and from 10:30 p.m. Sunday to 12:00 M. Monday. Quiet hours shall begin in the corridors at 7:30 P.M. Monday to Thursday inclusive. Reasonable quietness must be maintained all day Sunday.

CALLING HOURS
Calling hours are as follows: on all days except Friday, Saturday, and Sunday; 4:00 p.m. to 8:00 p.m. On Friday and Saturday 2:00 p.m. to 5:30 p.m. and 7:00 p.m. to 11:30 p.m. On Sunday, 12:00 M to 5:00 p.m. and 6:30 p.m. to 10:00 p.m.

LIGHTS
On Sunday to Thursday nights inclusive lights shall be out at 10:30 p.m.; on Friday and Saturday nights at 12:00 a.m. One light cut a week for an hour (longer by special permission) may be taken by each girl. She must register the light cut in advance. No light cuts are to be taken for spreads except by special permission. Girls desiring extra light cuts during the week should see the house mother for special permission.

PERMISSIONS

Permissions may be secured for the following purposes:

To be absent from the House for special occasions until 12:30 a.m., not to exceed four times a month for Senior women; three times a month for Junior women; two times a month for Sophomore women: and, once a month for Freshmen women. These are to cover formal parties.

Permission may be secured from the Dean of Women by one couple to be out of town after 8 p.m. provided the woman is a Senior or a Junior, otherwise there must be two couples. In either case the specific purpose for leaving must be stated.

Permission to leave the dormitory is not required for attendance upon authorized college functions. No permissions will be granted for girls to stay overnight in town. Out of town permissions must be secured from the Dean of Women.

September 18, 1928

Dear Family,

I am all registered and ready for school to really begin. It was quite simple—got over to the gym early and waited an hour or more and then pushed and jammed my way into the gym. They all seem a jolly crowd and I think everyone looks quite interesting. Had trouble getting in all the subjects I wanted to take, but ended by taking these classes: Greek—3 hours, Biology—4 hours, History—3 hours, Bible—3 hours and Philosophy—3 hours, for a total of 16 hours. I couldn't get play production in without making my course too heavy, so contented myself with the above. Perhaps I can take it next semester.

My expenses were $270.00. General fee $15.00, Gym $10.00, Biology $9.00, $65.00 for tuition and $108.00 for room and board, plus a few miscellaneous charges.

The Dean was lovely and gave me special permission to take philosophy. And when I went to him to have my schedule OK'd he said that it was quite refreshing to see someone taking things like Greek and Philosophy for a change!

Tonight we go to chapel at 7:30 to hear Dr. Seaton. Dorothy K. was rather blue today and wept copiously this morning. Registration was too much for her I guess. It's all wonderful, but I shall be very glad when my roommate arrives. Went across the hall this morning and helped one of the girls hang pictures. They are all very friendly and call us by our first names immediately. There are so many Dorothys that we have to use numbers to tell us apart! It is awfully cold so far and I am wearing a wool dress already.

Tell J.M. he can ship that candy along any time now. That's the way to be popular. I am going to run downtown now and shop a little. Hope I get a letter soon.

With bushels of best wishes and a heap of love,
Dorothy

September 19, 1928

Dear Mother,

Have had a strenuous day—going every minute. This was my schedule: Lecture 9-10 a.m., intelligence tests 10:00-11:15, lunch— noon—dancing, lecture (Dr. Goodrich) 1:30-2:00 p.m., lecture (Dean Williams) 2:00-2:45, recreation 3:00-5:00 (ran myself to death), dinner 6:00 p.m., then YWCA, circus at 8:00 p.m., and lights out 10:30 p.m. I never want another lecture on any subject! And my intelligence is simply minus.

Everything at the dormitory is lovely. The meals so far are fine—even the old girls admit it. My dresses look real nice and I have worn my new wool one already, it has been so awfully cold all the time. The only thing I seem to have forgotten is my cold cream. I wish you would send it to me and some dust cloths too.

I had a letter from Fleming Barbour yesterday—maybe you think it wasn't welcome!! I had another today from little Laura Garra- han and she sent me her picture. It's very sweet.

Would you mind getting me some more cold medicine from Uncle Dalton? I really need it, and about my money—I haven't enough in my checking account to get my books. I wonder if Daddy could get the $50.00 I have in my savings transferred to my checking account right away. I will send a note authorizing it, so he can surely get it changed. Too tired to write more now.

With heaps of love to you all,
Dorothy

September 20, 1928

Dear Mother,

The president's reception was tonight. I wore my new brown crepe dress and gold beads. The class was divided into two groups. I met all the notables including Miss Gray. Today we had classes and lectures and physical exams. I managed to clean my room, write a couple of letters and attend all the doings besides going downtown.

Am beginning to think I haven't any family at all, as I haven't had one word from any one of them. I would like to know if you are all alive, as this is my fourth epistle and, as yet, no answers have been received.

Please let me know about my checking account as soon as possible for I shall need money for books by Monday at least. We had a spiffy dinner tonight. Meat croquettes, mashed potatoes and gravy, squash, pickles and celery, milk, white and rye bread and butterscotch sundae. I just have about five minutes before they "douse the glim," so will have to hit the hay.
With love to my silent family,
Dorothy

Dear Dorothy,

I really need your typewriter, but perhaps I can manage. We must have picked up a tack back of the dorm, so we had to stop at Grass Lake and have a tire repaired. Reached Ann Arbor at 5:50, but Mr. Harding's antiques store was closed. My lovely platter was in the window and all the nice things displayed. Stopped along the way and bought a bushel of pears and some apples. We overtook a boy having trouble with his car, so we pushed him several miles. Finally reached home at 8 p.m.

John M. was at scout meeting but had left some soup for us which tasted good, for the house was cold. Went downtown this afternoon and bought some towels for the kitchen, a pair of hose and your collar stays. Lorene called up and visited a long time. She had a great visit with Mrs. Wolfe and Miss Gray and told them about you. They are going to have you read and be on some of the dorm committees and do everything to give you a lovely time. They thought you could have a job in Dr. Seaton's office or the dorm office next year—three hours a day paying for your board and room by doing a little this year to get ready for it. Also said if we let you know when we are coming, you can get tickets for us to eat at the dorm with you for fifty cents each— mighty reasonable I think.

We drove to Orion tonight, stopped on Perry St. and got the amber tray and three goblets. She would not sell the pitcher and I couldn't get the old chair. Paid her $1.25 and think I can get $2.50 for it. Wish I could talk to you tonight and hear all the news. I can hardly wait to see you. Somehow it's harder than last year, but I wouldn't have it different. I am so glad you are there and I do hope you will be happy. Don't work too hard. I would like to see your face a little more like a full moon! I don't want to be a nuisance, but if you knew how I want to know all about everything. J.M. has been especially good today. With a bushel of love for my little girl who can't seem to go to school without being away from home.
Mother

John Merritt Hill,
Boy Scout

Friday, September 20, 1928
Dear Dorothy,

Your letter came this morning—it made me so happy to think everything was so lovely. I have so wanted you to have that sort of an atmosphere. I am so glad your first day was all you could have hoped. My day has been very ordinary, except for your letter, which makes me weepy for happiness. I canned seven quarts of pears today and the rest of the time just worked. J.M. and I went to Birmingham with Daddy.

Am making something for you, but will not tell until I know whether it is a success or not. Glad the candles look so pretty. I am so anxious to see your room and meet Miss Gray, Mrs. Wolfe and Dr. Seaton. I hope you will go to the league reception. I don't like to have you lose your church all your college time.

Wish you had some of our pears. I don't see why we didn't get some fruit for you on the way over. I guess we were too excited. I want to go through the buildings, etc., next time we are there. Now I must pick up the house and get ready for bed. Your letter seemed so good, I guess I can stand it to have you away if you write like that.
Bushels of love from the family,
Mother

Dear Dorothy,

Did not get my letter written last night for Uncle George and Aunt Ada came over. Was very busy all day, but don't know what I did. I am so behind with my work I can't seem to see what I do. I had an idea that perhaps I could make you a coat out of the velvet dress. Mrs. M. thought I could too, but when I ripped it I was sure that we would not be satisfied with it, for sometimes Jo's things are pieced more than we like.

Went out in the afternoon and found a majolica mustache cup, isn't that good? Never saw one before. It is quite pretty. Also found a little blue cup plate. Canning pears again this morning and going to iron when that is over. Haven't your room cleaned yet. I ordered a tan blanket like your pink one for your bed, so we can keep you warm when you come home.

Your letter just came and I will attend to the bank matter, or have Daddy do it at once, also the other things. Daddy thought I had my nerve when I wished I could get a letter twice a day! John M. will make you some candy pretty quick. When I get caught up a little, we can do more. I think you have a wonderful course. Seems to me freshman week must be a great help to get all these things done before the crowd is there.

I called Uncle Dalton and he will fix something for your cold. He said for you to get rubbing alcohol and use lots of that. Then he thought if you would not eat sweets or starch for a few days you would feel better. He said if you were still hungry to get raisins and dates to fill up on.

I don't know where you post your letters. Lorene says if you take them to the 9:07 p.m. train they get here the next day, or one that goes just after 4:00 p.m. Send your schedule as soon as you get

it, then I'll know what you are doing. I am so anxious to see you and talk about everything. I'll probably write tonight when I am not so hurried. Lots of love to my little girl—your roommate will likely come today. I do hope you like her.
Lovingly,
Mother

Dear Dorothy,

Well, it is almost 10 p.m. and I have worked since 8 a.m. so I think I'll have a change, writing to you. Your letter came this morning saying you had had no mail. I felt awfully bad about it, for you have been so good about writing. I tried to do as well. Mrs. King just called me and said she had seen you today and that you had finally gotten your mail. I am sorry I couldn't get any eats to you this week, but it has been a very heavy week and I have such a bad cold.

I wonder if my blue coat would be of any use to you for a change. I could get along without it for a while. Last night Daddy and J.M. turned and washed the living room rug and I washed the furniture today so that room is all clean but the windows, which will have to wait till next week.

I am glad the eats are good over there. I think the board has been raised. I thought it was $65.00 a semester, same as the tuition, but perhaps I am mistaken.

Next Sunday is J.M.'s birthday and if Mother Hansler does not come, I would like to go to Albion. Of course I want to go all the time, but I can't. Mrs. King said there was some misunderstanding about your roommate and that she was rooming with someone else. I hope you do not care. For myself, I think I would be glad, but do not know how you feel about it.

Daddy is planning some changes at the office that will cut his overhead. It is time he was home—10 p.m.—and I have been alone all the evening with my majolica mustache cup.

Aunt Lottie is going to bring me some tomatoes and a crate of eggs. I am so glad for them. I won't need to be idle. I wish Albion was just a wee bit nearer home, but I must play the game. I have followed your program every day.

Just called Lorene and she said Brad would take anything over, so I'll send this letter with him and you will get it sooner along with a few of your clothes. J.M. is making candy for you. Do not know how it will turn out. I expect you can come home most any time with Brad. Someway Albion seems farther than Ypsilanti did. I am counting the days until I can see you.

Lovingly,

Mother

Sunday

Dear Dorothy,

It is Sunday evening. We went to church and Sunday school this morning. Our dinner was rather late—our first Sunday dinner without our little girl.

Bought some more pears yesterday and am going to make some pear jam for a change. Mrs. Barrett was picking up rummage and got me a blue and white coverlet. It is only in fair condition, but good for the price. Miss Perry of NY, who has the glass head plates will take the little old Sunday school hanky but would not set a price, so I am going to offer $2.00 for the hanky and the plates. Then I could sell one plate and get my money back. I expect the hanky is more valuable than the plate, but I prefer the plate.

We drove out to see the new airport today. It is near Watkins Lake. They are getting ready to build the hanger. There was a nice pavement all the way. Our yard still looks terrible. Thought perhaps we could get it seeded this fall, but I am afraid it is too late. If I have time I will get your dress ready to fit. I can't seem to get through cleaning and there is quite a little sewing I ought to do. Cheeri is a naughty bird and does not sing. Teddy has been a pretty good little dog. I hope the Albion church is homelike and that you will enjoy going there. Don't you dare to forget your little mother, cause, well, you know.

With a bushel of love for my little girl,

Mother

September 22, 1928

Dear Mother,

This is a glorious retreat—this little log summerhouse by the tennis courts. We have just had lunch and Margaret's mother and sister were here too. I got your letter this morning and was so glad, for letters mean a lot to freshmen (even freshmen plus!) I'm glad to know my money will be fixed up as I want to write a check soon for my books. I have another bid to a tea. Alpha Xi Delta, I think it is. Of course I don't expect to join any, but as D. Hawley says—why not have a little free tea!

I went to see the Dean this morning about work. She wanted to know when I wanted to work and I told her most any time. I figure what I have now will take me through one semester and then I'll have $164.30 toward next semester. She advised that I take a job in the dining room now if there is one open. You serve at one meal a day and get half your board. Then perhaps next year I could get in the office. I don't know whether you will approve or not, but I do so want to be independent and not have anything go wrong with my finances. I'll find out about the job tonight. I may call you about it.

We went to the league reception last night and had the high privilege of staying up until 12 a.m.! My roommate is here, but has decided to room with another girl, so I am alone and can only hope for the best. I don't know whether she saw me from afar and was scared away or what. I haven't met her yet anyway.

Am going downtown this afternoon and perhaps invest in some shoes and buy my books. I hope everything is OK at home. Don't work too hard nor worry about making me a coat. I shall get along nicely without it. I'll be glad when Monday comes.
With heaps of love,
Dorothy

September 24, 1928

Dear Dorothy,

I am ready to go to that band practice so will write now for if Daddy has time I want him to help turn the dining room rug around tonight. It seemed so good to talk to you. Perhaps we are wrong, but we hate to have you work this year, especially this semester and as long as you have had so much office experience we think that is the kind of work for you to do. I would suggest that you talk to the Dean or Dr. Seaton and ask for office work next year. If there are any odd jobs this year all right, but try to land it for next year. I would rather rent your room here than have you miss being in a sorority if they look good to you. I think there will be lots of girls in the sororities who have to be careful. I don't think you will be alone.

Have been fixing our elderberries ready to can. It is a slow job, but the pies will be good, I hope. I do hope nothing happens to prevent us coming over Sunday, for we can talk about things so much better now that you know all the details. Am anxious to know how you like your roommate but it is too soon to know.

I just called Lorene and she says your roommate is the worst in school and that you can't stand her, that she hasn't any background and just brags, so perhaps you had better watch for a chance for a change. Lorene wants to ride over with us Sunday and she said that she would go to Miss Gray and that she thought it was terrible for her to give you such a roommate. So you can be thinking about it and don't let Miss OK put a thing over on you. I am so mad about your roommate!

Last night we went over to see Dudley's pictures. He talked two hours. He surely does very well, if he had just a little fun in his make-up he would be a wonder, but he is deadly serious. I want Daddy to mail this so I'll kiss you bye.
Lovingly,
Mother

Sunday night

Dear Mother,

This has been a strenuous day, the worst I've had, but at last everything is settled and I am still rooming in 200! There has been a real mix up about rooms and last night Mrs. Wolfe called me downstairs after I was ready for bed and asked me how I would like to room with Olga (a sophomore) I can't take time to explain the whole mess, but the result was that Olga and I had no roommates and she wanted to room in 146 on first floor which is not as nice a room as this, and I wanted to room up here. Neither of us wanted to give in and after several sessions with Mrs. Wolfe and with the dean we were still far from a solution. This noon right after dinner the Dean called me into the library and talked to me about it and said that I shouldn't feel badly for I needn't give up the room unless I wanted to.

So finally Olga said she'd come up here. I feel rather selfish to let her do it, but on the other hand, I would have felt mean all year if I couldn't have this room. Anyway it is settled and Olga is moving in. She is a little blonde and rather sweet, I think, so expect to get along finely.

Went to chapel this morning and to two teas this afternoon. Had to wear my coat but didn't much mind. I had a lovely time at both teas and wasn't a bit scared. The girls were all lovely. We had a regular old confab at the Kappa Delta house and had difficulty in tearing ourselves away. My dress looked lovely and all the girls said it made me look lots shorter. I invested in some black satin slippers and am quite wild about them because they are so frivolous. Everyone likes them a lot. I wore them and my black felt hat which looked all right too. My cold cream and things came fine and thanks lots. I almost wish my winter coat were here, it is so beastly cold, but I expect it is almost too heavy to mail. Daddy's watch is keeping good time and I do so enjoy it. I wish I had time and space to write every little detail that happens, but I just can't so will have to tell you when I come home.

Next Saturday is a football game. Do you suppose there is any way I could get my winter coat by then? I may need it. I wish you could all come over soon, but I suppose that's too much to ask. I just have to get some sleep, so good-night.
Lovingly,
Dorothy

September 25, 1928

Dear Mother,

Thanks for the bundles. Everything was OK. We are still eating grapes by the cartload. The candy is gone, however, for we have had company all the time. They all appreciated the candy, especially when I told them who made it.

My roommate and I entertained seven last night and argued on the subject of souls. It was really quite thrilling. Today I only had two classes, but tomorrow I'm busy from 8 to 3. I am going to enjoy all my classes, I think. Tonight we'll take a light cut and study until late as we haven't done much today. I am invited to the

Kappa Delta parties this week and have accepted two of them. Last night one of the Delta Gammas invited me to a party Wed. night, so I'm going to that too. I have a slight chance of making Delta Gamma if I want to. The Kappa Deltas are being wonderful. They come down to see me and appear to enjoy it. Of course I may not get a bid, but I shan't worry about it. So I expect this week will be rather exciting.

I hope you can come over this weekend. You know, I'd rather like to see you all! Funny, isn't it? Have just been to a tea in the recreation room and feel that I shall never care for food again, but I suppose I'll develop a real appetite by dinner time. I bought some marquisette curtains and now all we lack is bedspreads and valances. Olga says she can't afford a spread for a month or so, and I haven't hurried about getting mine. I enjoyed Daddy's letter and shall answer it soon. Maybe I'll have a little surprise for the successful candy maker.
Lovingly,
Dorothy

September 27, 1928

Dear Mother,

Went to Delta Gamma lodge last night and had a simply wonderful time dancing. I danced all evening more or less successfully and even led! We played bridge too and had refreshments at little tables. (Daddy's favorite salad too!) We got the cutest little blue and white berets for favors and got in at just 10 p.m.

Tonight I'm going to the Kappa Delta party. I am enclosing the invitation they sent. Planning to attend the parties checked. So you see I am literally rushed to death between trying to study Greek and go out nights too. Greek is pretty fierce, I think. Hope sent me some candy yesterday. Wasn't that spiffy? I hope you can come Sunday and we can talk real hard.

It seems to me you've been cleaning house rather strenuously— getting rugs moved and everything.

Oh say, over at the Delta Gamma lodge there are two lovely old candelabra and the dearest little picture hanging between them. It is oval and shows three young girls grouped together with their

hair hanging in curls. I know you'd want to steal it! I must go to the
library now and get busy. More later.
Much love to you all,
Dorothy

September 28, 1928

Dear Dorothy,

J.M., Billy and Gerry are playing some game that I am not
sure they should be playing, but at least I know where they are. I
have had a rather strenuous day—trying to houseclean this week.

This afternoon the Persis class met at Aunt Ada's as a little
surprise on Mrs. Crawford. They gave her a pretty rose colored
sweater. She was so pleased. How wonderful to be so beautiful inside that everyone just loves you!

While I was there an auto full of folks came, and Mrs. B. sent
them to the office and then she called me. Daddy came after me
and by that time it was almost 6 'clock. I didn't know what to do—I
was all in and not a thing in the house to eat and five extra to feed.
I finally asked them to stay, but they decided to go. It was an old
schoolmate of mine, her husband and little girl and another couple. I
felt so bad about it.

I am planning to go to the convention in Ann Arbor in the
morning. Mrs. Voorheis is driving over. I ought not to go, but I don't
seem to know how to rest at home, so I guess I'll go for the day.
Aunt Ada wants me to stay over for Friday. It would be just lovely,
but I can't.

I am so sorry I didn't send your coat with Brad, but it needed
a few stitches and whoever thought it would be so cold. I sent your
sweater so you can put it under your coat. I had no box that would
hold your winter coat and I couldn't bear to wad it up when it had
just come from the cleaners. We'll bring it Sunday.

Mr. Waldron had a chance to lease Daddy's office and
came to see if he could get along with less room. It was rather
queer for Daddy had been trying to see him to see if he could
rent out some of the office or make some adjustment. Daddy is
going to move into Mr. W's suite and will sell some of his furniture. Will tell you all about it later. We are very much pleased to
have the overhead lowered.

Took this letter to Ann Arbor and thought I would be able to mail it there, but was not, so will finish now. Mrs. Voorheis, Mrs. Stalter, Mrs. Lyons, and I went over. President, treasurer, and secretary were guests of the church at the noon luncheon. That was unusual and nice. I received some very helpful ideas for my work as treasurer this year. Aunt Ada stayed all night. I would have liked to have done likewise, but couldn't think of it.

Have to clean house, iron and go downtown tomorrow. J.M. is going with me to pick out his own birthday present. He thinks it is a real treat to come to Albion for his birthday. Lorene will not eat with us, for she wants to be with Brad. She called me last night for Albion news. I was sorry I told you what she said about the roommate for I found out she doesn't know her well.

With lots of love till Sunday,
Mother

Sunday night

Dear Mother,

Your visit made me feel oh so much better. I guess I kind of wanted to see my family. Everything seems brighter and more fun. I have studied this evening and got almost through! Even Greek doesn't seem so bad.

I found a bid to the Delta Gamma formal dinner tomorrow night and am quite thrilled. I think I'll wear my black velvet formal—I hope that's all right. My coat looks awfully good, I think, and everything is rosy. I'll try and get home next week, but Saturday night is informal pledge night and if I take a sorority bid I'll have to be here, but could come home Sunday morning with Brad if he does as he thinks he will.

I do hope everything is fine at home and tell J.M. I'm getting him a present, but won't tell what. I must get to bed, but send bushels of love to my dear family.

Yours the OK Collegiate Student,
Dorothy

October 1, 1928

Dear Dorothy,

It is 9 o'clock and J.M. has not come from Scout meeting yet. I have been alone all the eve. This was the day of the P.W. Club luncheon. I was so tired it seemed as if I couldn't go, let alone make a fool of myself, but I did think the program went over well. The papers were all very clever and our rube band seemed to make quite a hit. The meeting was at Fox and Hounds Inn.

I wasn't quite satisfied with my visit yesterday. I wanted to stay all night or else have you come home with us. We arrived home at 9, and put Aunt Minnie on the Detroit bus. She enjoyed the day very much. I hope you will be able to get a little rest this week. You looked tired to me. I don't suppose there will be much rest until this sorority rush is over.

I asked Lorene what the Delta Gammas were like and she said they were very nice girls, but she thought you would be more at home with the Kappa Deltas. She said the DG's were more society girls and did no philanthropic work. She said the KD's would be dreadfully disappointed if you don't choose them.

I liked the looks of the girls as a whole very much, also Miss Gray, and I think you will be very happy when things get settled down a bit so it is not quite so hectic.

I hear J.M.'s bugle approaching. I can hardly wait until you come home. Lorene says you cannot come this week, for if you do, you will miss the sorority pledging. If trying to write home so often is too much for you don't do it. I don't want to be selfish about it. I'll probably get used to your being away before the year is out and I guess if the other mothers can get along without letters I can.

Tuesday a.m.—Well Daddy went away early before I was up so your letter didn't get to go. He moved into the corner suite on Perry and Pike St. yesterday. He has one small office and use of the reception office for $40 per and Mr. Waldron pays half of Mrs. Warren's salary, so that is quite a cut in overhead. Mr. Waldron has promised to buy his big desk and another man is looking at another one, so he is unloading some of his indebtedness.

Yesterday Mr. Spencer called him in to Detroit and wanted to make him some kind of a proposition to build the same sort of a plan there, but it looks to us as if it should be made a going concern here first and I do not want Daddy working both places. It's too hard. Anyway it pleased Daddy to think Mr. S. thought so well of his plan.

I thought your slippers were real pretty for party wear and think everything you have is just as good looking as the rest, but having so much doing, you haven't any too many changes, so I will make you more as fast as I can get time.

Now I must get busy. With heaps of love to my little girl who just had to go to school. If you get lonesome, just remember you wouldn't be happy if you were home and couldn't go. And as much as I miss you I am glad you want to go to school.
Lovingly,
Mother

October 3, 1928

Dear Dorothy,

Your letter just came and made me so happy. I came home from Albion so blue. It is hard enough to have you away and you didn't seem happy, so of course if you weren't happy, I wasn't. I suppose you just felt alone over there and it looked like a heavy load, but you forgot we are behind you.

Went to market with Mrs. B. this morning and got a bushel of peaches, so I am sure busy today. Glad you got the Delta Gamma bid. I am quite sure you will get a bid to both, but which one to take, I don't know.

If you can come Sunday with Brad I would be so tickled. You looked so kind of lonesome we thought maybe we would try to make it again Sunday, but if you can get a chance to come we would rather have you come home this time.

Just called the office. Daddy has gone to Detroit again. I would not be surprised at anything that might happen—even moving to Detroit, but I wouldn't want to. Guess I won't cross that bridge until I come to it.

Daddy is home, but sleepy tonight, so my evenings so far this week have not been very exciting. Would like to go to the church reception tomorrow night if Daddy doesn't have to work.

My birdie sang a wee bit for me today. Maybe Teddy wasn't glad to see us Sunday night! I have some mending I must get at tonight.

Hope you have a wonderful time at the Delta Gamma formal. Lorene said you would get a bid to the Kappa Delta formal too, so you will sure have a good time this week if parties will make one. I expect next week you will be a pledge and doing the shoe cleaning for all. Let me know if you can come Sunday.
Lovingly,
Mother

October 3, 1928

Dear Mother,
    Your letter came this morning—also the stamps—a gentle hint! Thanks, I needed some. The rush is not yet over and it seems as if it never would be, but am enjoying it all to the utmost. I went to the Delta Gamma formal dinner and had a very good time. I ate with Eleanor again, and we had a four piece orchestra, which was real peppy. We danced between courses and finally, the Sigma Chis came and serenaded us and we all rushed out on the porch. Then we sang the Delta Gamma song and we departed.
    My dress looked very nice and Olga water-waved my hair. Some of the girls wore elaborate party dresses, others black, and some very simple ones. Our favors were little pottery vases. Mine is pale blue and real ducky. You'll probably want it.
    Yesterday afternoon I went to Jackson with Frances, Hannah, and Margaret (in the coupe). We went to all the little gift shops and had a lovely time. We didn't get home in time for dinner, but didn't mind that. Tonight we are going down the river on a hike and roast. Must go to class now.
Lovingly,
Dorothy

Excerpts from the 1929 Susanna Wesley Annual
Reprinted with permission of Albion College

SERENADES

Out of the night we hear the sound of footsteps, muffled voices, a low murmur and then a burst of voices into song. Can you guess what it is? Sure—it's one of the biggest thrills of dormitory night life—a serenade!

Many nights during the year, whether there is snow on the ground or balmy moonlight, the court is frequented with fraternity men. They come to announce the engagement of a brother or merely to entertain us.

When the Sigma Nus visit us, we rush to the windows as we hear, "The girls are fair but they can't compare——." We jump from our beds to hear the Sigma Chis sing of their sweethearts. We envy the A.T.O. girls. Some of us are the sweethearts of Delta Sigma Phi's, but even when we hear the T.K.E.'s sing our heartbeats quicken.

The men can hardly know how we enjoy these surprises and how much we look forward to the traditional fraternity serenades.

October 5, 1928

Dear Dorothy,

Last night we went to the reception at the church. Don't know when I have enjoyed one more, as all the people we knew were there. Aunt Ada called me early this a.m. and said she had to iron and couldn't I bring my ironing over there, so I did. I had a big one too. Finished it and all my darning, also cooked some grapes, ready to make jelly. It had been so long since I had been over. I enjoyed the day very much.

I think I know how you feel about the sorority—if the Pontiac girls had not been loyal and invited you, you would have been hurt. They will be hurt if you do not go Kappa Delta, but I think it is fine for you to get bids to all the parties, for when rushing is over, it is all over. Yes, I expect I'll want the pottery vase, unless I'm lucky and find something old. Haven't seen anything so far this week, but you never can tell. I'm going to wash the kitchen windows and have clean curtains in the morning—get cleaned up for fear my daughter comes home.

With bushels of love,
Mother

October 5, 1928

Dear Mother,

It is a misty, moisty day with the wind rustling in the trees and the air damp with rain. It seems rather nice although it is cloudy and dark. Tonight is the formal party and I have yet to fix the bow on my dress, but will get that done this afternoon. Have been to philosophy and Bible classes this morning and enjoyed them. The Dean is certainly enjoyable and so is Dr. Goodrich. It seems I'll never get my studying done, but I suppose it will be that way all the time.

Last night I went to a spread after 10 p.m. with the Delta Gammas downstairs in room 100. Had a lovely time and were serenaded by ATOs in the court. It was hugely exciting. Tomorrow is the M.S.C. game and from what Fleming writes, I fear that we are to be beaten rather disgracefully. I wish I could come home this week, but I don't see it working out that way. Anyway, I'll come next week.

I must finish my Greek now. I got three letters yesterday—wasn't I lucky—from Helen, Hope, and you. Have found I have a roommate with Hope's own love of study and work. How life repeats itself!
Lovingly,
Dorothy

Dear Dorothy,

Mrs. King called me just as we were ready to leave for Detroit, saying you wanted your light dress. It wasn't washed and Lorene offered to let you have the one I am sending so I thought it would be better. Just heard Albion beat M.S.C. Hurrah for Albion. Fleming will be surprised.

Frances S. called her father this a.m. and told him they thought you were going Delta Gamma. They are pretty much worried. I am anxious to know what you have decided and everything else.

Daddy had to go to Detroit, so J.M. and Billy and I went along. We stopped at the zoo and did the cave end. Then we ate our lunch at Palmer Park. I stayed at the library while Daddy had his interview. Then we came home, went after the dress for you and now I am pulling things together and getting ready for bed.

J.M. is sending for material to build an airship—maybe that will keep him busy awhile. Next month he will deliver papers twice a week.

Made grape jelly this a.m. and cleaned up the house because you might be home tomorrow, but I know Brad can't come and I guess you are pretty busy yourself. I'll be glad when the rushing is all over, so you can get down to business, but of course you have been having a wonderful time, you have to think about that. Hope I have done all right about the dress.

Lovingly,
Mother

October 7, 1928

Dear Mother,

The dress came and your note. Thanks so much. I thought I would need it for formal pledging, but perhaps I won't. You might be pleased to know that I went Kappa Delta, after much thought and worry. It was almost a draw between the two and I could hardly decide, even after visiting the Dean twice. The atmosphere was electric Saturday morning and there was even some weeping by the girls who were torn between sororities. However, they all seemed happy at night and ate with their different sororities.

The Kappa Delta girls were a little surprised about me I think. They weren't a bit sure what I'd do. I had a wonderful time at the formal Friday night and my dress looked lovely. I felt most thrilled and happy. I like the KD pledges very much, better than those of the other sororities, I think. We have 25, which is more than was expected. The others haven't nearly as many.

Saturday night was informal pledging and after going to the lodge and being hugged and kissed all around and getting our green and white ribbons to wear, we all piled into cars and went down to Mitchell's and had ice cream. They lined the tables all up in a row and we ate. Then the Delta Gammas came in and we both yelled and sang and played the player piano and then had to leave, for the Alpha Xis were coming in to eat too. Today we wore our ribbons and went to church and the frat pledges were all there too (at least Sigma Nus were). Then all the sororities grouped at tables at dinner, so I guess everybody knows where we all belong now. The Delta

Gammas all congratulated me and were awfully sweet to me. So that's that. I am beginning to feel very much at home now and can hardly wait for things to get into full swing.

I wish you would write the Dean giving me permission for out of town and also permission to ride home with people. Make it general enough so that I won't get in wrong. I'll write more later—too sleepy now. Am coming home next week for sure and am quite excited.

With much love,

Dorothy

October 10, 1928

Dear Dorothy,

Don't know whether I can keep awake or not, but will try. Yesterday I cleaned around all day, but this morning when Daddy called up and asked if I wanted to go to Oxford, I just bunched everything and went. It was just beautiful—the trees are so lovely this year. I went to see Mrs. Purse and got a ducky little majolica fan, and then to see Mrs. Mitz and bought a milk glass bread tray and the little amber lamp for you if you want it. If not I'll sell it to Mr. Harding. It is very pretty, I think.

Your letter was a long time coming. I have been so anxious to know what you would do and Lorene and Veda were calling each day. You seemed to be rather important in this rush.

I knew it was going to be hard for you to decide. I wanted you to go Delta Gamma, but I doubted if it would be wise, for after all, this is your hometown. Am so anxious to see you and hear everything. Will you please write me right away and mail it on that 4 or 9 p.m. train, so I will get it the next morning, telling me about coming home. Are you going to have a chance to ride with Frances or Brad? I want to know because Mrs. King and Mrs. Luther have called me and, of course, if you came with them we will have to plan to meet or take you back to Ann Arbor or wherever we decide. They seem to be planning to come by bus to Ann Arbor. Lorene says it is better to go by train. Am so excited about your coming home, I can't think of anything else. It has seemed pretty long, but I'm okay if you are happy. Well, Daddy has just come and it is late so I think I'd

better trot off to bed, so I can get up and snap to it in the morning.
Your name is in the paper tonight.
With heaps of love,
Mother

October 9, 1928

Dear Mother,

Your letter just came this noon and I am writing my plans as well as possible. I can't come home until Saturday noon, so expect to go to Jackson by bus, then take the flyer either to Detroit or Ann Arbor. If you could meet me in Ann Arbor it would be nice. I'll try and let you know soon.

I can't remember what I wrote you last, but anyway I'm now formally pledged KD and have a pledge pin and everything. Mrs. Wolfe just came in and wanted me to help with some posters for the W.F.M.S. and I guess I'll do it.

I had a letter from Aunt Minnie this morning and she sent me a dollar bill to do something with—join the Y.W. if I wanted to. It was a real peppy letter.

Dr. Harrop gave me A- in my Greek notebook, so I'm feeling quite uppity! I'll tell you all about him when I see you.

This is a glorious fall afternoon, but I must get to studying so I can come home soon. You must be getting pretty good with the antique business.
With loads of love to my dear family,
Dorothy

October 19, 1928
Vassar, Michigan

Dear Dorothy,

Well, here we are. Left home soon as possible after lunch, came Baldwin road, then Oakwood, and it was a beautiful drive. I stopped a few times to hunt antiques, but had no luck. Reached here at 4:30. Pretty good for us.

Have been listening to the radio all the evening. Daddy is

going back home in the morning and then come up Saturday, then we'll go home Sunday.

We received an invitation to Homecoming from Albion and we would like very much to go but thought it all over and decided that it would be better to come later, when you might be getting a little lonesome. Also thought that with all there was to do, you would be pretty busy. Next year we will try to come and stay over.

Daddy deposited the $15 for you. We are so glad you are having such a wonderful time in the sorority.

I don't want to be an old crow and croak, but you will have to watch and pick out the things you can do easily, and when you know you are getting too tired, refuse to do things, because if you have to work next summer you can't afford a breakdown. It is just like any other kind of work—no one will look out for your strength, they will let you do all you will do.

Friday a.m.—Daddy has gone home and it is raining. Not very nice weather for Homecoming so far.

They have formed a dramatics club at the church and will put on something every other Sunday night and Lorene heads it up. I think John Merritt is included. I was so happy about it.

Everyone is well up here. Aunt Lottie sends her love and wishes you were along. Hope comes tonight.

Well I must get up and help Aunt Lottie with the work. J.M. is out gathering walnuts so you can have some at school if you want them. I am going downtown after a while and I may just look in at the secondhand store. Will write again soon. With heaps of love to my busy little girl.
Lovingly,
Mother

Thursday

Dear Mother,

Your box just came and I have been downstairs pressing the dresses and my room is cleaned and the new spreads on the bed. We look really spiffy!

No school today as it was cleanup day. However, I didn't do any cleaning up or raking, for Betty Harmon and I started out early this morning, gunning for an idea for the parade Saturday. We were to take a book for the idea of our float, but after choosing *Treasure Island*, we found that the DGs had that one. We racked our brains for hours and I finally suggested *The Iliad*—using the Trojan horse, but nobody thought it practicable. However, tonight everyone is happy for we have ordered the horse made (a huge white one) and have gotten shields and spears for the soldiers and are planning on having Helen of Troy in the procession too. (This sketch shows the idea—with a real black horse in front, then Helen of Troy on a chariot, followed by an eight foot tall Trojan horse pushed and pulled by pledges.) So everything is set and all we have to do is execute it. The parade is Saturday morning. I wish you could come for it. The campus is all raked and decorated and the frat houses trimmed. Have been working but will get a little rest now. No classes Saturday.

Later—just came from dinner—all is enthusiasm over home-coming. You'd better come.
Love,
Dorothy

October 23, 1928

Dear Mother,

This hectic weekend is finished and we are back at the old grind again. The football game was fine and so were the plays Saturday night.

Today is founders' day for KD and we are all wearing white rosebuds. The KD inspector is here and we are all on our best behavior. Tonight is a potluck at the lodge, but I don't see how I'll make it, for I have a bluebook in history tomorrow. I have another real A in Greek! I don't mind Prof. Harrup as much as I did. In fact I get a good laugh most every day.

The roommate business is rapidly coming to a head. I have broken the news to Olga that Dorothy H. and I want to room together. Of course, she didn't get the reason why, so I had to come right out and tell her that our temperaments were not congenial and that some sort of move would have to be made. It seems rather brutal, but she hasn't much sensibility, or sensitiveness, and is already trying to be good so that I won't want to change. She has been clean and neat around the room and oh, so very gracious in everything, but it won't work. She doesn't know her opponent! And I have stood all I can stand without going mad.

I must be at that studying now, so goodbye. Thanks for the $15. I shall be very careful that the rest of my money holds out as long as possible. I still have $9.20 besides some cash.

With heaps of love.

Dorothy

October 23, 1928

Dear Dorothy,

Have not seemed to be able to accomplish much today. Worked out in the yard a little while and spent some time with Daddy. He seems to need me most of the time.

Tonight I made six more of the new towels, so they are all finished, and I mended your old lavender pajamas which will do to wear when you are home.

Lorene called up and told me all she could about homecoming. Think you must have had a real time. She seems to think you are making a real place for yourself among both students and faculty. She said she had never known anyone to make such headway in such a short time and that the Kappa Deltas were very proud of you. Lorene thought your float should have had the prize.

It has simply poured all evening. Daddy has been home as it's too wet to go out. John Merritt just came in pretty wet from scout meeting. Will try to get the upstairs hoed out tomorrow. I don't have interesting things to write like you do.

Daddy deposited your check in your savings account, so that's taken care of.

There is a bunch of storage goods for sale down on Auburn and I think I will go down and look it over today if I can.

Am expecting a letter from you this morning. They seem a little far between, but of course I understand. Don't forget us cause we are still here big as life only our life seems a little tame with a fourth of our family in Albion, but of course we wouldn't wish it different. Had any more A's? Are you having any time for study? Perhaps there will be a little lull now.

I understand you play nights and sleep daytimes regardless

of meal times. Hope you won't get to sleeping in your walking!
Well I must get busy.
Heaps of love,
Mother

October 24, 1928

Dear Mother,

Have had a strenuous day with five classes, chapel, and an
hour and a half meeting of pledges with the KD inspector, so I have
not done any studying. Have merely written a few letters and loafed
this evening. We had a wing meeting and were reproved for too
much noise in our wing, so shall have to reform or be punished.

Miss Gray is not back yet and at present my roommate is in
a most repentant mood. I wish the Dean would hurry back while it
lasts. We had a blue book in history, which was very easy. Hope I
make a good grade on it. Tomorrow is my study day and I think I
shall arise early and begin the good work soon.

I like the KDs better all the time. They certainly are darling
and so very nice to me. I went to Eunella's room tonight and lay on
the bed and watched the dates go out. If only I could find the right
tall man, I'd step out myself. I must wash and jump into bed now.
Goodnight. Heaps of love to you all,
Dorothy

P.S. Philosophy is thr-i-lling!

Kappa Delta Lodge, Albion College
Reprinted with permission of Albion College

October 25, 1928

Dear Dorothy,

Did not get a
letter written last night.
I was just finishing the
dishes when Herbert
came over and wanted
me to stay with Veda. She
had a tooth pulled yesterday and went to pieces,
so my evening was shot
and Daddy was alone.

Yesterday morn I was at the office with Daddy, so I didn't have much of a day. Cleaned the little bookcase at the head of the stairs. Transplanted some of the plants into Mrs. B's fernery, but I am afraid I'm not going to like it. Worked a few minutes on your dress—do not know whether it will be a success or not.

Was so glad to get your letter. They are few and far between. I hope the roommate affair straightens out all right, sorry it had to be so. Perhaps she wouldn't annoy everyone as she has you.

Daddy left before I finished so I didn't get this mailed. It is eleven a.m. and I have cleaned the bathroom and most of the up-stairs, washed J.M.'s scout uniform and extra knickers and done my own little dab. Been to the store, so now it will be lunch next.

I have the rosewood clock ticking again. Don't know why I thought I couldn't fix it before.

J.M. goes to the dramatic club tonight and I am so glad for ev-ery night that is planned. He is so much better than he was. I don't know what has caused the change, but he has been like a different person. If we could only understand the causes, but I have no idea.

Have lunch ready—breakfast sausage, spaghetti, lettuce, and apple and date salad. Not so much, but all good, of course.

Uncle Charles and Aunt Elizabeth just walked in. I guess they will stay to dinner so my afternoon and evening are planned full now. Heaps of love,
Mother

October 29, 1928

Dear Mother,

Have finished classes for this day and have had a blue book in philosophy, in which I didn't make much of a mark probably. I have been awfully busy studying these last few days. We've had blue books in most everything and it certainly keeps me jumping.

Made a big hit with Dr. Goodrich when he found I was tak-ing Greek! I just got my history blue book back and was all prepared for the worst and then I got A-. Pretty good, eh? The freshman marks are out now I expect. I haven't much idea what I'll get but Miss Rogers told one of the girls I was doing well in Biology, so I'm not going to worry. We didn't do anything very exciting over the week-end except win another football game and I really did get to go to

Sunday dinner this time.

Our room is changed around again and looks real spiffy. We have our beds side by each with the little book case between. No change has been made yet but we hope something will happen pretty soon.

The afternoon is simply glorious today—so crisp and cold and sunshiny. I'm getting the biggest thrill out of my work this year. I fairly ache to learn a lot. Each class is interesting and I do so want to take more courses. I'm going to attempt to write an oration for the contest—just for fun. I haven't chosen my topic yet.

I'll rush downtown and mail this while the sun is bright and then come home and memorize some sorority stuff, eat, and go to sorority meeting afterward. I'm awfully keen about our lodge and everything.

Much love,
Dorothy

October 31, 1928

Dear Mother,

Thought I would get a letter off to you this afternoon, but stayed at the library instead and did some much needed work. Everything is coming along swimmingly, I think. I'm buckling right down to studying and really hope I'll make some decent grades. Freshman marks are out this week, but they don't mean much. We had a house meeting tonight and were duly scolded for not observing quiet hours, so we feel quite humiliated. Tonight D. Hawley and I took a late permission as it was the last of the month, and stayed out until nine p.m.!

I do so want you to come this weekend if you can. I really think Sunday would give us a little more time, although I am through classes at nine or ten on Saturday and we could have a real spiffy day. Well, do whichever you wish and I'll look for you. Our Thanksgiving recess has been granted, so I'll come home Wed. afternoon after three. Hurrah! If you come this weekend, will you please bring me a sheet or two? I'm all out of them and haven't had time to wash. I have to turn in now so goodnight.

Heaps of love,
Dorothy

Friday eve

Dear Dorothy,

Have your box ready and will take it over to King's tonight, then if we don't get to go over you will have that much. I put in one double sheet. If you don't want it, send it back and I'll get yours laundered and back to you. If we come it will be Sunday for Daddy will be busy tomorrow.

Mr. Bingham came this morning and wanted me to get the furniture together that the players will use for *Abraham Lincoln* Monday night. I am quite thrilled about it. Lorene and I are going to choose it. There are some things in Mrs. Hoffman's studio and we are going to see if she will loan them.

My glass plates came at last, just like Aunt Ada's. I think I made a pretty good bargain. I have been cleaning house. Cleaned out the secretary, the bookcase, and washed the woodwork in living and dining rooms. Hope I can get a little enamel on next week. Am sorry I cannot tell you positively about our coming, so don't look for us, then if we come, you will be glad and if we don't, you won't be so disappointed.

Hope you like the eats. I didn't have time to bake anything else, just the fried cakes. The cookies are not fresh, but maybe they will taste good.
Heaps of love,
Mother

October 31, 1928

Dear Dorothy,

If you could see this house and the ironing, I am afraid you would think I ought not to be scribbling to you. I worked all day Monday, just cleaning and feeding, the regular routine.

Yesterday afternoon I went to the County Federation meeting. It was not especially interesting. Hunted antiques on the way down and back, but did not find anything I could buy.

It was cabbage night. Billie and J.M. came in at nine bells, popped corn and made a mess of the house, but were real good. Tonight is Halloween. I don't know what they will pull tonight, nothing serious I guess.

Daddy finally sold Mr. W. some more furniture. Of course,

he would not pay cash, but his rent is paid for a year and that helps some. He has let Mrs. Warren go, as he really did not need her at all and it was quite an expense. He seems quite peppy this morning and is right out after business.

I am proud to bursting of your marks. I really did not expect much with all the parties you have had.

Daddy was out to Auburn Heights Monday for a few minutes and I went with him for a drive. Found a green majolica pitcher and leaf and a big round salt and ten little salts—none of them very wonderful. Of course the leaf will go to Aunt Lottie as she has wanted one.

Birdie is singing to me a little this morning. Daddy called and said he wouldn't be home for lunch, so I won't be able to post your letter until morning.

Have my ironing started. Think I will run out for an hour on a hunt for antiques although I do not seem to have much luck in Pontiac. I would like to get some place that had not been thoroughly combed. The dealers have just scoured the country everywhere. I wonder how I ever find anything.

Do not plan on our coming this week. We don't know yet whether we will be able to or not, but if we don't, will send your laundry with the King's. You know we always want to come, but we may not feel we can have the expense this week. If you were in Ann Arbor, I guess we would see you every week. That part of it would be wonderful, but I prefer Albion for you.

We are so glad you are enjoying your work. Think the oration idea is fine, and am anxious to hear what you get in your other blue books. Wouldn't it be nice if we could broadcast back and forth, but I am afraid we wouldn't get anything else done.
Just bushels of love.
Lovingly,
Mother

Sunday

Dear Dorothy,

It is the quiet time of the afternoon, but it is too dark and dull to want to drive or anything like that. J.M. is out playing. Lorene and Daddy are reading, so I'm going to write to my little girl. Uncle

George and Aunt Ada went to Port Hope Sunday, so Lorene came yesterday about 5 p.m. She brought me such pretty flowers.

We all went to church this a.m. J.M. and Lorene stayed to Sunday school, and I came home and pulled things together and had our dinner. Lorene and I have been visiting about everything. Soon now Daddy will take her and J.M. down to the church to get ready for the picture, *The Angelus*, which the dramatic guild is going to put on tonight.

We kept wishing you and Brad would come over today. I did extra baking yesterday because I knew Lorene would be here and I was in hopes someone would be going to Albion, so I could send something, but I couldn't find any one who was.

I have a new antique. Aunt Ada and I think it is lovely. It is another lamp—clear glass, but shaped very much like Ada's vaseline lamp. You will like it, I am sure.

Am wondering if the roommate question is settled yet? Lorene thought your pinch bottle filled with green water would be very pretty in your room.

I can't tell what I have done the past week. Haven't attended a meeting or been anywhere but I kept so busy. Did I tell you Aunt Elizabeth invited us there for Thanksgiving, but I told her we would wait till we knew what you were able to do? Aunt Lottie invited us for Christmas, so we are quite invited.

Read a book I enjoyed this week—*Forever Free* by Honore Willsie Morrow. I do so enjoy anything by her. It is a novel of the life of Lincoln in the White House.

I hope you are writing me a long, long letter with all the doings. I was so proud of your A in Greek. That was even more than I was expecting. I hope you get the weekend off for Thanksgiving so we can have a long visit.

Bushels of love to our little girl,

Mother

Tuesday

Dear Dorothy,

Received both of your letters. We arrived home about 8:30 Sunday night and were not very tired, but of course had a late lunch so I haven't felt especially fine since.

Monday afternoon I spent with the stage manager getting the furniture together. The stage looked very nice. Had our little walnut table and paisley shawl there. The play was very good and the church was just packed.

Went to vote first thing this a.m., washed your dress and will try to get ironing done tomorrow and then I can send your box Thursday.

John M. left a Pontiac Library book in the dorm library—*Danny the Freshman*. Will you get it right away and be sure to bring it when you come home?

Daddy went to Detroit today. Hope he gets home in time for dinner, which I must get busy and get right away. Aunt Ada wanted me to come over today but I was too busy.

I don't suppose you will agree with me, but I think the reason there is no dating with a certain class of boys is because they have an idea that all the girls are fast and they are not interested in them and, of course, some work and have very limited incomes.

I am glad if the roommate situation clears up. I was sorry not to have treated Olga nicer. She won't think we are very nice, I am afraid, and it is well to have even the respect of the enemy. Although I think most of the things that irritate you are things she cannot help—just a part of her.

If you change I do hope it will be very much better for you are giving up a lot to go on third floor.

The phone hasn't even rung tonight. John M. is working on his history. It won't hurt us to pay for all the A's he gets, I'm afraid.

If you can get an ad in the paper have it say—"Wanted small melodeon and old sampler and paisley shawl." Either list my name and address or you can have them give you a box number, then you would have to go after it. Do it any way you like and it will be all right. I am afraid it will be too late for this week.

With lots of love,
Mother

Susanna Wesley Hall—Room 214
November 7, 1928

Dear Mother,

It is the evening of an eventful day. Mrs. Wolfe has done a real favor for us and has had her own sweet time doing it too. I am now rooming in 214 with Lydian Halliday, and am simply enjoying it to the utmost! Our room is lovely and the largest on the wing and close to the phone, the dean's room and the stairway. Lyd is a perfect dear, so considerate and very interesting. In fact I like her more and more as I know her. I am truly happy now and college is really college and I love it all. Lyd has traveled a lot and is a Congregational minister's daughter from New York State. Her sister is here too.

We have had a busy day. Classes all day and all the moving mess too, but now we are all straightened up and look very spiffy.

Thursday afternoon—your letter came this morning—the material is very pretty, I think. It's a lovely color. The Dean just came in to visit us and see our room. I do hope you can come over with Lorene. I'll put the ad in the paper.

Fleming wrote me and said he almost wished he were at Albion—it all sounded so good and he said he'd like to come over some Sunday. I think it would be fun.

I must go study now and be real good. We have a birthday dinner next Wednesday and then it's just two weeks till Thanksgiving! Heaps of love to you all,
Dorothy

Dear Dorothy,

You will think this letter is from Milford. I went in to get my pen from Uncle Dalton and he filled it with green ink as you see.

Well your letter was a surprise. I am so anxious to hear all about it—how it was done, who is with Olga and how you got a nice roommate too. I am so glad. I felt so sorry for you since Sunday. But I was afraid they were not going to change you. I remember Lydian. I liked her the first Sunday we were over. Lorene is real crazy about her, thinks she is very clever, full of pep and generally lovely. Hurrah!

Saturday I worked around all the forenoon. In the afternoon, J.M. was at the office with Daddy. Aunt Ada and Lorene asked me to go out to the antique shops at Bloomfield. I got an odd candlestick from Dr. Chapman's home.

Daddy, J.M. and I were home all eve and were just thinking of bed when Mrs. Barrett came running in and said their house had been robbed, so we had to go over and the police came. They were evidently hunting for money. They broke a hole in the glass of the porch door and ransacked everything but fortunately there was no money in the house.

We just got home nicely, when she came again and said Connely's house had been entered so I went over there where the same thing had been done. The police came again and told us they had also broken into a place on Tasmania. They took the title of Barrett's car. You would have laughed to have seen J.M.—he had seven knives, his bayonet and a hammer, in bed with him and I do not think he slept much, he was so excited.

Went to church, on time too, and had a splendid sermon. I am planning to stay home every day this week and see if I can't at least get the velvet part of your dress finished.

I haven't decided about coming over with Lorene. I thought perhaps you would rather I would come when you have had a chance to know Lydian better, although if there is no one using the guest room I could sleep there. I feel a bit shabby too—you can write me what you think about it and then I'll do what seems best. Let me know right away.
Love from the family,
Mother

November 9, 1928

Dear Dorothy,

I am sleepy but I guess I can stay awake long enough to write to you, a note, anyway. Well we are surely happy over the election returns, aren't we? It was some landslide for Hoover, more than I dreamed of.

J.M. is over to Lorene's tonight. The drama guild is meeting there and they are going to have angel food cake. Wow—he even took a bath—he is quite thrilled over the guild and it sure is an opportunity for him.

I did not go to Detroit after all as it just seemed as if I could not make it. I baked cookies for my little girl this morning and packed her box. I hope they are good. I thought they looked wonderful, but I didn't dare eat one for I have been having one of my times since Sunday, when I am using mostly orange juice. But J.M. pronounced them great.

This afternoon the Seminole Ladies Aide Circle had a lovely time. They took over 150 ladies out to Cranbrook and went through the school and church. It was a real treat. The school is very, very nice, and the church is beautiful. They played the organ and the chimes for us then we came back and stopped at Mrs. Cloonan's lovely new home for tea.

Daddy will deposit $10 for you in the morning. I forgot to give him your bank book this noon. You can let us know if you need more before you come home.

I have a missionary meeting tomorrow afternoon. I want to go downtown before that as well as clean the house in the a.m., so I think I will be a busy lady.

Must go to bed. Teddy is asleep on his pillow and Daddy in his chair. J.M. is not here yet.
Lots of love,
Mother

P.S. Daddy got a check for $98 from the city case and will get two more checks during the year. That's better than nothing, isn't it?

November 10, 1928
Saturday night

Dear Mother,

Your box of cookies and nuts came Friday afternoon, as well as the rest of the needed and desired articles. The cookies are delicious and much in demand. Tonight I have been up in Margaret's room (eating as usual). She is entertaining her friends Gladys and Virginia this weekend. We've had a real good time today, but I haven't accomplished much.

We had our first snowfall last night and this morning the evergreens outside our window were lovely and white with a burden of snow. I love our room and am so very happy over the change in roommates that it seems that nothing could annoy me. We beat Hillsdale 27-0 today and added another star to our football crown.

Tonight we had a YWCA old-fashioned party so Phyllis and I decided we'd go for a little while. Phyllis had an old-fashioned costume and I made a colonial one in about five minutes. Used my black satin pajamas as knee breeches, tied ribbons on them, borrowed a black velvet jacket, did my hair in a tight pigtail, pinned a lace hankie to my bosom and completed the knockout with my white shirt and a black Windsor tie.

Sunday p.m.—I am studying up in M's room. Have a lot to do as I have loafed over the weekend as usual. Just two weeks and three days till Thanksgiving.

Heaps of love,
Dorothy

November 13, 1928

Dear Mother,

Have talked and giggled until I'm all tired out. Lyd is a scream when she gets started. We don't know what all the fun is over, but anyway it's a good time.

Freshman marks came out yesterday. I had all B's except philosophy, for which no mark was handed in. My B in Bible was a minus. (I wrote a C plus test) Margaret got a B and wrote the same kind of test, so I am rather disgusted at Dr. Goodrich. However, minuses don't count in marks anyway. My Greek is coming fine and I am hoping for an A in the semester mark, also in history. He gave no A's in history and only seven B's and told us he'd raise us later. If I could just get an A in biology, I think I could have ten hours of A. We have a mid-semester test in philosophy tomorrow, so I must get busy and work on that. Lyd and I are both taking philosophy and enjoying it lots. Tomorrow night is birthday dinner again, and also my busiest day.

Thanks for the deposit and the laundry. Everything is going finely and we are all looking forward to Thanksgiving. Wish you might come over with Lorene. Am so glad Daddy got that city money—it was about time he got something from it. I hope business is OK and that the Hill firm is functioning in great shape. I must go to class now.

Much love to you all,
Dorothy

November 20, 1928

Dear Dorothy,

We reached home safely. Stopped at Aunt Ada's and Daddy and J.M. were there waiting for us. Aunt Ada insisted we stay for lunch and we showed our antiques, told all the news and then came home.

Daddy had straightened the house, so everything was in perfect order except a few dishes, which I did not mind.

We had such a nice time. It seemed so good to be with you. Mrs. Springman said some lovely things about you. She enjoyed herself so much.

Found I had a hole in my stocking when I came home. I felt so bad about it. Don't know when it happened. I hope I wasn't around all day like that.

If you are downtown I wish you would run in to the antique shop and tell him I came to see the Godey's books and he was locked up. Tell him I asked you to look at it and price it. Count the pictures and see what the condition is. I think there will be some more answers to the ad. I am anxious to get them.

It seemed good to find you so happy and I hope you were able to get some studying done after we left. I think when I come again I will stay in the guest room, for it surely upsets your studying, and not only yours, but the roommate. It won't be long until you are home again. Thank Lydian for her little bed and her kindness to us. Hope you have a successful interview with Dr. Goodrich, but I am sure you will.
Lovingly,
Mother

November 23, 1928

Dear Dorothy,

Have a busy day ahead of me, for this rainy, snowy, weather spells mud for the housekeeper, and I will have to clean from top down. However, it is a beautiful sunshiny morning today and I shall not mind working.

Yesterday Aunt Ada came at 8 a.m. and brought her mending. We had a lovely day. It was so long since she had been here to stay all day.

We went to the corner store and found fresh fish and had that, with nice crisp lettuce, salt rising bread and custard for our lunch. I cut out and sewed up your slip in the afternoon. Lorene and J.M. had to go to the church at night, so they stayed for dinner. Aunt Ada cut some silhouettes for the little round frames. I had a brilliant idea, took out the old silhouette from the large frame and put it in another old frame and will sell it for $5, for I don't think it is pretty and then sometime I will find another old one.

Ada bought a green majolica pitcher from me yesterday. It is quite pretty—you haven't seen it— but you know we can't keep everything. I am so anxious for you to see my tea caddy, candlestick, etc., although perhaps you won't be keen about them.

Glad your party was a success. Sometimes if you want anything well done, doing it yourself is a good idea. Aren't you glad you had expression lessons?

Well, my dear, I could write a lot more, but I just must get busy. Heaps of love,
Mother

Dear Mother,

Today has been my busy day—five classes and chapel and the library. I haven't been able to see Dr. Goodrich, although I made an appointment for today. Feeling rather discouraged about my mid-semester marks, which will come out at Thanksgiving time. However I'm still studying and I suppose the world won't fall in if I don't get good ones.

Tonight we had chicken, mashed potatoes, squash in the shell, Jell-O salad (just like home), cranberries and plum pudding with lemon sauce and milk. Some food, I'll say! The best we've had yet.

It has been snowing hard today and the whole town is white with it. Our evergreens by the window are very beautiful and so is the campus. Wonder if I have any galoshes left from last winter? I certainly would like them if I have. I think I shall invest in some rubbers. That's about the size of my pocketbook at present.

I'm glad the frames and silhouettes look so nice. Am anxious to be home, but the time will be very short as it always is here. I'm

77

going to write a few more letters and study Greek for an hour and then go to bed.

My roommate just entered with a giggle as usual. She's singing and doing German. So goodnight.
Much love and a hug to my family,
Dorothy

November 26, 1928

Dear Dorothy,

Monday a.m. Breakfast over, dark morning—will have to make our own sunshine. Worked hard Friday a.m. and in the afternoon went downtown with Beatrice to do a little Christmas scouting around. I bought books for Uncle Doctor, Grandpa Hill, Auntie Steed and Bradley and stationery for Alice and Aunt Lucy. We don't have to buy three John Merritt presents as he is buying his own gifts this year. Isn't that fine? His paper route helps.

Sunday we went to church and the car froze up, so Daddy missed the service. Daddy did some church calling in the early afternoon. Aunt Ada came over and then Lorene and J.M. came and wanted some lunch quick, so we fed them and they went back and then I fed the older bunch of us. We went to the evening service. The Thanksgiving pantomime was lovely. I only wish you might have seen the stage and the costumes.

You will probably write telling us your plans. If we do not hear, we will take it for granted you have a way to come. Must get busy and work.
Lovingly,
Mother

November 26, 1928

Dear Mother,

Have just eaten Sunday dinner and am going to run downtown to mail my letters. I have been in bed since yesterday afternoon with a cold. Friday afternoon I cut Greek and came home and went to bed, but couldn't seem to get rid of it. I'm feeling better now though. I'm sorry not to have written sooner, but I just haven't felt like doing anything, not even study!

Thursday afternoon I went to interview the lady about the antiques and she had lots of things, some too high priced, others were fairly reasonable. I'm bringing a list of them, along with prices, when I come home and I'll tell you what they're like

I think I shall have to come home on the train, as I have not yet found any other way to come. Can you meet me in Ann Arbor? I'm almost broke. I can hardly wait to get home, but it won't be long now, for the days fairly fly. Have lots of exciting things to tell. I must get busy on studying now and make up for lost time. See you all soon.

Much love,
Dorothy

November 27, 1928

Dear Dorothy,

We will meet you unless we get message to the contrary. Wait at the station for us. I will bring your galoshes. I hear the bugle approaching—scouts must be coming. We are counting the hours.

Lovingly,
Mother

Saturday p.m.

Dear Mother,

My laundry arrived and I was certainly glad to get it, as well as the delicious eats. M's mother sent a cake, so now we have all varieties of food. The meals have been rotten this last week. I guess they're saving everything for the birthday dinner this month.

Have cleaned my room, closet, and drawers, washed and ironed clothes, pressed my brown dress, put my clean clothes away, and mended all my hose and underwear, besides going to class this a.m. The Alma game is at Alma today and it certainly is miserable weather for it. I can hardly wait for the scores to come in, for Alma is a real enemy and has been undefeated this year, as well as Albion. They have taken the championship away from us twice, so here's hoping we win this battle.

Don't expect too much on my freshman marks that come out this week, for they are marking exceedingly low, so we won't get all puffed up! These marks won't count anything and are merely given as an indicator. Also mid-semesters are not recorded, only the final semester grade. I wrote a rather punk test in Bible, so am not hoping to get much on that. Also wrote a bad test in philosophy, but am not going to worry, just get busy and "show the ladies and gentlemen."

Hope you come Sunday. Boy those fried cakes are good! Am going to run down "quick like a rabbit" (as D. King says) and mail this. Much love,
Dorothy

December 4, 1928

Dear Mother,

I have just been to gym class only to find no teacher. Ha! To begin at the beginning we arrived here about 7:45, having left Ann Arbor at 6:20. Had a real nice trip, but didn't get any studying done that night.

Yesterday everybody was sleepy and all of us wished we were home in bed. I got my history blue book back—with B+ on it. Not so bad considering how fast I wrote it.

Tomorrow we have a quiz in philosophy. I haven't studied at all yet, but expect to dig in hard today. It seems there are a million things to do and only two weeks!!

Miss Gray liked J.M.'s candy and said to tell him that she didn't know any boy, or girl either, who could make such good candy and that she was going to save it and just eat a little every day. She told me all about her vacation and we had a real visit Sunday night
With much love to my dear family,
Dorothy

December 3, 1928

Dear Dorothy,

Well it is eight o'clock and I guess I'll call it a day's work. I have been a busy lady today. Cleaned the basement, and that, with the regular housework, was all I could manage, but it is a good job to have behind me.

Daddy has felt pretty well today. He sold a thousand dollar policy and a membership, which he will follow up on tomorrow, so he is happy tonight.

Have my missionary report about finished, have written to Aunt Lottie and must write Aunt Elizabeth, so you see I am hopping right to it. Will finish your dress the first day there is any sunshine. I am going to wash all the windows downstairs tomorrow and shake the new curtains and will try to tint yours.

Hope you had a nice trip back and weren't too tired. I was sorry we had quite so much to do. I wanted you to have a chance to rest, but we packed in a lot in a short time.

I have to be the hired man in the family album at the church bazaar. Expect I'll be a scream. J.M. is at scout meeting. Did he tell you he won a prize selling tickets for the church entertainment course? He gets it tonight—a book I think.

J.M. is home and not too pleased as he has to make the boy's toast at the father and scout banquet December 11. I admit I am sorry for him.

Lovingly,
Mother

Tuesday

Dear Mother,

I am having a glorious time, for I have studied long and hard on philosophy and Greek. I didn't quite master them, but I guess I won't work anymore on them. Oh, it is so wonderful to be able to do this. I feel as if I had been let loose in a wonderful garden with beautiful flowers just waiting to be picked. You'll never know how I appreciate my family's helping me to have this privilege. I only hope I shall be able to repay it a hundred fold someday. I wish I might be someone you could all be very proud to own.

My home grows dearer in many ways as I am away from it. I hope we shall live in a closer, dearer harmony because of my having been away and all that that has meant.

Tonight I went to hear Dr. Gray, who is to be here for a week to speak to the student body. I think he is very good, but not quite up to his predecessor. I must go to bed now. It's two a.m. (and I love it) but I have an 8 o'clock class.

Heaps of love,
Dorothy

December 6, 1928

Dear Dorothy,

I'm surely tired but perhaps writing will rest me. In the evening Beatrice came over, and then Dalton, and you know how he likes coffee, so I made some and consequently didn't sleep much and got up so tired this morning.

I finished painting all the baskets, have the sherbets for Aunt Lottie and will try to get everything mailed this week, if possible. It will seem good to have them mailed so then I can concentrate on our family if there is any time.

Next week I have to work at the father and scout banquet, take that part at the church bazaar and attend the missionary meeting. But you know I may get everything done and it would seem queer to have everything done ahead of time.

Glad Miss Gray liked J.M.'s candy. He was real pepped about it. He has to give a toast Tuesday at the banquet and of course doesn't know how. I wonder if you could write a little to help him— just a toast and welcome and short bit. I don't believe he'll ever get it done.

Daddy is home tonight. He thinks a warm house a pretty good place after being out in the bitter cold all day.
Heaps of love to our little girl,
Mother

December 7, 1928

Dear Mother,

The weekend lull has come, but doesn't seem much of a lull at that. We got our marks yesterday. They are rather disappointing, but not bad—all B's. Of course I made my sorority average which is 1.7. I got 2.0.

Last night we had a wonderful time, Lyd and I, just talking. Later Lyd went into the bathroom for a shower and Laura and I stole her kimono and hung it on the fire gong in the hall, so that she wouldn't have any clothes to put on when she came out. Then we had another inspiration and pinned hose to the bottom of the skirt and put shoes underneath the hose and topped our creation with my black hat.

Finally we conceived the idea of putting arms on it, so we

took the handle of the sweeper and put it through the armholes and it certainly was a ghastly affair in the dim hall. We called some of the others to admire it and just then the fire gong honked right from within the ghost! We all screamed at the very reality of the thing and ran. In the confusion, everybody forgot Lyd, who was still in the shower. I had a sudden thought and went to rescue her. She is fire captain and is supposed to take roll at fire drill and here she was dripping wet and no clothes. I finally got her dressed and outdoors. We spent the rest of the night laughing and explaining the joke to everyone on second floor.

The orations are set for Tuesday afternoon and they gave so little notice that I don't believe I can enter. I may try, however. I'll see.

With heaps of love,
Dorothy

December 8, 1928

Dear Mother,

The day is gone and it doesn't seem that I have accomplished one thing, but I have started on an oration. Don't know whether I'll be able to get it done in time or not. I'm afraid your daughter isn't worth much—she's an old softy! No spunk—or nothin'.

I had a check come back—the last one I wrote for $2.30. I have checked back my figures and can't find anything wrong with them. I paid it in cash, and am a little worried for fear another might come back. If possible I would like a little money to tide me over. I can't seem to get a job and earn any money as yet. I applied to Mrs. Wolfe for any dorm job, She says she has very few changes, but will keep me on the list.

Harriet and D. Hawley and I went downtown and window shopped this afternoon. At least D. Hawley and I did, while Harriet did Xmas shopping. Everything looks nice in the stores and the crowds aren't so great here. Only three or four people in the stores at once. It's sleepy time. I'm pretty well tired out tonight.

With love to my dear family,
Dorothy

December 9, 1928

Dear Dorothy,

This morning we went to church and Sunday school. Early this evening we went over to Ben Church's. They certainly have the dearest family, the babies are walking and little Jeanette is adorable. She came over to me and said "Mrs. Hill, I enjoyed the book you gave me very much." She is so dear and quaint. I think we have a number of books we might give her.

Daddy is writing a little business right along now. I feel quite encouraged. While there is not much cash right now, if he keeps getting applications the money will soon come in. He is encouraged and working well.

I had a letter from Grandmother Hansler. She is dreading Christmas and wishing we could be with them. Of course, it is out of the question, we can't go there, but I wondered if we ought to ask them to come here. What do you think about it? Would you be terribly disappointed not to go to Vassar, if they should decide to come? Please write what you think so I can answer her letter.

I think your marks were pretty good. They will likely be all A's by semester end.

Lovingly,
Mother

December 12, 1928

Dear Mother,

So many things have happened thick and fast that I hardly know where to begin. Tonight was the Christmas party and birthday dinner combined. It was lots of fun. I wore my taffeta dress and we had chicken and mince pie to eat. Afterwards we went to the first basketball game of the season with Battle Creek. The score was 26-32 in our favor. Then we came in and talked with Hannah, Frances and Eunella. I just love them—they are all so lovely and sweet. Hannah is a regular cut-up and can "take off" the Norwegians to perfection.

It has been my heavy day and I am very tired, but I will attempt to tell you of the colossal failure I made Tuesday. Miss Hill got what was coming to her for not starting to write her oration soon enough. I was discouraged with it, but finally decided to give it. I worked all day Monday on it and had very little sleep and only one meal (aren't you horrified!!) and then Tuesday was too busy finishing it and attempting to learn it so I didn't eat that day either. I took an aspirin tablet and departed to the chapel with great foreboding and the queerest feeling I ever had. I was fatally calm and composed, was handed a program and found that of the six orators, I was third on the program. Mary D. was nearly in tears because she didn't know hers and was determined not to give it, but after she noticed how quiet and composed I was as I sat waiting—she suddenly decided to give hers too.

Well, to make it short—my oration was "Price Tags" and rather good I thought, but no sooner had I gotten to the platform than I knew it would never be given. I started out though, and got through a part of it and suddenly—my mind absolutely refused to function! There I stood—I was never so calm in all my life! I started on again and finally realized I should have to give up. I paused, then said "I am sorry" and walked calmly off the platform. I sat down and thought, well, Mother said I'd do this someday and now I have. I didn't feel like crying or anything. When the orations were over and the winner named, I congratulated them and then left.

As it happened, the judges were Dean Gray, Dr. Harrop, Dr. Goodrich, and Prof. Hendrickson, and Prof. Weiss! (A fairly complete list of my teachers it seems.) Don't feel too badly about it, for I believe it was one of the best things that ever happened to me in several respects. Dean Gray called me into her room that night to talk about it and asked me what was the trouble and I told her. She was perfectly adorable and told me that she was interested in me from the standpoint of the judges. She told me that when the judges met, Dr. Harrop said, "I wish we could have heard the rest of Dorothy Hill's oration, she had a winsome way of speaking." She made me promise that I would work up my oration and give the same one next year and win first prize. Dr. Goodrich and Dr. Harrop also talked to me yesterday and told me that I had great promise! Dr. Goodrich offered to help me with mine next year and said that he had had the privilege of training Albion's first state (woman) orator and he thought I could be a state orator if I would.

So perhaps after all, I have aroused some interest at least. So don't please feel disgraced! My oration is going to be a WOW next year.

About Christmas, I am willing to do anything that will be agreeable. Of course I hate to miss going to Vassar, but I guess I can stand that. The thing I am wondering about is whether you have room to sleep the Toronto folks and whether you are feeling well enough to tackle all the preparations for Christmas dinner and entertaining or not.

Thanks for the money. I shall go downtown today and do what shopping I have to do. It's just a week now until I "blow in." Janie thinks her family will meet her in Ann Arbor and has asked me to ride with them. If that works out it will save you a trip.
With much love,
Dorothy

December 15, 1928

Dear Mother,

My classes are over for this week and this afternoon I must do all the necessary odds and ends and study a little on the side. We had a hard blue book in biology this morning. Monday I have one in history and then that ends them. Only five days until I come home.

I have Daddy's present and like it quite well. Having a time trying to stretch my money to pay for everything. I guess I owe a lot. I haven't the rest of my pictures yet—they will come to $3.75 and I must have $2.12 to get home on. I think I will come out even when I get my pictures and then I can bum home. I have $6 left after buying Christmas cards. After the pictures I will have about a dollar to get home on. My watch is at the jewelers being cleaned and will cost me $2.50, so I guess I will leave it there till after the holidays. It's great sport when you get used to having your watch in hock!

Everybody is in the same boat, so it's really rather fashionable. I like the picture very much—as well as I ever could like a picture of myself. I think you'll like it too. It looks natural and grinny!

I shall try to get busy now and get some studying done and my washing and pressing finished. Planning to wear my velvet dress Sunday.
With heaps of love,
Dorothy

January 3, 1929

Dear Dorothy,

I ought to go right at my work, I know, but I am sure a letter will look good to you. We reached home at seven last night, pretty well chilled. I am not sure I am warm yet. Had one near accident—skidded all over the road just as we were coming in town, but fortunately there was no traffic and Daddy kept the car out of the ditch.

This morning I am going to get all the dishes washed and the kitchen cleaned a bit, then this afternoon I will iron. Tomorrow I'll clean and have the house looking so nice, but no little girl to enjoy it. Seemed pretty lonesome last night and this morning. With all the Christmas rush I do not believe we were as tired as at Thanksgiving, so I am hoping at Easter we will not be tired at all—although I expect to see you before then.

I unwrapped your box to put your shoes in and Daddy is mailing your boxes this morning, so you will be all set. We forgot your marmalade, but perhaps I'll get a chance to send it sometime—it isn't easy to mail. Was going to write a long letter, but Daddy is on the anxious seat, so I'll write again.

Don't take a 6 o'clock job for steady; you would lose too much sleep. Please try to sleep some, so you will be well. With heaps of love to our little girl.
Lovingly,
Mother

January 4, 1929, 7 a.m.

Dear Mother,

I am down in the office writing this. Have finished my morning's work except the guest room, which is still occupied.

I either left my pen at home or it is in my laundry case—so I am quite at a loss for writing implements.

We arrived at 7:45 and I went to bed at 9:30, but couldn't sleep because of the noise, and then woke up at 3 a.m. I guess the bed didn't agree with me. We had a busy day yesterday and last night Dorothy H. spent the night with me. I have been up since 5:30! Believe it or not!

The cake is all gone and the crackers are few and far between. I think I'd better go now and study a little philosophy. I'm going to work hard this weekend and try to get caught up with everything. It's just three weeks until finals.

With much love to my dear family.

Dorothy

January 5, 1929

Dear Mother,

The packages came all OK. Everything is going well, except that I still can't find my pen. Perhaps it's at home. We dissipated last night and went to the show and saw Bill Haines in *Excess Baggage*. It was really good and we were all feeling funny anyway.

Later: I just got back from lunch, have had a full morning and am wondering which of my many important duties are most urgent this afternoon.

Well I shall have to plan my work—first study, then wash socks, then go downtown, then do collateral readings and clean the room, go to dinner and then study some more and write some of the many letters I owe. Would you please send me my salve which I left in the bathroom and also my pen when you find it? My pillows look very nice on my bed and I don't need any of Lyd's now.

I hope the family isn't working too hard and that you are all keeping your New Year's resolutions.

With heaps of love,

Dorothy

January 8, 1929 – Midnight

Dear Mother,

Have just closed the good old Greek book with a sigh, wishing that I knew more about tomorrow's lesson. Tomorrow is my full day again. I am getting a real kick out of my work, even though I don't study as much as I ought.

I did enjoy calling tonight for it seemed so good to hear your voices. I wasn't blue, but just rather restless and wanted to rush home for a little while. It seemed that I was almost at home when I heard what you were all doing. I should like to caution you, though, on the evils of too much card playing—it is not good for the morals!

Tomorrow is the birthday dinner and I am going to wear my black velvet and my new hose. I've had more compliments on them!

I gave my history report on Napoleon (800 pages of collateral!) today and am glad to get it done. Now I still have my Greek and Biology to review thoroughly and then I shall be ready for finals—come what may. Am dreadfully sleepy, so will close now.
With love,
Dorothy

Dear Dorothy,

I think our little girl must have been homesick or else the cold, stormy weather got you—anyway we were mighty glad to hear your voice, and isn't it nice to be near enough to call when you feel that you would like to. I had been thinking about you and wondering if you were able to keep warm.

Did you know I was a "junk snupper?" Well I am. Found a book at the library called *The Junk Snupper: or The Adventures of an Antique Collector* and it quotes Mrs. Roosevelt as saying "Snuppers are born, not made," and the art of snupping as she defines it, is "the art of finding quaint and valuable things in junk heaps and the ability to get them cheap."

Now the junk snupper has to get to the kitchen, do dishes and you know the rest. Lots of love to our little girl—so glad you are not any farther away.
Lovingly,
Mother

Dorothy wrote this story about her mother years later, after Blanche's death. It is a loving and humorous tribute to one of Blanche's passions.

A Junk Snupper's Epitaph
Mother's Antiquing Gloves

Mother always wore gloves. "A lady," she said, "was no lady unless she wore a hat and gloves." At church Mother's gloves were invariably white and without flaw. But her antiquing gloves were another matter. Black, slightly worn at the finger tips, with a telltale scrap of pink finger peeking through; they characterized her role of genteel poverty to perfection.

You see, Mother was an artist as well as a lady. The gloves were just a part of her technique in the art of wheedling family heirlooms from old ladies.

When Father took a short business trip to any small town, Mother always went along And you could be sure that her antiquing gloves were tucked away in the corner of her purse. Father and I soon learned the danger signals for a quick stop. No sign listing "Fresh Eggs" could be ignored, especially if the farmhouse looked old, or there were plants in the window, or an old chair on the porch.

Mother's frugal nature reasoned that you could always use a dozen fresh eggs, and it was the easiest way she knew of seeing at least one room in the house. If there were suspicious signs such as an old clock, a chair, or even a quaint old beaded pincushion, Mother saw it. If it could be done tactfully, Mother would admire the object, if not she guided the conversation to plants. By the time the woman had given Mother two rare slips, and she had promised to return the favor on the next trip, the ice was broken. They were no longer strangers, and the rest was easy.

"Eggs are a protective food," Mother often said. Some weeks when antiques were scarce, Father and I thought our diet a little overly protective. In fact, we preferred antiquing in the towns, as it did not fix so rigidly the menus for the coming week.

However, this town technique was a little harder on Father. Suddenly he would be flagged to a stop by Mother, who was already drawing on her antiquing gloves.

"Stop right here, John." Mother had been peering down the street, and a good block away, had spotted an old lady out sweeping her walk. For all such encounters, Mother must get out of the car, start strolling down the street at a leisurely pace. You get the picture. She was simply walking around this delightful little town, enjoying the air, while her husband did business there. A sweet good morning, a remark about the weather, or an inquiry about some other old lady whose name Mother did know, would usually start off the conversation.

Father and I, a block away, would try to catch a word or two. Usually all we could make out were the two figures engaged in talk. I would go back to reading my mystery story until I could stand the suspense of Mother's adventure no longer. By craning my neck out of the car window, I could sometimes see the two of them going up the walk to the old lady's house I would pull in my head, sigh with relief and go back to my book. She'd made it again! If she came out in ten minutes, no sale. If it was half an hour, one could be hopeful. If it was an hour, and still no sign of her, and Father, the world's most patient man had begun to fidget, you could depend on it— she'd struck a treasure.

"Unearthing the treasure took time," Mother said, "because no well-bred old lady will willingly display her treasures—much less sell one, unless you become a friend first." Mother's way was to be artless, friendly as a stray puppy, eager, and appreciative of all the cherished objects in the house. Thus led on, who could resist the admiration showered upon her possessions? Sometimes Mother found herself on a stepladder, reaching for a dusty, forgotten piece of china, which the old lady hadn't looked at in years. Of course, there was often a story about Uncle Ben or Aunt Sophia, a lengthy narrative which wandered interminably, while Mother clung precariously to her dizzy perch.

But Mother never for a moment lost sight of the treasure in store. As the old lady reminisced over an old piece Mother was deciding just what she should offer for another item. This one Mother hadn't even admired.

The final bargaining was a delicate matter. She must not offend by offering too little and, on the other hand, she must not frighten her prospect with a large sum, even though the item might be worth more. Mother had learned, to her own chagrin, that to offer too much was worse than to suggest too little. Too big a price indicated to the old lady that if it was worth that, it was doubtless beyond price, and nothing would then induce her to part with it. Quite often the friendly feeling which Mother had inspired would get her a lovely old piece simply because the frail little woman had no one to leave it to. It pleased her to think how much Mother would cherish it.

91

The welcome sight of Mother beckoning to us from the front porch indicated the triumph of a big haul. It might be a "pig-in-a-poke" such as the set of old blue dishes that were literally black with dirt. But Mother's antiquing gloves never showed the soil, and furthermore, she would never embarrass another lady by wiping the dust off in front of her.

So off we started, with many friendly good-byes, and Mother never noticed when Father speeded all the way home. She was far too intent on her find. Once at home, the antiquing gloves were tossed aside as Mother bustled around with warm water and soap suds, washing and exclaiming over each perfect piece. This climaxed the adventure. At last she was sure she had gotten a bargain.

The meal that night would be no bargain, but no one seemed to care. Mother's enthusiasm was contagious, and for a meal or two she could have stuffed us with sawdust for all we knew. Often we were all too busy with varnish remover to know that it was mealtime.

"I knew it from the shape of those knobs," Mother would exclaim. "It had to be cherry and maple under that black coat of varnish." And sure enough, a few strokes of varnish remover, and the color of the old chest was revealed, a birds eye maple and cherry combination under the dark crackled exterior.

Yes, it was exciting digging up old treasures. Many years later I can see the rooms in our house as they used to look, filled with the fruits of Mother's antiquing adventures. The brown Bennington dog that it took two years to buy, the signed sampler that said "My Name is Mary Snell," the tiny pewter porringer, Annabelle, the papier-mache walking doll which leaned forward as it walked and pushed a baby buggy. It would take too long to name them all, but they proved beyond doubt that what Mother started after, she got. And rarely did she pay too much.

Mother's antiquing gloves are gone now, and her adventures here and her beloved antiques are left behind. But I am convinced that her lively spirit is busy elsewhere. The oldest, rarest treasures in heaven have no doubt changed hands—that is if Mother has really gotten down to business and found herself a pair of antiquing gloves.

Dear Dorothy,

It is nearly four and I have trotted all day and am so tired. Neale has been here with John Merritt all day. They have been good, but it is rather strenuous at that. Have never tried this typewriter before and do not know how to operate it.

After writing a note to you Thursday I went to the kitchen and tackled the dishes, then upstairs to your room and cleaned it all nice, put away all the Christmas boxes and had a real cleaning time. Even went after the old bureau drawers and felt terribly righteous when I got through. Then I went at the ironing and did part of it, but had to stop and play games with the two boys of the family. Daddy beat us, of course.

Daddy and J.M. wanted to play games at night so I called up Mrs. Smith and she was so bored she was making fudge and was glad to come up. She brought her fudge along and we popped corn, played rummy and hearts and beat Daddy for a change. It is just pouring. Aunt Ada called early this morning and invited us over to dinner tomorrow—isn't that nice?

I washed J.M.'s scout suit, pressed and cleaned his good suit also and lengthened the sleeves—all jobs I hate.

If it freezes tonight I guess everyone will need to be on skates. Daddy got his license plates. He has not needed them before as he had the car in the garage being overhauled. I would like to go to the library tonight if it is not too terrible out.

Monday morning and all is well. Cold, cold. We went to church and Sunday school, then home with Uncle George's and had such a nice dinner—baked ham with raisin sauce, baked potatoes, celery stuffed with cheese, wonderful apple salad, biscuits, macaroons and coffee.

Then we sat in the den with a nice fire, read and talked, had a little lunch at night and came home before ten. I guess no one even went to the telephone. It was a very restful day. Lorene showed me her hope chest things.

Aunt Ada and I are going to make the gowns for the drama guild's performance of *The Ten Virgins*. It will be quite a lot of work, but fun too. We have a missionary meeting on Friday.

We enjoy your picture. It seems sort of company when we are missing you. The next three weeks will be busy for you and I do hope you will get marks that will satisfy you, but don't forget that after all you get out just what you put in. They cannot take away what you have learned even if they do not give you credit for it.

With heaps of love to our little girl,

Mother

January 9, 1929

Dear Mother,

Have been downstairs dancing at the birthday dinner and had a lovely time. My eyes are all tired out, so I am using that for an excuse not to study. Please don't be too disgusted with your little girl.

We received notice today about registration, so I am sending you the information, as we must be registered and have our fees paid by Jan. 28th. Lyd and I are going over to the business office and get permission to pay half our board in the middle of next semester. That will bring down the immediate expense a little.

I went up to Dr. Goodrich today after class to find out what I got on my blue book which I wrote before vacation. You could have knocked me over with a feather when he said he was keeping it to read to the class. He said my grade was B- (not so startling). Your good-for-nothing daughter has at last become a working woman for at least four or five hours a week typing for Dr. Randall at thirty cents per hour. If I don't feel that it's worthwhile, I'll quit and let someone else toil and moil away for a mere pittance. (Ha!Ha!) In the meantime I'll wait and see if anything comes up in the dorm or at the desk, but I don't expect it will.

I feel rather elated tonight, but don't know what it's all about—except that there's a thrill to be living and studying and having fun—and calling up my dear family at all hours of the night!

Well, I feel more like studying now, so perhaps I can "bone" for an hour before reclining on a bed of ease.

With heaps of love,

Dorothy

Dear Dorothy,

I am waiting for Daddy to come after me to take me over to Mrs. Alexander's to the missionary meeting. Not to waste a minute, I will start a letter to you. Uncle Dalton just called me up and asked if I was too busy to do his book work, so maybe I'll get a little job.

Glad you are finding out about your fees and hope you can arrange to have part of the room and board due later, for we have a lot to meet during January and February. You had better write to the bank or us authorizing the transfer of your account to your checking account. We had to draw fifty from your account for an emergency about the house. There was no other way, except Mr. Spencer.

Please do not be blue about it for Daddy has money coming in right away to cover it. He has quite a number of applications out and the policies will begin coming back any day now. I feel quite encouraged. He feels well and is working hard and has some good prospects, so everything will be all right. We must not lose the house, for we would have twenty-seven hundred clear to pay on another place any time we sell at a reasonable price. We have had our rent all this time; you have to think about that, so we certainly made a good move when we came here.

Daddy is going out to Sylvan Lake to interview a man and Mrs. Hungerford asked me to come along, so I guess J.M. and I will visit with her while Mr. Hungerford and Daddy make their interview, for we get lonely evenings. J.M. has been so good lately. I do not know what to make of it, but appreciate it anyway.

You will have to use your common sense about the typing job. I know you could use a little more cash than you have, but on the other hand, you must not overdo or fall down in your work. I wonder why Dr. Goodrich does not give A's for work excellent enough to be read before his classes.

Home again and dinner is ready—baked potatoes, corn, sausage, cabbage and pineapple salad, gelatin and whipped cream—as soon as Daddy comes to eat.

Let us know about the fees right away so that we will be sure to be prepared. I think it is best to use yours first so Daddy will have a chance to get his policies delivered. It is satisfying to think we are fighting it out among ourselves. I hate to be obligated to other people.

I guess you had better destroy this letter as I have talked about our business matters so much, but I like you to feel you know where you are. Daddy says any fees that you can have thirty days

on, take it. The next thirty days will be his hardest. Will try to get time to fix you some eats soon. Enjoy your letters so much.
Heaps of love,
Mother

Dear Dorothy,
Well your letter was not mailed so will write some more. I wonder if it is as cold at Albion as it is here. It's very hard to keep the house comfortable. We went to church this morning and have been home all by our lonesome the rest of the day.
Daddy made $130 yesterday and he was tickled pink and thinks he has some good ones lined up for next week, so you see pretty soon we will be OK.
J.M. has some history to do, so I must get him at it. Wish you were here with us, but then we always wish that. Hope you are nice and warm.
Bushels of love from the family
Mother

January 10, 1929 – 12 p.m.

Dear Mother,
Tonight was a concert at the high school, one of the numbers on the Albion College Artists course—Ralph Leopold, who is a prominent pianist. Peter and Lyd and I went and quite enjoyed it. His last two numbers were marvelous. Now I have been trying to study a little, and then shall go to bed for want of something better to do. Your two letters came today. All I can say is that you must keep your mind on Albion while you address my mail!
Today we had health lecture! More bad luck—and fritters for lunch and pork for dinner. Aside from these minor difficulties everything has been going well.
I wanted to do something exciting tonight so I wore my new dress down to dinner. It fits like a dream and feels awfully good. I had heaps of compliments on it.
I simply must go to bed, much as I hate to. Much love to the "junk snupper" and all the family of the "junk snupper." Your letters sound as if you were having a good time lately.
Dorothy

January 12, 1929 – 8 a.m.

Dear Mother,

Have had breakfast and am sitting in the alcove, about to review biology. I'm going over to the chemistry building to see Dr. Randall about typing and then going to Biology class till noon, then type in the afternoon, study in the evening. Everything is going beautifully and I think the job will be quite fun. I never saw such an absent-minded man as Dr. Randall. He's simply a scream! After being used to business men who know what they want done, it's just too funny. I think the job will give me some good experience as well as getting me acquainted with some new people. I'm awfully busy, of course, but you know that top speed is best for me with my procras-tinating temperament.

Yesterday afternoon we had a cozy at the lodge given by the pledges. I dropped in late, just in time to help. We had two Kappa Delta visitors from other chapters so everyone was on her very best behavior—almost formal in fact. Then last night Lyd and Peter and I went to the Alma game and saw some good basketball. We won 33-13. Not so bad for ancient rivals! Then I came home and spent an hour on philosophy review. And so to bed.

I have a schedule planned for next semester, but don't know how it will work out, or whether I'll have a conflict. I'll continue Bible at 8:00 a.m. and take Philosophy of Religion at 9:00 and History of Philosophy at 10:00 and then Greek at 2:00—Monday, Wednesday and Friday. Biology on Tuesday, Thursday and Saturday, and if possible, Play Production (a two hour course) on Tuesday and Thursday at 4:00. This will make 18 hours if I can arrange it. Time will tell, as usual. In haste—with much love,
Dorothy

Susanna Wesley Hall
January 15, 1929 – 11:00 p.m.

Dear Mother,

At last I got some mail! Your letter came today, the first for six days. I felt absolutely cut off from the world. Also had a letter from Fleming today, so I guess after all I have a few friends in the world.

I've had an eventful day. Went to classes this morning, washed my hair, my clothes, etc., cleaned the room, wrote a letter and have finished my Greek for tomorrow. I'm going to sub for Marian again tomorrow morning. I worked for her four days last week when she was sick and also did three and a half hours of typing, so I'm beginning to feel a little self-supporting—even if it is a mere pittance!

Monday night the pledges gave their party to the actives. It was a sleigh ride party and, if you remember, Monday night was perfect for a sleigh ride. The snow was freshly fallen and sparkled like diamonds (or ten-cent store snow) and it was still and there were stars and it snowed big, soft, white flakes. We met at the lodge at 7:00 p.m. and had two sleighs loaded. I wore all my shirts and sweaters as well as a pair of wool socks and Wesley's suede jacket. We were all tucked in warm in the hay and didn't get very cold.

I got out and ran once and it was gorgeous. We went to a farmhouse out near Parma and had a lovely lunch—chicken sandwiches, coffee, fruit salad and the most luscious homemade chocolate and white cakes. The actives all seemed to enjoy it. Then we presented them with stocking caps of green and white as favors and we piled into the sleighs once more and drove home. It was all like a picture, two sleighs, one drawn by white horses, the other by black ones, and the lanterns casting shadows on the sparkling snow. The trees were half covered with white and stood straight and silent in the night as we slipped by them, singing all the songs we knew. The sleigh drew up right at the steps of the dorm and how we did laugh and shout as we shook ourselves and our blankets and then rushed to sign in.

With loads of love,

Dorothy

January 17, 1929

Dear Dorothy,

You will be looking for a letter, I expect. Lovely winter day, the sun has shone so brightly that it made everything seem right. I guess I was lazy this morning. I wanted to play with my antiques, so I moved the furniture around all I could, put up the little lacquer bracket I am so fond of, dusted, and painted the pleated lampshade. It is surely a gaudy affair, but I was tired of seeing it white, so I did it. Have my rag rugs upstairs again—thought perhaps I could at least get one done. Yesterday I typed on the family history, so you see I am a very busy lady. Then I scrubbed the hall and dining room rugs. It does them good and they do not seem so doggy now.

Daddy and Mr. H. are out after them again tonight. Daddy is working full speed these days and that will eventually bring in the bacon. Hope your typing continues to be funny for then it will not be quite such hard work. Staying home is my middle name, but I am rather enjoying it, for there are so many things I want to do and when I gad, I can't accomplish anything.

Wednesday a.m.—your laundry just came. I wonder if I can get it back to you in time. You should always send it the last part of the week, then it goes Monday. This will not go until next Monday, but you probably know that.

Daddy did not get home to dinner tonight as he is really working. Now you know what that means—I have a widow's life, but am not complaining. You cannot have your cake and eat it too. Seems like years since you were home.

J.M. has gone to the library, so I am alone. He played basketball at the church after school tonight, and will again after supper tomorrow. I am glad to have him play and be where they are under supervision.

Going to work on my rag rug awhile tonight, then iron tomorrow. Please do not count the typing mistakes—it isn't done.
Bushels of love,
Mother

January 18, 1929

Dear Mother,

Tonight is the Hillsdale game, but it is so icy out that I'm glad I'm safe at the dorm. It has been almost impossible to walk all day. Your letter came this morning and I was certainly glad to get it. It seems that I never get any mail anymore.

I have written a couple of letters tonight and have visited the infirmary to cheer the sick, have studied a little and am planning to take a bath and then climb into bed.

I went to see about paying half my board later and had to deal with Mr. Gregg, who is about the type of the Wilson Foundry, and he made it all very difficult for me and finally had me fill out an application blank, giving everything about me and my affairs except

whether I had false teeth or not. (I can't imagine why that was neglected!) Anyway, I shall find out about that Monday afternoon and
write you.

    The fees will be almost the same as in the fall, with the ex-
ception of the $10.00 reservation fee, and if I could delay paying half
the board that would take off $54.00 ($280.00 minus $64.00). That's
approximate until I know just how many hours I can take.

    My exams are scheduled quite conveniently—I'll be through
Friday morning at ten (February 1). I don't know just what arrangement to make about coming home, but I'll see. I am hoping I can
get a lot of interesting subjects in next semester.

    I must go spring into the bath!!

With heaps of love & soap suds,

Dorothy

January 20, 1929

Dear Dorothy,

    Well I have been to the store and done the Saturday shop-
ping, also to the garage. Baked a cake and some cookies, cleaned
kitchen floor and made beds. Still have to clean the bathroom, go to
the barber, and get lunch. Then I am through till dinnertime.

    Maybe I will go to Birmingham with Daddy this afternoon.
The sun is shining and I have spring fever and want to go somewhere. J.M. is going to the show with the boys. I went with him to
the play at Eastern High and it was real good. We went in the pouring rain, but did not fall. Mailing a little package with this letter—do
not know whether it will be worth the bother or not. Saturday is not
a good day to mail things.

    Wish you were home today. I miss my little girl although I am
so happy you can be away.

Lots of love,

Mother

January 21, 1929

Dear Dorothy,

    Yesterday was a cold icy day and I was only out at night. The
drama guild gave *The Ten Virgins* and it was very good, although
not comparing with the Christmas pageant. Had a very quiet day

alone. This morning I went into the Detroit Art Institute with the club women. Did not feel too good today and would not have gone, but I had made a reservation. We had a very nice day. I suppose I need to get out with the ladies once in a while.

Daddy is working tonight and J.M. is at scout meeting. I am so sorry Mr. Gregg made things so difficult for you. I do not know why he should. That is the way Uncle George did with Lorene—gave a note. We can do that, I suppose. But if we can just keep up our courage and fight a bit longer I think we will be all right. Daddy's mental condition is so much improved. He is not afraid anymore and is ready to fight things through.

He has a very fine man working for him. I think this Mr. H., who was a contractor, called Daddy up to come out. He wanted more insurance and while he was there said he would like to work for him. He looks good to me—is older than Daddy, has some property, is a worker, goes out and sets up the dates for the interview. He has spoken of a partnership, but I don't know whether that will be or not, but the association is very helpful to Daddy and I think they will make money whether he buys an interest or not.

Daddy is so busy. I am going to the office in the morning to try to help him so they can get off to Detroit. I haven't heard any more from Dalton. I was rather hoping he might have work for me for a little while.

Played with my scrapbook awhile yesterday and enjoyed it. I had not looked at it for a long time. You surely get some dumb letters! I do not go out enough to have any news and have not been having company lately, so there does not seem to be anything to tell you about. I ought to write something thrilling about my daily work. J.M. says all I do is study the cookbook that Good Housekeeping sent me. It is a good one too.

We had ham with raisin sauce yesterday and I'll say our dinner was better than our luncheon in Detroit today. We played going in, had a special car, it was quite fun even if I did have to play the fool a lot of the time, but I did not mind.

Well, darling, I will say goodnight and mail this in the morning so my little girl will get a letter.
Bushels of love,
Mother

January 22, 1929, 4:30 p.m.

Dear Mother,

It is very cold, snowy, and wet out and I have just come in from the library where I have been studying for a couple of hours. Your package was in the post office, so I grabbed it and ran upstairs and now I am all cozy and warm in my clean room, eating cookies—yum—they taste so good and I can look out and see the evergreens laden with snow, all overhung with a gray winter sky.

I think that at last I have things pretty well settled for next semester. I went to Mr. Gregg for the third time yesterday and finally got the $54.00 delayed until March 15th. I have had a hard time deciding on my courses as there are only two I can get from the dean and one of them has to be by permission. I was planning on carrying more hours, but don't know that I can do it now.

Miss Crosby asked me if I would like to wait table at noon next semester and I said I would, so that will take care of the other $54.00 board. That means that I won't be able to get Biology in my schedule, but it does allow me to take a second course of the Dean, two Bible courses, Greek and Play Production. So I am all set for next semester with a good schedule of subjects that I like, and no Saturday classes, and my board all taken care of until March 15, when $54.00 is due. The approximate amount now due is about $152.00, not counting books.

Dr. Goodrich is thrilled to death because I'm taking religious ed.—I think I could have the moon from him, if I'd just mention it. My schedule will be: Philosophy and Psychology of Religion, Optimist and Pessimist, Bible 102, Religious Ed 222, Greek, and Play Production. Marvelous schedule!! I have to do my Greek now. It's 11:00 p.m. Much love and many hugs,
Dorothy

January 22, 1929

Dear Dorothy,

This morning I went to the office to help Daddy awhile. Early this afternoon we had a real blizzard. The snow must be eight or ten inches deep. I was glad I did not need to go out, but was worried about Daddy getting home. He called me about eight and said they had been home some time. Now it is pouring rain and he will have to ride the streetcar.

Uncle Dalton called me today and wants me to come in to-morrow. It may be too hard for me but I would like to try it. Daddy does not want me to do it, so I do not know just how we will come out. Did not get home until nearly noon, so have had to make beds and clean the house this afternoon, then I got out my old green satin dress and have been working on that. I don't care so much what it looks like if it will just give me a change.

Lovingly,

Mother

Dear Dorothy,

Mother has a little temperature this morning so I am keeping her in bed, although it is hard work. I shall keep you advised just how she is.

My business is coming along very nicely now.

With a heap of love,

Daddy

January 24, 1929

Dear Dorothy,

Mother wanted me to write you about your dresses not being ironed. She is sick I guess with the flu. Not very bad. She had a little temperature this morning. I got out of school at 2:30 today and do not have to go back until Monday. I just got through making custard and Spanish rice for dinner. We had exams yesterday and finished them today. I think that I got through all right.

Your loving brother,

John Merritt

January 24, 1929

Dear Mother,

I hope that you are not sick now and that everything is going well. We are terribly rushed, but aside from that, are all fine. I just remembered that we must wear white Hoover dresses (or something white) while serving in the dining room. Perhaps you could get me a couple of Hoover dresses at home, or if I come home February first, I could get them then.

I have decided to carry 18 hours as I can get a 2 hour course in advanced comp., which Lyd is taking. She says it's not bad at all, and it would give me those extra hours credit I need.

I must go to bed now and get rested for a change. Oh say, would you send me Aunt Nellie's address?
With much love & many hugs,
Dorothy

January 25, 1929

Dear Dorothy,

I washed my hands good with alcohol so I don't believe you will get any flu bugs off me and Daddy is so busy I am afraid he won't get a letter to you in time.

I feel pretty limp and Teddy is sick. J.M. just went all to pieces and screamed and cried. I didn't dare go down, so I told him to call Daddy and get Mrs. Barrett and some castor oil, so Mrs. B. helped him give Teddy the oil and then Daddy came and released her. He isn't well yet, but is better.

I guess I have been having the flu, but lightly—no cold— just sore throat and achy, temp 102. I hope perhaps I can get up to-morrow. I was so thankful J.M. happened to be home from school Thursday and Friday. I can write better, but only have a big carpenter pencil. So glad to get your letter and think your schedule sounds wonderful and it is so nice you don't have classes Saturday. I am sorry to have you do the extra work, but if it is not too much for you, it is a wonderful help to us right now. Daddy is feeling fine and working hard. He will deposit $60 to your account, then if you will write to the bank to transfer your savings account, you will be all set for the next semester. I figure you have $114 in your savings plus the $60 will give you enough for your books and some to use. If that isn't all right call us up and Daddy will take care of it. You will enjoy all your subjects and instructors the coming semester. I think it is just fine.

Wash your hands good after you read this and I guess it won't hurt you. So good you can come home Fridays next semester. Heaps of love—everything is coming fine here.
Lovingly,
Mother

January 25, 1929

Dear Mother,

I have just come upstairs from phoning you. Somehow I had an uneasy feeling that you were sick. I do hope you will be very good and not work at all until you feel much better. The old "flu" has to be treated carefully.

Tonight was Dr. Seaton's birthday and we had a special dinner and candles and everything. I got the hiccups just before the dessert and had to leave! More bad luck! And as soon as I got upstairs, of course my hiccups stopped. So I consoled myself by playing solitaire. Then who should pop in, but D. Hawley with a big piece of luscious cake with gooey frosting on it. Then Frannie, M. Nash, D. King, Peter, and others were all in here for an hour or so and we had a real gossip time.

Everyone is so looking forward to next semester. The Kappa Deltas are giving a formal either March 2nd or 9th at the Hayes Hotel in Jackson (my kingdom for a man!). It's going to be a gorgeous affair.

Last night we heard Dr. Jackson of Chicago, a Negro, speak on "What It Means to be a Problem." He's a graduate of Harvard and a banker. He was wonderful and presented the facts so clearly that never again will I have quite the same feeling about Negroes.

This afternoon we had a cozy at the lodge and I took D. Hawley with me. We had a nice time playing bridge by the fireplace and also had a lovely little lunch. I wish you could be here when we have a cozy some time. It's very pleasant and refreshing and seems to give you a wonderful feeling of belonging somewhere and being a part of a real organization.

Dr. Harrop has at last ascended into his glory! For today he gave me a real compliment. I went after my notebook and he said "Miss Hill, you write beautiful Greek." I was so pleased and thrilled that a rather dull and sad day was changed into glory! He said my script could almost be printed in a book. So I shall study doubly hard for the exam now, spurred on by a little sweet praise.

Must study for Biology now. Is J.M. keeping house while Mother's sick? I wonder if he did that ironing for me? It was fine. Heaps of love & many hugs,
Dorothy

January 27, 1929

Dear John Merritt,

Received your letter OK yesterday and was glad to hear from you. You seem to be the general manager around the house now. Keep up the good work and I know that Mother will feel lots better because you're home. When does school start again and what subjects will you be taking next semester? It won't be long till you'll be over at the good old high school where I spent many, many hours. I think you'll enjoy it and will get a real kick out of senior high school. I wouldn't have missed it for anything.

This is Sunday morning and Lyd and I were tired, so we slept in and now we are ready for dinner, and after dinner we begin "boning" for exams. We're going to put a busy sign on our door and then get to work. I wish our exams were all over as yours are.

Yesterday afternoon I spent typing chemistry exam questions for Dr. Randall. I'll bet those chem. students wish they knew the questions.

I must go to dinner now, so farewell. Yours for better and bigger chief cooks.
Heaps of love,
Dorothy

January 27, 1929

Dear Dorothy,

Well, here it is Sunday and we still have Mother in bed, but hope it won't be long. I had thought that she would be up today but while I was at the office Friday, Teddy was taken sick and "threw a fit," which frightened John Merritt and threw Mother into a panic. I rushed home when J.M. called me and Mrs. Barrett came over and she and J.M. had given Teddy castor oil, but he was still a mighty sick dog. This was before noon and J.M. worried over him most all day and finally pulled Teddy through OK, but the whole thing most tired Mother out so she didn't sleep well that night and Saturday morning she was not so well. I felt that someone should be here with her, so I drove over to Davison and brought Aunt Lucy home with me yesterday afternoon. Mother feels much better to have Aunt Lucy with her. Of course J.M. shall be in school tomorrow and we cannot depend upon him as chef any longer. It was very fortunate that he was at home these last few days, and of course, we'll get along fine now that Aunt Lucy is here.

I'm in hopes that Mother will be much improved by tomorrow and shall try to get a letter to you every day telling you just how she feels. My business is quite "rushing" just now and I feel sure that we shall have a nice year's business. Mr. Hungerford started to work for me this week and I believe that he will be very successful in this work.

I have also made a contract with Hascall & Hascall in Birmingham to represent us and they look mighty good too. These two connections ought to feed into my office a sufficient membership to keep me busy with analysis and interviews and that means at least $10,000 of insurance per week and should provide a splendid income for us. At present, we have plenty "in the mill" to keep me busy for about two weeks and Mr. Hungerford says he can keep me in this situation continuously without the Hascall agency. I am enjoying your picture every day.
With much love & a big hug,
Daddy

January 28, 1929

Dear Mother,

Everything has turned out splendidly today. I went downtown this morning and bought a white smock for serving and in the meantime got another job from Mrs. Wolfe, which pays the other half of my board. I am extremely happy in spite of exams. I have Hildegarde's job of dusting the recreation room and she says it is very easy and doesn't take much time. So now you won't need to send the other $54.00. I also am taking eighteen hours, which I am crazy about, and have all new classes but one. I registered in an hour and a half this morning and finished mimeographing some exam questions for Dr. Randall this afternoon, so you see I feel quite important.

I went to get my eighteen hours okayed with fear and trembling for fear they wouldn't let me take it. The prof. turned to the Dean and asked him if a sophomore with a B average could take eighteen hours. He said no, and then asked who it was. The prof. told him it was Dorothy Hill and he said— "Oh that's all right—she's

an all A student." (Imagine my embarrassment when I had just said I had a B average. I chuckled all the way down the line and am still laughing cause I'm an all A student, it seems. Am so sleepy.
With heaps of love,
Dorothy

January 28, 1929

Dear Dorothy,

We received your splendid letter today and enjoyed it so much. In fact your letters are all and singularly quite some inspiration to us. Well, Mother is quite a little better tonight. This is Monday and John Merritt has gone to scouts. They went out to a skating party tonight. J.M. has just been elected troop leader for this year and is having quite a wonderful time. Then too he's very fond of Aunt Lucy and she is doing the cooking and housekeeping (for you know we are keeping Mother in bed) and J.M. is helping Aunt Lucy and doing the buying for the house and otherwise managing things. Yes, he did your ironing and helped me to get it packed. We were all sorry that we could not send some eats with it, but now that we have Aunt Lucy maybe we can treat you a little better.

We were very much delighted last night when cousin Florence called up and said she was in town and would I drive down and pick her up. J.M. and I rushed downtown and brought her home and she will be with us for a day or two. She sure turned up just at the right time, for we all feel that Mother is getting the best care that can be had for her. She will probably be in bed for three or four days, for the doctor says it is a real case of flu and we shall keep her under Florence's care until she is feeling fine.

Tuesday morning—well, Dearie, Mother's temperature and pulse are normal this morning so we are all quite happy about the situation. I'll get this in the mail and try to write you every day.
Heaps of love to my dear little girl,
Daddy

January 30, 1929

Dear Family,

Daddy's nice letter came this morning and I was so glad to know that Mother is getting along nicely and that Aunt Lucy and

Cousin Florence are with you.

I hope to come home Friday as my exam will only last until 9:00 a.m. I shall have to look up trains, or perhaps I can get a ride home. If there is any reason why I shouldn't come, please call me or let me know some way before then. I have been so rushed with exams and everything that I haven't had time to write any newsy letters home. But the worst is over now and I shall either flunk Biology or pass it. Only two more exams and I'm through.

We cleaned our room today and it looks gorgeous and is quite the envy of the corridor. The old problem of roommates is disturbing a good many people now. Peter is going to room with Dot M., who is returning this semester. I must go to bed now.
With much love & many hugs,
Dorothy

February 3, 1929

Dear Family,

Arrived OK about 7:30. Met Frannie and Janie on the train and arrived at the dorm feeling as strange as if I'd been away for months. I found Lyd in bed with her same old cold, and everyone changed as to roommates.

I am so glad I could come home and feel much better after having seen you all. I would give detailed instructions for everyone to follow in my absence, but I don't think you pay much attention to them anyway, so I will refrain. I have taken a hot bath and am going to bed and get a good sleep and then tomorrow, classes. Sweet dreams to you all.
With heaps of love,
Dorothy

February 5, 1929

Dear Daddy,

I have been having an easy time since I got back, with hardly any classes meeting. By Wednesday we shall probably get started. Last night was a supper at the lodge and the whole fraternity went to the show together. It was quite exciting and lots of fun because we didn't have any studying to do. I haven't bought any books yet.

Lyd is in the infirmary with a bad cold, but I seem to get

along without going to bed with mine. Everyone has colds, it seems. Miss Gray said that Mother's flu sounded just like the flu we have had here—with a high temperature going up and then down. Do make her be a good girl and be careful of herself.
With heaps of love to you all,
Dorothy

February 5, 1929, 10:30 p.m.

Dear Mother,

After a more or less busy day, I've managed to take a bath and spent a few minutes studying Greek and Bible. The new courses are going to be interesting, I think. I went to Play Production class today and quite enjoyed it. Also went to Advanced Comp., but only stayed long enough to sign my name.

This afternoon was lovely, so crisp and sunshiny out. D. Hawley and I went downtown and mailed my bathrobe to you and did some shopping. It was too glorious to study and besides we didn't have much to do. Real work probably won't start until next week. I have invited Hope over for this weekend, but don't know whether she'll come yet. Tomorrow is my busy day, so will make a bee line for bed.

If I didn't know how futile it would be, I should endeavor to advise the whole family, but instead am trusting to your good judgment. Heaps of love to all,
Dorothy

Wednesday afternoon

Dear Dorothy,

Miss Pink Jacket is sitting up in bed. The doctor has been here and dismissed himself after repeated warnings for me to be careful. You would think I was some baby, the care I get.

Aunt Lucy went to Detroit today to her lodge. I expect she will have a wonderful day. She and J.M. went to the show last night. Cousin Florence leaves tonight or tomorrow. I hate to see her go—she has been so good to me, but I am so thankful to have had her.

I hope you won't miss your bathrobe for two or three days until I get back into clothes. Expect to sit in a chair for 20 minutes

today, so you see, I am coming along. It was so good to see you.
With bushels of love to my darling girl,
Mother

February 11, 1929

Dear Mother,

I just returned from a potluck and pledge meeting at
the lodge. Today has been a red letter day for me, and I just
remembered that it is the last day I shall be twenty years old.
It doesn't seem at all possible. I should be sorry if I were not
so happy and full of the joy of living. Isn't it queer that such
days come when you need them most, for tomorrow I shall be
twenty-one!

Instead of letting it make me old, I am going to be younger
and peppier. I think I shall even go to the length of bobbing my hair
and eventually buy a new hat.

For my birthday I should like very much an excellent con-
valescent, who is very good and does not do anything unwise
or contrary to her "bosses" advice. I should also like a carefree
Dad, full of pep and vim and vigor. Aunt Lucy is requested to
spend a wild, reckless night at a show under the supervision
of Daddy. John Merritt is to be given an extra piece of cake on
February 12th and then I shall indeed feel that I have had a real
birthday celebration.

Today was my lucky day in letters too, for I received a long-
anticipated one from Jo and a lovely one from Fleming, who never
seems to forget my fatal birthday date.

Tomorrow I have more interesting classes. I am simply enthralled with my work and fairly eat up Dean Williams' lectures. I
think I'm going to make my marks all right. Am getting a B+ in Biology, which is all right, but doesn't look too much like the A I would
have liked. I got B- in Greek and the other marks haven't come in
yet and I am not expecting more than B's anyway.

My weekend with Hope was lovely. We did very little
in the way of seeing sights, but just had a real good time, eating, sleeping and talking. I am quite crazy about Gerry (Hope's
roommate). She seems just adorable. She impresses me more
favorably than any of Hope's friends I have met. It was a real

111

vacation I had, and now I'm all pepped up for school. I found your letters here Sunday night and enjoyed them so much. Till I'm twenty-one,
With heaps of love & some big hugs,
Dorothy

Friday a.m.

Dear Dorothy,

Well, it doesn't do any good for me to write to you. I sat up and wrote to you Wednesday & Thursday and Aunt Lucy just found the letters. Cousin Florence said she would have them mailed. Also wrote two others. I am sorry, but I did all I could do and told Daddy I had written to you. I am gaining each day—walked to the bathroom this morning. Haven't had any callers yet, but I guess it is a good thing for me to be quiet. Cousin Florence went yesterday morning. Lucy is doing some of the laundry and Mrs. Gray the rest, so I guess you'll get your laundry some time. I'll be so thankful when I can be on the job again. I guess you will have to postpone your birthday till I can get going again.

So glad to get your letters—glad everything is OK. I know you will have a wonderful time if you have Hope there.

I'll put this note in with the other ones and hope we can get them mailed. Your bathrobe came. I won't keep it long. Hope to get downstairs Saturday or Sunday. Have no news, of course.
Heaps of love,
Mother

February 11, 1929

Dear Dorothy,

I am downstairs, sitting up awhile and then lying on the cot. A sort of a lazy mother you have. Saturday J.M. went on his fourteen mile hike. I didn't want him to go very bad, but he came home safely, tired and stiff. Friday night Aunt Ada and Uncle George came to see me, but it tired me. They have a new ice machine. Saturday afternoon Beatrice came to see me and brought me some ice cream.

Sunday morning Daddy took me downstairs. Aunt Carrie and Uncle Joe walked in and surprised us. They brought me a lovely pot of tulips and raspberry jam, but I was so tired I had to go back to bed. Then Mrs. Smith came, but she would only stay just fifteen minutes, she was so afraid of tiring me. Aunt Ada & Uncle George came over later, but Aunt Lucy wouldn't let them see me. But I got rested and came down and lay on the cot all the evening. I expect you had a lovely time with Hope.

I feel so sorry for tomorrow is your birthday and I can't even bake anything for you or go downtown to get you anything. But I try to think nothing matters as long as you can stay at school. Some girls have had to leave school and come home to take their mother's place, so after all you are rather lucky. Aunt Lucy is still working although it is easier since I am better and cousin Florence is gone. It makes the family smaller, although we miss her. She was so good.

Expect your work will begin in earnest now. I'm anxious to know what marks you got. Think I feel pretty good today. I will send your bathrobe back soon. I wear it over my pink jacket.

The birthday dinner will be in your honor this month. I had so wanted you to have a new dress for the dinner, but you know all about it.

Heaps of love,
Mother

Feb. 13, 1929

My Dear Family,

Another happy, full day has come to a close. It seems that I have been showered with good things lately. Yesterday Lyd gave me the dearest wide gold bracelet and I received a package from Aunt Lottie containing a lovely pair of gray hose and some peanuts. Also, Aunt Minnie sent me a nice birthday greeting and enclosed a dollar bill. Then today my spiffy clean laundry came and apples too.

Tonight was the birthday dinner, and I thought my day was quite full, but to cap it all, in walked Dot with a box of candy from Daddy, on which we have been feasting.

The birthday dinner was lovely. The tables were decorated with red tapers and tulle bows and valentines were used for place cards. We had little heart candies and some very good chicken.

I think I have a date for the formal party with Evan, the one that all the girls have been urging me to take. It's all going to be a gamble I guess, but I'm rather fond of surprises and am expecting to live through. The formal is March ninth. I think I shall put a new bow or new top on my taffeta dress, or perhaps both, if I can match the taffeta. What do you think about it? It's the waist which is soiled and marked with perspiration.

Oh yes, and I have another surprise. The Kirby-Page Conference is held in Ann Arbor. It is the YM and YW conference of the college. I rather wanted to go, but felt I'd better not spend the money. But now they are planning to send one delegate and have asked me especially. It is held the weekend of February twenty-second and I will have practically all expenses paid. Do you advise me to go?

This semester is so full, and yet I seem to have as much time as ever. Today I mimeographed some work for Dr. Randall and Saturday I expect to do some more. It doesn't leave much time for long, newsy letters, but I will do the best I can and hope you will all forgive my shortcomings.

I made my marks for sorority and came out with a 2.18 average. I don't know how that will rank with the rest though. I am rather disappointed in them, but here they are Philosophy B+, Biology B, History B+, Greek B-, Bible A. I must sleep now, so goodnight with love and valentines for you all, including my dear Aunt Lucy,
Dorothy

February 14, 1929

Dear Daddy,

I guess I have a Valentine sure enough, or was my candy a birthday gift? It came yesterday just before the birthday dinner, so I guess I shall call it both. I certainly have been showered lately. Everything seems to be coming my way. We had a lovely birthday dinner last night and didn't get to bed until about twelve, then Miss Gray came in and sat on the bed and talked. She said I had been made art editor of the Susanna Wesley Annual, which the dorm girls edit every year. Isn't that fun? I had a poster down in the Green Shoppe advertising posture week and I guess they liked it and that was the reason I got this job.

How is the Pontiac Conservation Club (P.C.C.)? I think the initials must mean the Public Can't Croak without life insurance. How's that for advertising? Don't you think I'd make a good advertising manager for you?

This year is certainly the richest one yet, in learning all the things about life that have puzzled me. I simply revel in classes and figuratively "eat it up." My two philosophy courses are stimulating and make me at least attempt to think all the time. Advanced Composition consists of play writing, and I also have a class in play production, so you see how well my courses correlate.

More excitement yet! I have a date for the KD formal with a boy I have never even met. Ernie got me the date and from all the tales concerning him, I think he's quite the thing! He doesn't know me either, but says he would love to go to the formal. He is a junior and comes from a college in N. Dakota. He is very tall, I think, and just terribly quiet. So your dear silent little daughter will have to do all the talking, I expect. (Can you imagine that?)

Oh yes, and besides all that, the Dean says I am an agnostic. Doesn't that tickle you to death? He read my definition of religion and then couldn't classify it in any group with other definitions, and has concluded that I am an agnostic. The funny part about it is that this agnostic is majoring in religious education!!
Lovingly,
Dorothy

P.S. Did you deposit some money for me? And if so, how much? I'd like to draw some for books.

Thursday noon

Dear Dorothy,

I suppose you will be looking for a letter and the dumbest one around seems to be the one to write. Yesterday Aunt Ada offered to stay with me, so Aunt Lucy could go to Detroit for the day. She went and had a grand time. I am so glad, for Daddy is taking her back to Davison this afternoon. We shall miss her terribly, but I am trying not to fret about it. We will get along some way.

Aunt Ada baked a cake for us yesterday and I wanted to send it to you. J.M. was willing too, but Aunt Ada didn't think it was nice enough to go to the dormitory. J.M. wanted to make candy to send to you, but I thought he had better not mess up the kitchen until I was back on the job.

I am sitting on the cot and the sun is so shiny and bright. Enjoyed your dear letter so much, all unless it was getting your hair bobbed and, of course, I don't care about that. I expect you are tired and want a change.

It doesn't seem possible that you are twenty-one and it is the first time you have been away from home on your birthday.

I am trying to be good. Haven't done anything yet, only sit and lie around. Daddy is working hard, but feeling good.

Lucy is cleaning up my room before she goes. She will work till the last minute. Daddy will miss her as much as I. Aunt Lottie said she sent you a parcel. It wasn't what she wanted to send, but Doctor is so busy she can't get out. She said she hoped you would understand. Teddy is well again. Well, shut-ins don't have much news.

Write often as you can and be happy while you can. Isn't it queer Dean Williams did not know you were from Pontiac? He was here and Lorene was visiting with him and inquired about you. He spoke very highly of you, Aunt Ada said, but did not know you were a Pontiac girl, so I guess you made your own reputation with him. Must stop.
Heaps of love,
Mother

P.S. It's Friday a.m. I am alone today, but all right. Daddy went before I was up, so he didn't know there was a letter to go. The house is so upset it seems as if I can't sit around, but I expect I can.

February 16, 1929

Dear Dorothy,

Daddy just came and brought in the mail, including your letter, so I will answer it and then he can mail it when he goes back to the office.

This is still a secret, but Bob and Boqueen are married. They went to Toledo December thirty-first and just told their parents last week. Bo is still in school, but as soon as her grandfather finds it out, there will be no more school for her.

That last deposit Daddy made was $10.40. I thought you wouldn't know when you were out of money. Lydian certainly was a dear to give you such a lovely gift. I am glad you have been so happy about everything. I was so disappointed to think I couldn't do anything.

I don't know what to say about your dress. I would like you to have a new one for the formal, but I can't plan anything definite yet. If we had lace enough to cover the top of the dress I would think that might be practical, but do not remember what is left. I'll see if I can think anything through. I would like it to be a very happy date. I don't think the taffeta would need to be an exact match—the skirt is so covered. It would probably be a good idea to send it home and let me have a look at it. I never heard of Evan L.

Seems to me you couldn't help but gain something helpful and pleasant too, out of going to the conference if you can some way trade your jobs with someone. I think I'd go if I could manage it. I wouldn't be disappointed about my marks. If you never get below a B you should worry and I think you'll get higher marks when you are no longer a freshman. It seems Dr. Goodrich has come across. You can't very well improve on that.

We are so happy to get your nice letters. I made out my missionary report today and got my own breakfast this morning and am going to try to dust this afternoon so you see I have started. I didn't feel that I saw much of you when you were home, but next time I will, won't I?

Lovingly,
Mother

February 19, 1929

Dear Mother,

Received your nice letters yesterday. I was quite anxious as I hadn't had any for some time. Please forgive me for not writing before, but I have simply been swamped by a multitude of things, and although I am enjoying them all, it leaves me little time to write.

Saturday I spent on my sorority exam and it was no picnic.

Then came back from the Lodge late in the afternoon, all resolved to clean my room and write a million or so letters and get my studying done.

I no sooner had the words out of my mouth than Margaret poked her head out of the dorm window and called me to come up in her room. She was all smiles and I thought something must be up. I went up and found that she had a date for me with Evan to go to Battle Creek or Jackson, and double date with her and Ernie. Of course I went. We scrambled around and I tried to get ready by seven but didn't quite make it.

I wore Dot M.'s darling black hat and it looked very nice with my coat. You should have seen the assistance I had in getting ready. Frannie fixed my hair while I dressed and powdered my nose and Dottie went to hunt up a real hot scarf. We hurried so that I didn't have time to be scared and so was quite cool and comfortable. The boys had been waiting half an hour when we finally came down.

I don't wonder that you haven't heard of Evan. I hadn't until just lately and both Frannie and Margaret were determined that I should take him to the formal. I hadn't even seen him, but they said he was very nice looking and tall and rather quiet. He is new here this year. He is a senior and comes from Jameston, N. Dakota. So Ernie asked him if he'd like to go to the formal with me, and although he didn't know me, I guess he thought Ernie's recommend was enough, and he said he'd love to go, that he hadn't been to a formal this year. I hadn't expected him to be as nice and as good looking as he was. He has blonde rather curly hair, blue eyes and dark eye lashes, small features and is very tall, six feet or over and he doesn't date at all, I guess.

We went to Jackson in his car and heard the vitaphone in Old Arizona and then stopped at the Green Cottage on our way home and ate. We stayed out until the late hour of 12:30 and I had a lovely time. If he only likes me as much as I do him—oh, well, I should worry. He'll come to the party anyway.

I think I shall send my taffeta dress home. I think if it had a new taffeta top and a big bow in back it would be cute, or if you could get some taffeta and send it to me I could fix it over a weekend.

Initiation comes March third and then our party March ninth. So my name will be on the program as an active. Don't I feel puffed up though?

Yesterday was rather hectic as well as Sunday. I attempted to type a term paper for a girl Sunday afternoon and evening and it was terribly long, but I finally finished it. It will cost her $2.00. Then last night I typed two hours for Dr. Randall, and had a chance to do some more typing, but just couldn't arrange it.

We had second degree initiation last night, and everyone wore white. It was quite lovely. There were fifteen of us who made our marks. Then after that we went to the Alpha Chi pledge party for a little while and I made everyone lead me when we danced, so I'll get practiced up for the formal. After that I did ten pages of typing and was so sleepy, I couldn't even write a letter home.

With heaps of love,

Dorothy

February 21, 1929

Dear Dorothy,

Had such a nice letter from my little girl this morning. You seem to be having a wonderful time. I didn't know you had to take sorority exams. Surprised that they are stiff. I am so glad you made your other marks all right.

Wasn't it nice to have the date before the party and get a bit acquainted with Mr. Evan? I should think he would like my little girl, and if he doesn't he'd better trot along for I wouldn't think he had very good judgment. Although you may not be his type, he sounds rather good. It must have been a real thrill getting ready for the date. I guess the girls enjoyed it as much as you.

You must hurry your dress home, for I may have to send to Detroit. I know Gray's are going over Friday, so you can send it back with them. They offered to take anything over for us, but your lazy mother is not baking yet.

I darned the stockings today, got my lunch, dusted a little bit and went to the phone a few times, so you can see what a worker I am.

I wish you would watch your weight. If you begin to lose weight I think you ought to give up some of your work, for we don't want any more sickness than we have had.

Dorothy K.'s mother called on me yesterday afternoon. Wasn't that nice? I was so surprised and pleased for I am having a good many hours alone. It is a good thing that I'm not the kind that just has to have company. I have had no temperature for two days and have gained a lot since Sunday.

How is the weather with you? It was twenty-two below here last night. I am afraid you need your bathrobe. I am through with it, but haven't felt up to washing it yet, but perhaps I can tomorrow.

Terrible scrawls you get, but I write on my lap and everyway, but my fingers work much better than they did.

Lucy bought one of Mrs. Judd's old chairs and wants three more. All my friends get the antique bug. I had a letter from Aunt Minnie today. They have certainly been good to me. You have to be sick to know who your friends are. (Mrs. Barrett hasn't been in yet.)

Veda came over this morning for a little while and just called up to have J.M. come after a pudding she made for our dinner. She ought not to have done it as she is doing all her own work again. I think it is too much for her. I appreciated the sunshine so. Staying in is not so bad when it's shiny.

Hope I can soon go to a barber. You ought to see my hair. Have you had yours bobbed? Wish you could run home and spend the evening with me. I would just be so still while you told me all the news.

This little girl is tired and will have to go to bed. When is Easter vacation? You just needn't plan to see anyone else. Oh, perhaps I won't be so selfish after a day or two, but I feel that way now. Heaps of love to our little girl,
Mother

February 21, 1929

Dear Mother,

Have just finished my studying and now this day's work is done. I have decided not to go to the convention, as I have plenty of things to do and am afraid I'd be more tired than I want to be.

Initiation is next weekend and then the formal the following one, so I think I'll be busy a little while anyway.

I wanted to come home next weekend, but don't see how I can make it. I sent my formal home and if you could match the taffeta near enough, I can fix it. I thought the waist could be even tighter than it is and I could put a new bow on the back. The old one is rather dilapidated.

I hope you are feeling lots better and not working. I wish I might be at home for a while so that you wouldn't worry about things.

Lovingly,
Dorothy

Dear Dorothy,

Monday morning and all is well. Saturday was a rather hard day—I didn't feel very good and no one to do anything. Aunt Minnie walked in about 4:30, loaded down with *The Life of Bishop Quayle* for me to read, a loaf of homemade bread, fresh green peas and some candy for John Merritt. She stayed an hour and then back she went.

Sunday Daddy and John Merritt went out for their dinner and brought my dinner to me and Ada ran in for about five minutes and the rest of the day we were all alone so it was a very quiet day and I felt much better.

This morning I have a girl helping me, someone who helps Florence Church. She is very nice. I want to get her to give the house a thorough cleaning—woodwork, windows, etc., then I won't have anything but the regular work to do.

I am glad you are so happy and having such good times. Send your dress home and I will try to match it and fix it up for you, if it can be done.

Four weeks tomorrow since I went to bed—all that time wasted and money enough spent to fix us both up, but I am trying to be sensible about it.

Lovingly,
Mother

February 25, 1929

Dear Mother,

Arrived OK last night after stopping at the Kappa Delta house in Ann Arbor. I had time to get my studying done and then found that we don't have Greek today. Hurrah! Have such a lot of studying to do in all my subjects that I can see that I won't be able to waste a minute, but you know me when it comes to time.

This afternoon Peter and I are going downtown to do a little shopping and then I'm coming back and going to the library to study. The weather is perfectly gorgeous—just like spring.

The Dean was too funny for words this morning. He even told a couple of jokes and appeared to have a royal good time all by himself. He says there's always a reason for a person's being either an optimist or a pessimist, and the condition of a man's liver has a great deal to do with it. So remember don't let your liver bother you—it's fatal. I won't want a real hardened pessimist in the family, as we are already overwhelmed by agnosticism! Will go mail this now. Heaps of love and watch out what you do. I may hop in and surprise you.

Lovingly,
Dorothy

February 27, 1929

Dear Mother,

After an exciting, strenuous, but enjoyable evening, I am at last undressed and at rest. This week is supposedly "Hell Week" for the pledges, but I think it's rather fun. We have to do something for each active and make formal calls on patronesses as well as making candy for our sorority mothers and scrubbing the lodge. I have done all those things today except the calls. D. Hawley and I made three batches of fudge tonight. Also tonight was our special Wednesday night dinner and a lot of the ATO's were invited over, so the occasion was quite festive. Then we danced and had a good time. I'm tired, but still going strong. My cold has disappeared and I have purchased a new pair of lovely brown rubber galoshes—as "orders is orders."

Dr. Harrop has been ill, so the Greek is rather easy this week, which helps a lot. The province president of Alpha Xi Delta has been here for several days and tonight Lyd had her up here in our room and I met her. She is very charming. The Alpha Xi's had a formal at Parker Inn tonight, so that added to the festivities of the evening. I hope you don't mind the writing as I am doing it lying down in bed.

I wonder how everything is at home, and how my formal came out. Please don't be too much worried about the initiation fee, for if you can't do it, I'll understand

I wish I had more time to write to my dear family, but just living seems to take up so much time. Today has been a glorious spring day with blue skies overhead for a change. I don't believe even your hard-boiled daughter can be an agnostic in such surroundings.

I must tumble inside the covers now. You know how I love to go to bed.
Lovingly,
Dorothy

February 27, 1929
Dear Dorothy,

Not quite nine o'clock and I am in bed. Have worked today quite enough for an invalid. Yesterday Aunt Ada invited me over for the day and the family for dinner. I went and had a very restful day and good eats, of course. I think it did me good. I weighed 120 lbs.

Will try to get your dress off to you tomorrow or next day. I think it looks very nice after cleaning. I will get the hose. Have sent to Detroit about the silk, and do hope they hurry it out.

We enjoyed having you home so much. Hated to have you kept so busy, but I won't have to be waited on after this week.

I saw Lorene's new dress. It is very pale blue taffeta, very short in front, with a bustle in back and skirt to the floor, very plain. Saw all her linens too.

Daddy is so busy. I wish I could help him. Maybe I can a little later. Had a letter from Aunt Lucy. She may be back to make us a little visit soon.
Lovingly,
Mother

Feb. 28, 1929—7 a.m.

Mother asked me to mail this with mine this morning and she is still in bed, so I'll tack on my little note and let it go forward so that you may receive it on time. I was mighty glad to receive your letter and shall make the deposit for you of the $35.00 so that you shall be able to give your sorority the check at once.

Mother and I want you to enjoy your sorority now and from now on, so let your old Dad know if you should need anything more.

With heaps of love & a big hug,
Dad

March 2, 1929

Dear Dorothy,

You have been neglected this week, but I could not seem to do any more. Daddy has been so busy he could not take me downtown, so Mr. Hungerford is going to take me this afternoon. Then I will mail your dress tonight or in the morning.

Went downtown and could not find anything to suit me, but if Daddy can take me I will go down in the morning and try again. Found some handkerchiefs, but colors are not right and they just had rolled hems, so I may get material if I can do no better.

Walked as far as the corner yesterday and have done some work yesterday and today. Trying to do the ironing this week, but I can only do a little at a time. Thought maybe typing would be easy, but it is not.

Daddy said he managed your fees. We hated to have you disappointed at the last minute. Daddy is working on a big case in Detroit. I do not feel that he has much chance to get it, as there is so much competition, but he could not resist trying.

Aunt Lottie sent me such a pretty house dress for my birthday, but sent it ahead as she thought perhaps I could use it.

Your semester marks came today. They look good to me and I think they will be better this semester if you are not working yourself to death.

124

Well it is eight o'clock and I have the shirts ironed, but will have to stop for tonight. Will send this in the morning along with your dress. I did not starch the lace as I thought it looked better as it was.

Heaps of love. Hope "hell" week is not too much for you.
Lovingly,
Mother

March 4, 1929

Dear Ones,

It is late, but I must at least write a note to my dear family. It seems I've been too rushed even to live lately. It was certainly fine of you to come to the rescue with my initiation fees and you don't know how much I appreciate it all.

I can't write you everything that has been happening tonight, for I am too tired, but it certainly has been one round of lovely good times—the kind you dream about but never really expect to be a part of. My sorority mother sent me roses after initiation and I am wearing Eunella's pin until mine comes. It means quite a lot to everyone here and is the real subject for congratulations it seems. I am very proud of my pin and love to wear it. And now, Saturday, comes the climax to all the excitement and good times. I haven't studied much this semester, but I believe I needed these other things even more than the study.

My dress came today and looks lovely I have borrowed Jane's coat for the formal. It's black with pretty light fur collar and cuffs. It really looks lovely on me. I would love to write miles tonight, but really mustn't. Don't any of you work yourselves too hard!
Love to you all,
Dorothy

March 7, 1929

Dear Dorothy,

I really don't know what I wrote in my last letter. Anyway, I sent your dress and I expect it will be a mess. I got fussed as Daddy was standing, waiting for me, so I know I didn't get it packed the way I should. Kern's are sending you a yard of material which is

125

a pretty good match and will surely be enough for a bow. I did not like the handkerchief I got. They all had heavy lace, which did not look well with your dress. So I went down last night and bought some peach georgette and will have it picoted tomorrow if I can. If they cannot do it, I will have to roll hem it. Some of them are that way. Forgot to send the thread, so will put some in this letter.

Hope you get everything fixed to suit you and have a wonderful time.

Lovingly,

Mother

Dear Dorothy,

My family is not up yet, so I will write to you, for I may not get another chance today. I did not rest very well last night. It was so windy; you could not but wonder whether you could stay in bed. Toward morning it turned very cold and the house is like a barn, but we have a good fire.

Intended to send J.M. back to school today but think I will wait a day. Hate to have him miss so much. I don't know whether he had a touch of flu—he acted like it, so we have played safety first. He has been so good, just so different when you are alone with him.

Finally sent your hanky yesterday and I was so wishing I could get you a coat, and your letter came and you had it, so now I guess I can relax.

Daddy has been working extra and is pretty tired. He stayed home last night and we covered him up on the cot with the hot water bottle and he slept all the evening and all night and isn't up yet at 9:30, so I think he will be feeling tip-top.

How I wish you had time to write all your lovely times and otherwise, but Easter vacation we can get caught up on some and then during the summer.

I am glad you liked your dress. I cleaned it myself for the cleaners said they couldn't remove the stains, so I did the best I could myself. Wish I could see you when you are ready, it will be like a group of wonderful flowers. I am so happy to think that our little girl can have this beautiful year—for while there have been some disagreeable spots it seems to me you have gotten much happiness in a short time.

Have you seen Evan L.? Hope your party will be all the joy you have looked forward to. Anyway, isn't anticipation as much a joy as realization? I believe so.

Aunt Katherine wrote that they had a delightful trip. Isn't it lovely she has so much and can do such wonderful things, but she has no John Merritt or Dorothy, so I couldn't exchange with her at all.

Have gotten along this week without hiring any help. Just finished last week's ironing yesterday, but what difference does it make? My family is crawling out and I'll have to get out in the kitchen and see what I can find to eat. I haven't done any baking yet.

Perhaps now that you are really a sorority member and after the party, you will have some time to study. I hope so, for you have such a hankering for good marks. It is hard to have everything isn't it, where there are only twenty-four little hours to each day?

I feel so queer and shut in. It is so long since I have been anywhere or a part of anything. Well Daddy is going and I must stop.

Lovingly,
Mother

March 10, 1929

Dear Mother,

At last the excitement and rush has at least partly subsided. I have had a glorious weekend and have been so happy over every-thing. It seems that I have had all the happy little excursions, parties, and all the joys that I can conceive of.

I will begin with Saturday and then work back to other events. The day dawned bright and Miss Dorothy definitely and completely loafed! Slept until 9:30, then got up and did my rec-reation room work, washed, pressed and bathed. Then I really splurged and bought a garter belt and a compact, and had a finger wave Saturday afternoon. Still I didn't seem to get thrilled over the party. D. King and I came back from the beauty shop about 5:00 p.m. and we remarked upon our lack of excitement, but we had no sooner reached the dorm than I was informed that I had some flowers!

Immediately my interest mounted. I ran upstairs and opened them. I had the dearest corsage of pink roses with little lavender and blue sprinkled in among them and pink ostrich feathers forming a background. They were tied with yellow and pink ribbons and it all harmonized beautifully with my dress. The new bow on my dress is huge and swishy and is on the left side, so I didn't pin the corsage on, but carried it. I wore my hair parted on the side and had little curls low on the left side and wore one earring. I believe I looked quite all right.

We went downstairs and the lobby was full of men in tuxes. Jane's coat and my corsage looked lovely, I thought. Margaret, Ernie, and Evan and I parted from the crowd and went out to find a brand new Chevy waiting. Mrs. Daugherty went with us, but the Coach couldn't come over until later. So we had five in our car. Evan drove and Margaret and Ernie and Mrs. D sat in back. Mrs. Daugherty was charming and pretty. When we arrived still I was calm, cool and collected (that's what comes of being 21.) We went in and found ourselves at the head table and Evan and I were at the very head of it. The dinner was wonderful and we had such a jolly time at our table.

Then we had our picture taken with us in the middle of the front row. We were there not by choice, but by chance—Evan says we rated!

After that we waited for the music to begin and Evan remarked casually that he hadn't danced for

Kappa Delta Formal Party

a long time and I was tickled to death! Well, we all started and I held my breath—absolutely—but by the time the first dance was half over, I knew I could dance with him and enjoy it. He claims he is a rotten dancer, but I didn't notice it! In fact, we only exchanged one dance and I didn't enjoy that one.

At midnight we left for home and I certainly hated to leave. The Rose Room where we had our party is quite lovely—all white and gold with rose drapes and many mirrors. It was lovely and I was so proud of my partner. We didn't do anything spectacular, but just had an easy, friendly time. I don't ever expect to see him again, but I shall always remember the charming time I had at my first formal party.

I was just interrupted to hear the Sigma Nu's serenade. It was the loveliest serenade I have ever heard. I feel sort of at peace with the whole world tonight. I don't feel the least bit like studying, but I must get at it.

Lovingly,
Dorothy

March 12, 1929

Dear Dorothy,

Was so glad to get your letter today. I haven't had many letters the last two weeks and have not written many this week. I thought you were almost too busy and excited to know whether you had letters or not. Aunt Lucy came Friday afternoon, and then at night we went to hear Dr. Rice. I went to the missionary meeting in the afternoon and got too tired and had to come home.

The family all went to church in the morning, but I stayed home because I wanted to go at night to hear Stanley Jones. Aunt Lucy had a bad spell with her heart in church, so we put her to bed at night and J.M. stayed with her. Yesterday and today we have done the work and chattered. Before we know it Sanford will be back and she will have to go home before we want her to go.

J.M. sang in the glee club wearing his first long trousers. He looked so nice when he was ready to go and was quite pepped over them.

I am glad you enjoyed your first formal and had such a happy time and a partner you were proud of. You did not say who sent the flowers.

I will tell Daddy about the deposit. The expenses will not be as heavy from now on. The last six weeks have been more than all last semester, but I expect it is the sorority and that will be over now. A little bird whispered to us last week that you had the blues. We wondered why, but perhaps you were just tired for your letters sounded happy, or have you been keeping things to yourself? Or perhaps your liver was like mine sometimes is.

You will soon be home again—less than three weeks now. We have had two or three beautiful days, just like spring, but we will get snow and cold days again.

Daddy said he would make the deposit for you this a.m. Cousin Florence just called and wanted us to come in for the day and go to the show and I guess we will try to do that.
Hastily & lovingly,
Mother

March 14, 1929

Dear Dad,

Again I take my pen in hand to let you know the state of affairs and, incidentally, the state of my bankbook. I have not heard from home since I found out about my $3.00 check being returned. I think my account is all straight now except the $3.00 I still owe to Harriet. My sorority pin, which will be $13.00, is to arrive after the sixteenth—C.O.D., so I would like to know how I stand about that. It seems that all I do lately is write home for money. I'm beginning to get the point of those "college letter" jokes! However, I hope after this there will be no more expense.

We have a petition going around to let school out a week from tomorrow for Easter vacation. If that goes through, it won't be long till I shall be there at home. Before that, however, we have mid-semester exams and I have a short story and an essay to write, so I don't see much loafing for this girl.

I am having a glorious time though and am thrilled through and through with everything that happens. I am surely having the happiest year a girl could have, with work and play and excitement mixed in perfect proportions. I feel intensely and vigorously alive and full of pep!

Yesterday I was busy all day and Lyd's father was here. We had a formal dinner at night, at which he was a guest. We had an exclusive little party in the private dining room and I wore my taffeta formal. Half an hour before that, I bought a gallon of naphtha and washed four of my dresses and another half hour after the dinner, I was all undressed and had done another washing consisting of all the rest of my clothes and my white serving dresses. After that, there being nothing else to do, I studied! So you see the days are plumb full. I am sorry I don't get more time to write all the good times, but it seems I just can't do it all at once.

Heaps of love to you all,

Dorothy

March 17, 1929

Dear Mother,

At peace at last! The turmoil of the last month seems to be about over. Our room is clean and shining and cozy. My studying for Monday is all done! My washing and mending are finished, my drawers and closet in almost perfect order and I have a box of red, cold, juicy apples under my bed. What more could any sane person want? It is a lovely, sparkling, tingling cool spring day and the tree by our window stretches old gnarled branches as if it too were completely enamored by the sunshine and blue, blue sky.

Our vacation begins Wednesday, March 27th and before that time I must write an essay and a short story, so I shall have to step on the gas!

I wish I might be at home today. It is so glorious, but I guess I can wait as I have vacation still before me. Did I tell you that Lyd's father was here on account of the death of her grandmother? He is very pleasing to meet, and is everything that Lyd has raved about.

Across the street I can see a boy about J.M.'s size running and jumping into a car waiting outside the house—the rest of the family follows. It looks just like us going for a drive. The sunshine makes a white birch tree in their yard fairly sparkle. Within the dormitory someone is playing a violin. The music floats out. Now the car is gone—but they didn't take me!

I shall go downstairs to serve in a few minutes and have lots of fun. Then afterward will walk downtown and mail my letter and come back and perhaps write my story.

If I never have another year in college, I shall never forget what this one has meant to me in a multitude of ways. It seems that it is equivalent to about three years in the strides I have taken in every way. I shall never forget how loyal my dear family has been and how they have sacrificed that I might be perfectly happy. I hope someday I can give back at least a part of that debt. In social, religious, and intellectual ways, I cannot even measure what college has meant.

Kappa Delta is very proud because we won both scholarship cups available on the campus. We are all immensely elated over it, and are resolved that KD shall rate high in every respect. My pin has arrived, but is at the post office, so I shall have to get a check cashed and go after it tomorrow. I feel badly to have that expense now, but didn't know just what to do.

You asked where my corsage came from. It was from Evan. Wasn't that darling? We weren't supposed to have corsages, but as long as neither he nor Ernie asked us about the color of our dresses, we didn't have a chance to refuse them. There were only about five girls with corsages. I wore mine right over the bow, on the side of my dress. I must go serve now. More again soon.
Heaps of love,
Dorothy

Dear Dorothy,

We are pretty busy sewing, but I guess I can stop long enough to write to our little girl. Lucy and I have been making my house dresses from the fabric Aunt Lucy brought me from Detroit, the piece you gave me last year, and the rest of the pajama cloth makes a fine house dress, so I am going to have a plenty to wear at home.

When you come home, I wish you would bring your spring coat and give me a chance to see if it has any possibilities with a change of collar, and anything else you have that can be fixed up a bit.

I am sorry not to have Lydian come home with you, but it seems as if I am not able yet. I am much better but still have to be careful. Sunday Mr. and Mrs. Hungerford and the children came to call here an hour or so and when they left I was all fussed and my temperature was up. I would like to get the house papered before she comes and things at least clean. I called Delbert Rich today to come and look at our front yard and see if he could seed it for us. That will help some. I am so glad this year means so much to you. That is the way I felt about it—I wanted you to have everything possible while you were there your first year, then if you had to stop and work you would have the wonderful year to look back on and also to inspire you to make the effort to go back.

The Mosures ran in for a few minutes last night. You ought to hear them tell about their new maid. It is so funny. She thinks their house is filthy, says her knees have been black ever since she has been there. She calls Dudley "What you me call him," but she cleans all the time. I wish I had her for a month.

Daddy expects to go to Detroit early in the morning. Aunt Lucy and I may go with him. She wants to go see her doctor. She is not at all well. I do not know how long she will be staying with us, perhaps till after you come home.

Teddy was sick tonight and had an accident. It was so funny—he got up on a chair and turned his face to the wall and hung his head. Then he would peek around at us and look so ashamed.

Wish you were here tonight, but as long as you are well and happy and coming soon, it's okay. With bushels of love.
Lovingly,
Mother

March 21, 1929

Dear Mother,

I just received your letter after Advanced Comp. class. It seemed so good to hear from you again and I am so glad that Aunt Lucy is with you. You must make her stay till I get there.

Today is simply gorgeous out—windy, sunshiny, blowy. I could almost fly on a day like this, but instead I must stay in and bone on a short story and an essay—both of which must be done before vacation. Also have two exams before I come home. But I don't care—everything is OK and I love living! You don't need to feel bad about Lydian's not coming with me, as I think her mother will be in Jackson during vacation.

I gave my play which I had to direct for play production Tuesday and it went off very well I think. Miss Champ seemed quite pleased with it. Oh yes, and more news, I am running for vice-president of the YW for next year. The election is to be very soon. I don't expect to get it because I'm running against an Alpha Chi, who is quite well known. However, I'm doing it anyway, just for fun. Never having done anything for YW, I think it's a huge joke!

Last night I drew a big KD crest and arranged the pictures on a huge cardboard for the annual. Also I am art editor of the Susanna Wesley Annual—so you see time hangs heavily in my hands!

My pin is here and it is adorable. The girls like it so well without a guard that they are almost inclined to dispense with their own guards. I can hardly wait to see you and tell you everything.

Oh yes—and I think I'm dating this weekend. Evan hasn't called me yet, but Ernie was talking to him and he thought it would be nice to go to Jackson again. He told Ernie he liked me and would like to date with me. Can you imagine that—after I had it all settled that he was a thing of the past! His sister wants him to date Alpha Xi's, but he said he'd rather date me. (Ha!) It would happen that way, when for the first time in my life, I've been perfectly happy in the springtime without dating. Isn't it funny, how things come when you don't seem to need them? I've felt that lately—so many nice things have just come to me without effort on my part. Maybe it's just a culmination of all the effort I've put out before.

I do hope Evan will like me and that I can go out occasionally. He is not too young and not at all the type who tries to hand you a line so you'll be crazy about him. In fact, he seems to be just about my speed. They are having a Senior Prom this year if all goes well, and I wouldn't be surprised if he should ask me to go. It would just seem too heavenly to go out enough to feel like the rest, and yet to be sure that it was just a congenial good time and nothing serious.

Poor D. Hawley has been dating a boy for about three weeks and he's so much in love with her that he doesn't know what he's doing. She doesn't know what to do, for she doesn't feel that way a bit and in fact, doesn't even want to be engaged to anybody until she's about 25. She said she wished she were at home, so she could ask her mother what to do, but said that even her mother wouldn't understand. I wish she might talk to you. I couldn't advise her and she's worried to death.

We sat on the bed and laughed to think how different our plight was last fall when Dot used to come to me for consolation because she didn't have any dates. Now she has them and then doesn't know what to do! It all proves that it's a great life, if you don't

"week-end" too much (as Dr. Harrop says.) Big kiss for Aunt Lucy.
Heaps of love & good wishes,
Dorothy

Wednesday

Dear Dorothy,

Have worked "lickity cut" ever since I arose, so for a rest period I will write to my little girl. I did not rest very well, so Monday I did not do much except a whale of a washing. In the evening Florence and Earl came in and wanted me to go over to Sim's, which I did. I had not realized that Tuesday was the Nims' golden anniversary, so Florence said I could go with them. It was a very ordinary affair, but I think it has made them very happy.

Came home and J.M. had the house all nice and a lovely fire for us. He played his mouth organ and it all seemed cozy and lovely after the hubbub we had been in.

This morning I stepped some. Want to know? Dampened the ironing, finished cleaning the bathroom, cleaned your room—windows and everything—ritzy—cleaned kitchen window and put up clean curtains, washed living room and hall windows, house thoroughly dusted and in order. Doesn't sound like much when you write it, but it does when you do it. Tomorrow I hope to sail into J.M.'s room and give it a real housecleaning. I think I can get the house all in order by the last of next week, then I won't have to do that kind of cleaning again until we know whether we move or not. How I do wish I were twins—there are so many things I want to do.

Guess I have told you every weenie thing that has happened since you went. Do hope you will be able to get all your work done—at the last minute—ha ha! I feel quite pepped up. I seem to require sunshine in my business. The birdie is singing and Teddy is sitting for a minute.
Heaps of love,
Mother

April 12, 1929

Dear Mother,

Just a little minute to dash off a note to you. My laundry came all OK and thanks so much for the money. Did you know that Lyd has been sick in bed with the curse and is now in the infirmary?

Your welcome letter came yesterday and I was glad to hear the news. Nothing exciting seems to have happened lately here. I almost had a date last week, but Evan couldn't get hold of me on the phone. I seem to be one of these busy personages who are always out.

I have been elected secretary of Kappa Delta for next year and am World Fellowship chairman in YW and am going to read a week from Sunday in the dining room at dinner.

It's so cold here now that I'm wearing my winter coat again. My dresses you sent were fine and it seemed good to have them back again. Must tear off to class now.
Heaps of love,
Dorothy

Dear Dorothy,

Hope you are so busy you have not missed my letters. I have been going some. Thursday we went to the art institute and the library. Friday morning we arose at 5:00 a.m. and arrived at Ambassador Bridge at 6:00. Of course it was raining, but we didn't mind. We went to Kingsville to see the whistling swans on Lake Erie, then to Jack Miner's to see the geese. You can imagine how much Dr. Wellemeyer enjoyed it. We were home at noon.

Saturday morning, Doctor and J.M. cleaned the yard and J.M. got their lunch—pancakes. Lottie and I went to Iris' for lunch. They came after us about 4:00 and we drove out to the zoo. It is not open but we drove around it, then back to Palmer Park through the log house and on to John R for groceries.

Doctor has been very happy here. He mended everything he could find, but is ready to go home now. J.M. has the porch screens on—summer is here all right today.

Rhea is laid off. Uncle George said they did not think it fair for a man and wife to have jobs when so many men were idle. Bradley has his pickle job for summer.

Your laundry is washed and I'll iron tomorrow so you will soon have it. Have to feed my son now. Don't forget to rest once in a while.
Heaps of love,
Mother

April 7, 1929

Dearest Mother,

It seems I have tried without much success to write you, but finally have found a quiet moment in which to write.

Lyd's mother, aunt, two cousins, and an uncle have been here today, besides Dot M's people, so you see peace and quiet have been at a premium. I enjoyed them very much, however, and I expect I wouldn't have done much anyway. There are just nine weeks left of school and I have two term papers, two short stories and a play to write, besides finals and the art work on the annual. Also expect that Hope and Jo will be here a weekend as well as Fleming, so I think I'll manage to keep from being bored.

My new coat went over big and is a real success. I have seen several on the campus very similar. I hope you aren't working too hard at home. Today we heard that 30 people from home had died from the epidemic in the last few days. So please be careful not to get too tired!

I hope I shall hear from you soon as I haven't had a bit of mail since I got back. I must finish studying now—so much to do and I am so happy to be doing it all!

Oh yes, I almost had another date with Evan. It seems he called me again and again last night but I wasn't in. So I hope he'll try again and I'll try to be at home.

I went swimming yesterday afternoon about 5:00 p.m. The water was wonderful—not a bit cold.

Lovingly,
Dorothy

April 9, 1929

Dear Dorothy,

Sent your laundry case this morning, was so sorry not to put in eats, but Daddy was in such a hurry I did not dare ask him to wait. Mr. Batz gave me some cash Saturday so I sent you a little change in your coin purse. I think Daddy will have things cleared up this week. The other company is very anxious to have Daddy, so I think Spencer would want to do most anything rather than lose Daddy.

J.M. went on an overnight hike Saturday. It was so warm I was quite content to be at home out of the sun. Sunday morning we drove out after J.M. and it was lovely. The park where they were is ideal—how the birds did sing and the air was delightful. I wanted to swing a hammock and stay there all day. We had a puncture on the way back and stood on the street over an hour getting it repaired.

I finished all my mending Saturday, so I am caught up and ready for this week. I want to wash my dresses and fix them up a bit.

It is a dark, rainy morning. I do not know whether I am going to get ambitious or run away. So far it looks as if Daddy's big case would go through.

Your lovely birthday card came and I was so pleased that you remembered me, for I did not have any celebration this year. The card was lovely, but it would be, when you chose it.
Lovingly,
Mother

Dear Dorothy,

I am all ready for the missionary meeting and am waiting for Daddy to come after me. Yesterday I went to Detroit with the missionary bunch—24 of us for a conference at Metropolitan Church. We had such a nice time.

I would not say anything about business, but perhaps you worry, I do not know. Mr. Spencer did not come across, but Mr. Durant is taking care of the house matter until we can turn ourselves around. He advised Daddy to put it up for sale right away for he does not want to handle it. We are going to do that and see if we can sell, so the strain is lifted a little, although nothing much is changed.

Cleaned out the bottom of the secretary this week—you ought to have seen me throw away things. I am going to start in the attic and go right through disposing of everything possible, for if we have to move it is such a job. There is so much around that really is not much use, so you will be lucky if you have any treasures left.

Hope we can go to Clarkston tomorrow to take some of our spirea and iris to our cemetery lot. Daddy will deposit $10.00 in the morning. Please write.
Lovingly,
Mother

April 18, 1929

Dear Mother,

Such a lot of water goes under the bridge between my letters home that I hardly know where to begin. We got our mid-semester grades and as usual, mine came only up to the old record, with Phil. of Religion A-, Pessimism & Optimism B, Adv. Comp. B+, Play Prod. B, Greek B, Religious Ed. B, Bible 102 B, Phys. Ed. B. My average is 2.16.

I am hoping to come out with a few more A's in June, but am afraid I'll go down in Greek. Today the Susanna Wesley Annual Staff had their picture taken. I hunted the town over for a pair of black pumps with medium heels, but couldn't find any.

Later—midnight—Georgia and I have been working on the artwork and are in a fair way to finishing it. I am very much pepped up to think that we'll soon be through. I must tumble in bed. Thanks for the $10.00.
Lovingly,
Dorothy

April 19, 1929

Dear Dorothy,

Your letter came today and a good thing, too, for I was getting fussy, although I know you are busy and tired too. You must have gotten my letter before this. The mails are slow.

I am cleaning the attic, ready to move if we do. Yesterday I had my uniform on ready to go up, when the telephone rang and Mrs. Gass asked if I would like company for lunch and I did. We had such a nice visit. This morning I went above again and I think two more whirls at it will finish it and then for the basement. I just love both jobs so much I would not think of letting anyone help at it, even if they wanted to!

J.M. is all pepped up tonight and has gone over to the school. He has been invited to join the HiY and they meet tonight. I guess I am just as pleased. Tomorrow the Glee Club sings at the Hotel Roosevelt at noon and will be served ice cream and cake. He has pressed his long trousers and been down to get his shoes soled and is quite delighted at the prospect.

Glad Fleming is coming over and do hope the weather is in your favor so you will have a good time. Yes, we would like to have driven over Sunday, but we just could not. Of course you know we would like to be with our Dorothy every Sunday and then some. Lorene was visiting with me the other day and she said Miss Gray gave good reports on you. She is betting you will be Dormitory President before you are through. Says you are the type.

The house is a little cool tonight so I went to the kitchen and ironed awhile, everything done but the sheets and shirts, but the shirts are a plenty this week. Guess I will iron a white shirt for J.M., eat an apple and go to bed. Don't work too hard.
Heaps of love to our little girl,
Mother

April 22, 1929

Dearest Family,

Just home from a sorority meeting, where we had installation of officers, and Jo Gray announced her engagement with little sweet pea corsages. Everyone is thrilled about it. As a result the Sigma Nu's will serenade—and the Teke's are also serenading tonight, so we expect an eventful evening.

Today is also the first day of class scraps and the freshmen have to wear slickers and carry umbrellas all day, also market baskets for their books and wear green bow ribbons. It's a perfect

Class Scraps fun on the roof

scream! They burned the sophomore flag and I joined in the fray to rescue the second sophomore flag. It's all real good sport. Tomorrow they must wear their dresses backwards and serenade at night as well as entertain us at dinner. Dear, good, happy times—it seems I haven't been so rollicking and young ever.

I hope you won't feel badly if I don't get many A's this year, for these other things and experiences are new and different and

140

give me all the happiness that I've always longed for. I can get all A's and have done it, and now I'm not quite so anxious just for marks because I know that I'll never drop too low, because I am essentially serious and interested in my work. I feel I need this other emphasis and oh, how I glory in the little sociability and the riotous good times of a bunch of carefree girls! Every day fulfills some dream that I've treasured and I find myself doing the things I always longed inarticulately to do—the things I've always watched other girls carry off with ease. So please forgive me if I wax frivolous now and then!

Tonight will be a busy night as I am finishing the artwork and studying for a quiz besides writing numerous letters. But if I can get that work off my mind, I intend to buckle down to two term papers in philosophy and get them out of the way by May 20. Think I can do it? I've got to, that's all!

Freshmen wearing dresses backwards

About money matters—I have $9.85 and I owe $8.00 to the sorority and simply must have some sort of shoes pretty soon. And do you suppose I could have maybe a sleeveless summery dress—very inexpensive? If you don't think I can, just say so. You know one can have a marvelous time without many clothes and you can do things and be recognized without even having new shoes, so I have seen, so don't let money worry you too much. I am so very, very happy and I owe it all to my dear loving family.
Love,
Dorothy

P.S. Miss Gray said that you reported my letters were too short! Shame on you.

Dear Dorothy,
Well I am lonesome for my little girl, so guess I will write to her. It is Sunday eve, we went to church this a.m. We went out for

a little drive, out around Bloomfield, Seminole and Sylvan. It was bright, but cold and raw. John Merritt is getting us some lunch.

Yesterday we went out to the cemetery and took quite a lot of things out. Do hope the things will grow for it was hard work and I have not gotten rested yet. I guess I tire easily and rest slowly.

Sorry Lydian is not well. This semester has certainly not been very pleasant for her. Will she be able to keep up her work?

Be sure to let us know the weeks you have company because any time we were coming over we would rather come when you were alone. It seems like quite a hard day there and back.

If it warms up any tomorrow I am going to the attic and the way I will throw away things will be disturbing. I am sure we have too much stuff up there. J.M. is helping Daddy with the dishes, so I am sure being the lady tonight. He wants us to play Anagrams, so that will be the next thing. I know it is not long since you went back, but it seems like two months.
Heaps of love,
Mother

Saturday night

Dearest Mother,

Received your letter this afternoon and it did seem so good to get it. All day has been topsy-turvy. Lyd's father came this noon and we packed all her belongings and this afternoon she left for home for an indefinite time. She hopes to come back before school is out. There were letters to write and details to attend to and it rained steadily all day, while I washed and cleaned and puttered around.

Fleming did not come today on account of the weather—so I had to cancel the canoe and lunch I had planned. Then tonight I got reckless and went to the show to see Buddy Rogers in an awfully cute picture and got home to find that Lansing had called—so I judge Fleming was calling to say he couldn't come tomorrow either. He is to call me when he gets in tonight.

At 10:30 I went to a spread in Dotty P's room in honor of Virginia, who is her guest. Everyone has been so darling about my being lonesome with Lyd gone, that I have at least three offers of other sleeping partners.

Tomorrow I'm getting up early and making up for lost time. I am quite in love with life in spite of the disappointments of today.

I wish I might peek in and see you all tonight. It seems a long time since I've been home. But it's glorious and gorgeous—this college! All of it and I must save every morsel so that I can give as much as possible of it to my dear family. Bear hugs for you all.
Sleepily, lovingly,
Dorothy

Dear Dorothy,

Here it is Sunday night and I have not written to you yet, but I have been thinking of you so much. It rained all day yesterday and so hard I thought about Fleming and wondered if he would come and if he did what you could do. Was in all day, had an early dinner, drove out to Sylvan to see some places that had been advertised, then to Birmingham on business. I did the grocery shopping there. We were sure glad to get home, for it just poured.

So glad to find the sun shining this morning. We went to church and Sunday school, then home for dinner. Went for a drive this afternoon and wished you were with us or had a car so you could go out, but perhaps you did. Saw Miss Gray at church and she said you were a busy girl. Miss Gray told me that Lydian had gone home. Will you miss her or are you so tired and busy that you will not mind being alone? Too bad she has to miss school.

Friday night it rained, so J.M. called up Mrs. Smith and she came over. Then Mr. Sager walked in, then Daddy, so we played games and ate candy awhile.

Did I tell you that Spittin' Glaspie finally let me have the little old sugar bowl that I have wanted so long? Also the other little blue plate and I found out that she has a sampler, but she could not find it. I told her to hunt it up and I would come to see it someday when I was over. Of course she would not sell it, but that is up to me whether I get it or not. Well this family has to go to bed for they plan to get up early and clean the basement. I got my part done Saturday, but the Pa will have to do his share now.

Hope Fleming came and you had a dandy time. Wish I could visit with you for two or three hours, but we will have to make up for lost time this summer.
Lovingly,
Mother

143

April 25, 1929

Dear Dorothy,

Well I am a tired woman, but not too tired to write to my little girl, I guess. Your two letters came yesterday and then one again today—pretty spiffy, I think. Yesterday morning I tore around doing the regular work, also the garage. Then decided to wash the curtains upstairs, so took them all down and washed and hung them out before I went to Mrs. Kelly's funeral. We drove out to the cemetery, Aunt Ada and I, with the Crosslands. It was a wee country cemetery and such a beautiful afternoon. While we stood around the birds were singing and it all seemed so peaceful and not so dreadful as when a younger person is taken.

Came home and after dinner I ironed all the curtains. That was fine, but then could not get to sleep, which was not fine. Today I have washed all the windows upstairs and cleaned in a fashion, so in the morning I can hang the curtains. I was afraid someone might come to look at the house although we have not had a nibble as yet. Do not know what we are going to do, but why worry?

We are so glad to have you happy that if you never get an A we will not mind. Youth is not so lasting. We covet happiness for you and have been able to give you so little, but you know how much we would do for you if we could. Sorry Lydian has to be away, but I really think you are just as well to be alone while she is gone, for I think a little of being alone will rest you.

Lorene plans to come over about May 19 and wants to take the mothers over again, but I am not at all sure that I can go but I cannot plan ahead.

Mrs. Gamble just called me saying she had a party to bring over who might be interested in the house. We have just driven all over looking and thinking about houses but cannot really get down to business until we know something definite. Rents are terrible, but there are practically no houses to rent. You are almost forced to buy something.

You spoke of Oakland County being quarantined. I have not heard anything of the kind. Another death in the paper tonight from meningitis, but I just try not to think about it. There is nothing one can do. I will try to manage a dress for you. I wish you could be home to plan it, but it will cost almost as much as the dress for you to come, so I will see what I can do without you, unless you get a chance to come.

I think Daddy will have some money in tomorrow. I will write you right away about it. Wish you were home while your room is all so nice and clean—curtains and everything. We are so glad you are happy and we love you so dearly. Do hope it will be easier for all of us next year and I think it will. The big case is not settled yet. Daddy may get it. Here is hoping.

Lovingly,
Mother

Dear Dorothy,

Have been pretty busy all week, trying to keep the house in order for people to go through, but so far no one has been here. Mrs. Gamble thinks she will bring someone late this afternoon. We will see.

I sent your laundry yesterday morning. Hope you got it today. Thought I would make macaroons and I did, but had bad luck, so tried cookies. Do not know whether they will go over very well, but it seemed to be my off day.

Hope to send you money the first of the week. Had some I had saved, but had to help Daddy. Will try to get some to you soon and will try to manage a dress and slip just as soon as possible.

I am going to give you something to think about, you know I have always been opposed to you working for Daddy. Well, I am going to suggest that this summer instead of getting a job that you work not for him, but with him. It is the only way I see that you can earn big money and I also think it will save Daddy.

When you were three years old, I made over a hundred dollars in one month, did the work and took care of you and at that time, was not so much older than you are now and you are far better qualified to do the work than I was.

I feel sure that if you will put in as many hours a day as you did at the treasurer's office, you can, in your three months, earn enough for your year, and then every vacation you have a job waiting.

You know Daddy has never failed to make good money when he worked, but he is always building a new plan or discouraged because his plan has not worked. I have known him to make $700.00 in a month.

You could help him with the clerical, which is not much, and he could help you close. I hope you will think about this seriously, for I think it is the solution to your problem and I also think it would give Daddy the mental uplift he needs to put him on his feet. I cannot seem to do it for him and you would be learning one thing more to add to your list.

Of course it is up to you to do as you like and I have not said anything to Daddy about it, but you know if I did not think it would help you to get to school I would not suggest it. Daddy averages $20.00 on every thousand he sells, so it does not take many to count up.

I have never felt you could do it before and to just go in the office as a typist, I would not risk. Well I have said a lot, and perhaps I am wrong, but I do not think so.

It is such a beautiful day that perhaps Fleming will come this weekend or maybe he has to wait until someone else is coming. J.M. is at the church practicing for the pageant tomorrow night. He is improving a lot. I think the year has made quite a change in him. With heaps of love, wish I could send you something else too for a change.
Lovingly,
Mother

April 29, 1929

Dearest Mother,

I am brim full of the joy of youth and living! The sun is just setting—I love my western room—I can see the streaked mauve and pink "cloudlets" so well. My room is clean and shining and neat. I wish you might see it in all its serenity and colorfulness.

Just got in from our sorority meeting and brought a stolen red and gold tulip with me. It looks charming in Frannie's little red and black vase on my dresser. I went into a garden at dusk and plucked it because I thought I needed it more than the lady who owned it. (It wasn't a question of morality, but one of beauty.)

I suppose I had better begin at the beginning and tell you all about my exciting weekend. Saturday morning I went to Jackson with Frannie, Eunella and Harriett in Joyce Maples' car, which has a rumble seat. It was a glorious sunshiny day and we started about 9 o'clock. I thought I might look for shoes, but decided I didn't have the cash. Harriett bought a dear little black coat and we all tagged along and window shopped and tried on sweaters and had a gorgeous time. I sort of wanted a scarf for my coat and we went into Field's, where I picked up a scarf that was all red with designs in it. I tried it and it looked all right, but I thought it was too expensive, when Frannie suddenly unearthed a three colored scarf of tan and red and navy blue. It is rather different looking and quite tailored and it was exactly right for the coat and cost a dollar less than the other, so my scarf was purchased for $1.95 and I just love it. It makes my coat look like a million!

It was near noon and as we passed a store I saw the most glorious array of pansies and immediately thought of you—and I couldn't resist them, so I went in and bought a long box of them. Then Eunella & I bought a little half pint of strawberries and half a dozen rolls and then ran for the car as fast as we could. Frannie and I in the rumble seat ate rolls and strawberries, while Eunella drove down Main Street. The sun shone and the wind flung my brilliant scarf ends to the winds, and we went on eating rolls and biting strawberries—and throwing the stems away as happily as the little boy in the rhyme, who went down the street "just slinging pies forever and forever." The dear good time of it all! Frannie was making faces all the way home. I laughed till my face ached and we hurried to get me home in time to do my little noon day duties. I didn't have any tables to serve so it was very simple.

Then in the afternoon I just tore around because I expected Fleming—we were going canoeing up the river and planned to cook steak. I almost gave him up for lost, but about 4 o'clock he came. I had decided to wear my little wool dress that you like so well and Frannie's leather jacket. Just then my laundry case came and I got the cookies! It was a most opportune time. I was in a terrible rush, with about five girls helping me to get ready and I took some of the cookies in my little basket for the picnic and did they taste good!

Then I went downstairs to meet Fleming. I was sort of shaking in my boots, but when he stood there looking quite natural and very nice in his grey top coat, my mind began to function—and within two minutes we were on our way over to the lodge to get the coffee ready. I was just a bit uncomfortable, but it wore off when we started getting things ready. Fleming made the coffee while I went

147

to the store and when I came back, he was playing the Victrola and seemed very much at home.

After that we had just a jolly good time and he was such good company. At 6:00 p.m. we were on the river and at 7:30 had finished eating. At 8:30 we had to give up the canoe and then we took a long walk, ending at the dorm. By that time I really began to know him as a person—not just a letter writer. I invited him to the dorm for Sunday dinner, and although he claimed that the thought petrified him, his curiosity got the better of him and he came. Oh, yes, and we also attended church! Then we took some pictures with a new arrangement of his, which allows you to both take the picture and

Dorothy and Fleming Barbour

be in it. It was all fun—and a real experience for me as I had never entertained anyone here before. We went downtown and ate in the afternoon and bought a new film and then it was so lovely we went for a long walk and took more pictures.

Then came back to the dorm and met Isabel MacVicar and Ben Brines, who is also from M.S.C. and the boys found a way to get a car and ride back to State together. I quite liked Ben. The funny thing was that Fleming had to come to Albion to really get acquainted with his frat brother!

Then your cake came, and the rejoicing was great. We told the boys about it and suggested we cut it and bring it downstairs and eat in the beau parlor. They didn't think we'd do it, so we did! It was so good and we had such fun eating it. The rest was soon gone when a few girls were summoned to partake of it.

It was about 9 o'clock when they finally left and when I figured it up I had been with Fleming 18 hours altogether! Quite a record for me. And now he wants to come over again the 25th of May.

In fact he rather seemed to enjoy my company. He even asked if he might come down to see me this summer—speaking quite ahead of time, I'd say. But I'm sort of jealous of you, for he thinks you and Daddy are just all right. In fact he told me very frankly that he liked my family awfully well. He feels quite at home with you and says that you are a dear and of course I didn't dispute him on that point at all.

Then to cap the climax today, I came home from classes to find a letter from him, written after he got home last night, so I was quite elated.

By this time you will think I am the complete letter writer! But I have tried to produce the whole weekend with clearness. I could write a lot more things tonight, just to show you there is no limit to my loquaciousness, but one must sleep sometime. Thanks for all the things you sent me. I have indeed a dear family!
Loads of love,
Dorothy

P.S. Now aren't you ashamed to say my letters aren't long enough?

Dear Dorothy,

Here it is Wednesday afternoon—almost dinnertime. The sun is shining so brightly after the rain, the air is much warmer, and altogether everything is very pleasant. We had a wonderful letter from our little girl, so heavy we had to pay postage to get it, but that is a kind of postage we like to pay. Never thought my daughter would steal! I am so glad Fleming came and that you had such a lovely time, it just sounded perfect to me. Sorry the cake was not better. It seems everything I try to make for you I have bad luck with. I guess I am too anxious to have it good. Anyway, it surely came at the right time, didn't it? Well, it seems that Fleming and I have a mutual admiration society. I would rather have you with him than anyone else. So glad you found a scarf that looks so spiffy with your coat.

Of course it is very poor taste to say "I told you so" but when a really worthwhile chap is with you long enough to know you a little, you seem to go over all right and I hope the others do not like you.

We do not know anything here only "sell the house" and what then, but I am beginning to get used to it, so I do not mind so much. Had another real estate man up here today, listed it with him, so we have two working on it. We feel in a way as if we are getting nothing out of it but Daddy says the things the house will pay are the only real things that are bothering him, so perhaps it is all for the best. It will be a real relief when it is over with.

We cannot get out and look for anything for we do not know when we will need it. Yesterday toward night J.M. and I went to Oxford with Daddy and had our supper there. Daddy seemed to think I needed the rest. I have been working pretty hard cleaning the house and getting it in shape to show. Have also packed everything for moving as I cleaned, so the attic and basement are ready to move any day. Then I went at the stove. I wish you could see it while it is nice. I cleaned it thoroughly, then used the aluminum paint wherever I could. It looks good to me, but tired me to the limit.

J.M. and I sat in the car last night while Daddy talked to customers, then we drove home in the pouring rain. We did not mind. I finally flopped in the back seat and let the men drive.

Hope to have a little cash this week to send you, also to get your dress with. It is so dear of you to write of all your good times. It means so much to us to know you are having such a happy time. It really has been a full year for you, I believe.

Daddy will deposit $10.00 for you Thursday morning and I think I can look for material for a dress, but I hate to do it without you.

Will the $10 get your shoes and leave you a little spending money? Hope things will loosen up soon so we won't have to be quite so cramped, but you are having a good time in spite of it, aren't you? Bushels of love from us.
Lovingly,
Mother

May 4, 1929

Dearest Dad,

How does it seem to have a birthday? Or had you forgotten all about it? I won't let you do that though, for I don't want my dad to miss a thing! In fact, I am so anxious that he shan't, that I am living long enough and having enough fun every day for two people. And when I get home, I shall make it a point to let you in on everything I have done, so you'll feel as if you've been to Albion too. I feel pretty selfish about getting all these advantages, and I sit in class and wish I might share them with you. Why, after all the things I've gotten a hold of, I ought to be able to live a first rate life.

How would you like to have your collegiate daughter sell some insurance this summer and keep your life happy by taking care of your office detail? Of course, you must realize by this time how eminently suited she is to the work—with all her wide experience of life. (Believe it or not.) But don't you think we could make some good money, really? I'm really not so slow when started properly. The only way to get me started is to get me up in the morning. Regular hours and plenty of work is what I thrive on, but I'm like the old donkey, I have to be pushed to it sometimes. I hear we're going to sell the house—whoopee! Perhaps we'll be all moved when I get home. Here's to the very best birthday yet! From your future co-worker.
Heaps of love,
Dorothy

Friday evening

Dearest Mother,

Received your nice letter today and didn't have to pay any postage! It has been another busy week. I understand that you might come over the nineteenth with Lorene. My, but that would be nice. I sort of miss you sometimes, you know.

I am planning on Hope's coming next weekend, you the following one, and Fleming on May twenty-fifth. So I am trying to get a couple of term papers done this week, besides sundry other things. We are having initiation tomorrow at 7 a.m. and breakfast at the Poll Parrot afterward. Then Monday evening is an informal Panhellenic reception at Parker Inn, which I don't think I will attend. Wednesday is our Spring Formal birthday dinner and I have invited Helen Fleming to be my guest. She is a town girl and very sweet.

Monday is Lyd's birthday, so I went down and bought a little owl inkwell for her. I think my $10 can't go for shoes, as I just have to pay some sorority dues. I owe $12.00 counting May and we are having a new plan of collections whereby you can't have your pin if you owe two month's dues, so I guess I will pay as much as I can on that.

I bet it has been a lot of hard work getting ready to move. You mustn't let yourself get too tired!! Perhaps when I come home we will no longer live at 69 South Shirley, Pontiac. Sort of exciting, isn't it?

About my dress—if you haven't yet bought material, I wonder if it could be a sort of fluffy flowered one, or maybe a coral color with a rather big collar. You see we may have an informal yet and that sort of dress would be all right for it and I could get along without others, but if you have already bought something, don't let it worry you, for I don't really have to go anyway and anything you do will be OK.

I am so glad J.M. made the HiY. I'm real proud of him.
Heaps of love,
Dorothy

May 11, 1929

Dear Dorothy,

I did not realize how long since I had written, so instead of going to bed just yet, I guess I had better get busy. Friday night after school we started for Vassar. Daddy had a stop in Lapeer, so it was supper time when he got through and the folks coaxed us to stay all night and we did. It was a nice visit. Margaret and Del took J.M. to the show with them. In the morning we went on to Vassar. Found Aunt Lottie fighting a sick headache, getting ready for a club meeting that afternoon. She kept going, but felt wretched. After she rested, we had the usual good time.

I bought material for your dress in Vassar, but when I got your letter I knew it was not what you wanted, unless you could have had two. Aunt Lottie was crazy about it and said if you did not like it, she would buy it, so I am letting her have it. I bought a pattern and may get up early and go to Detroit for material.

The house at the lake is still for sale. He called us again and wanted us to come out to see it. They are doing a lot of decorating—I am afraid they will spoil it, but we should worry, we will not get the chance to be bothered. Everything is just the same, no buyers for the house. Do not know what we are going to do as yet.

Will send money for shoes soon as we can. I am sorry we cannot do more and faster. Do not plan too much on my coming the nineteenth for I am not at all sure that I can come.

I saw Mrs. Barbour at the club meeting and she came right over and at once began telling me what a wonderful time Fleming had at Albion. After he had written her all about it he said, "Well I will have to come down to earth and study," so in some way you surely gave him a good time even if you did not know it.

Hope to get your dress on the way very soon.

Heaps of love,
Mother

May 13, 1929

Dear Mother,

Just a note to tell you that everything is OK here.

Much later—just as I wrote the above words to you, the fire gong honked and excitement began! And how! It is now 2 a.m. and we just got back from the kimono parade. We rushed the theatre and saw *Sorrell and Son* and had ice cream cones to eat—and then had our pictures taken. Pretty full evening, but we enjoyed it all—the excitement and everything.

My laundry came today and I also have a clean room. Aside from that I have accomplished very little. I'm so sleepy for once, that I think I'll really go to bed.

Heaps of love,
Dorothy

Excerpts from the 1929 Susanna Wesley Annual
Reprinted with permission of Albion College

OUR ANNUAL ESCAPADE

"Heavens, another fire drill. Where are my coat and my shoes and socks? Dorothy, close the windows and pull up the shade. Say, do you suppose that this is the way that they are getting us out to go on the Pajama Parade? Oh, dear, I don't want to go out tonight."

Well, we got downstairs and nearly shivered to death while we were waiting to go back in, as we supposed, to our nice warm beds. However, everybody was stopped in the drawing-room, and there we were told that the Pajama Parade was to be that night. Some were glad and some were not, but we got ready.

We paraded downtown to the show, singing at the top of our voices, and accompanied by numerous vehicles of young men who seemed intensely interested in us. Sam gave us a treat of ice-cream cones and we enjoyed the show immensely. Now and then the silence of the audience was broken by various sniffles and blowing of noses. The show happened to be one that was quite sad.

On the way home we serenaded the fraternities and the Dean and the President. We arrived home about three o'clock more than ready for bed.

May 22, 1929

Dear Mother,

My shoes came tonight, just after I had dressed all up, so it was very pat. They are very pretty and I like them so much. Thanks just heaps. I feel quite the society lady now, hat, shoes and dress to match. Oh, and wait till I tell you what happened to my hair. I had about three inches cut off the bottom of it and a huge handful thinned out underneath, so that it felt almost as if it were bobbed. It is so short I can hardly do it up, but I rather like it that way.

I had a letter from Fleming and he is coming Saturday, I guess, all by himself. We have also decided to have our informal party and now I am wondering if Fleming will come to it if I ask him. If he won't, I don't think I'll go, as I don't care about asking anyone else.

I still have loads to do, but am quite cheerful considering it. I even had an idea for a short story pop into my head and now all I have to do is write it.

Do you think I will be able to pay my nine dollars dues before May 31, which is our party date? We can't go unless our dues are all paid. I'd better not ask Fleming until I find out, I guess. So tell me what you think.

I suppose you are as busy as a bee with all your big girls' sewing and all your other work. But don't forget to take care of yourself, for you belong to me.
Heaps & slathers of love,
Dorothy

May 29, 1929

Dear Dorothy,

Daddy is just leaving, but I want to at least get a note to you this morning. We think we can get the dues to you by the 31st, at least, we are trying to, so you do not need to give up the party yet. Daddy is going to Detroit today and thinks he can make a collection.

Do not know for sure about moving yet. May possibly get in the three apartment building on Washington, across from the school. Have not been in it, but it has a fireplace and is fair, so I rather hope we get it.

Went to church Sunday and drove out to the cemetery in the afternoon. Most of our plants grew. We had an unusually fine sermon Sunday.

We are all feeling fine and hope our little girl is also. I expect you are so busy. I did the mending yesterday. Has summer come in Albion? It arrived here yesterday, but rained last night. I am looking for a letter and am anxious to know how you liked your outfit and if Fleming came. I have material for a dress for you—like the lining. I thought it was so pretty and would make a change with the coat. Be sure to let us know when you are coming home.
Heaps of love,
Mother

Monday evening

Dearest Mother,

My jacket is the admiration and pride of the school. Everyone raves about it and Harriett wants one just like it. It has been felt of and asked about until it is almost funny. My dress is a big success too. In fact, the whole outfit was the answer to a maiden's prayer. And it did look so good to me when it came, all wrapped so nicely, Friday afternoon. The little beret is darling and I look quite startling when I get all dressed up.

Fleming came, according to schedule, about four on Saturday and I took a late permission and we went up the river and ate our dinner and met Shirley, Ernie, Pete and Rex and were with them part of the time. We just had a jolly good time. Took a Victrola and got back at 12:30 exactly. The moon was nearly full and very orange and didn't come up until about 11:00 p.m

155

I had a lovely weekend. I got my short stories done Saturday noon. Then we went canoeing and Sunday morning went to church with Fleming and to the Green Shoppe for chicken dinner. Of course, I wore my flowered dress and feather hat and everyone said it looked lovely—also my new shoes. In the afternoon we fooled around and talked and Fleming went back at 6:00 p.m. He got a ride right from our door to Lansing. Today I got a letter from him, so I guess he had a pretty good time.

I can't thank you enough for my dresses. I just love them both and my newest one is quite the talk of the dorm! Orange seems to be my color, all right.

It's just two short weeks now until it is all over. In some ways I will be glad. My last exam is Monday, June 10. I guess I'd better go to bed as it is after midnight now.
Love to all my dear family,
Dorothy

Thursday a.m., Memorial Day 1929
Dearest Mother,

This is my first Memorial Day away from home. It seems very queer but I have such a lot of work, and I expect to keep busy all day. It has been terrifically hot and I was certainly glad to get my little pongee dress. I'm wearing it now and there is a nice breeze coming in my window, so I am quite comfortable.

I hope it was all right about my not serving any more this year. As I didn't hear from you, I concluded that it must be. It is such a relief in this hot weather. Just that one added thing tired me out. I think I shall come through with flying colors now. Not serving is costing me about $6. I figure that my actual expense for the rest of the time will be about $17 or $18. My present exchequer is twenty-five cents!

Oh, yes and the news! Lyd is back. She walked in Tuesday morning with her father. We were all so tickled to see her, but she has to be very careful about overtiring herself. We are taking Room 208 on this wing and are going to be very happy in it, I think. Lyd is dying to have me go home with her and work there and go to the Cape with them. I'd love to see it all. It would be a real experience, but I guess it won't work out. Two term papers

yet to do, so I will get busy. Wish I knew what you were doing.
Heaps of love,
Dorothy

Thursday evening

Dearest Mother,

I went to Convocation tonight at the chapel to hear Dean Williams speak. He spoke on Religion and Experience and I enjoyed it as I always enjoy him.

It was beautiful there in the chapel at that sunset hour when it is still bright outdoors. Even the old chapel didn't seem bad. The pipes of the organ with their gold bands gleamed softly and radiantly. Everything was alive, even to the green leaves which peeked in at the windows. It was a dream fulfilled just to be seated there. It seemed as if the opportunities for real living just tumbled over each other in a riotous tangle of ideas.

You know if I should die tonight—just slip out of the cosmos—I should thank God for giving me all the love and joy I have, for nothing can take from me what I have had, and life is only more full when touched by a little sadness—a little disappointment.

I have a queer feeling that no matter what happens, I have a place of retreat—no—not retreat, just a sense of holding the world in my hands whether it offers pain or pleasure and of lifting up my head and knowing that nothing can take from me the joy of living life to the full.

For as long as I can take life and hold it off a little distance— gain a little perspective—see its defects and its purpose—as long as I can look at life—see its problems and love it—so long as I can do that, I am free. For who can feel defeated by a world which he recognizes as imperfect and which he knows he cannot make perfect, but which is still a world in which his influence may count for little or much—as he wills it.

If we are but specks in a great cosmos, of which we can know little, at least we are living, reasoning specks, and it is our very consciousness of our smallness that makes us, in reality, great. Whether we attain our ends and purposes is a matter for conjecture, but the very purpose which makes us rational progressive creatures, makes us lords of the earth.

Men and women have such infinite capacities for living that there cannot be good and bad people—but only degrees of wisdom and folly.

It all seems a great enterprise in which we are all seeking something, perhaps not the best thing, but always seeking. We don't know that we are right, perhaps there isn't any real right. We can only do what seems best.

Curious, isn't it? How we do get cheated sometimes, but then most times we have another chance.

I didn't get this raving from Dean Williams—it just came out all of a sudden. Today Mr. Hillman read my story "Black Branches" in class—and I found that he had given me an A on it, which quite elated me, for my creations somehow lie close to my heart. I don't know whether you'll like it or not.

I wonder if you could find a description I wrote for my correspondence course, of Carleton Chapel, called The Vesper Hour. I think it was in Lesson 13 and maybe in that envelope in the box in the attic. I would like to have it real soon if you can find it. Hope to see you over here soon.

All my love to my dear family,
Dorothy

P.S. Haven't received that letter from my co-worker yet. I'll bet he can't write.

Dear Dorothy:

We arrived home from Albion in good season. I stopped at Aunt Ada's and waited for Daddy to come after me. They got along very nicely even if I was not here to run things. I surely had a lovely time. It was so restful and nice in every way. I went downtown first thing Monday and bought your shoes and sent them out. Hope they fit and you like them. They were the best I could do right now anyway.

Also bought material for dress and coat and finished them at 11:00 last night. As usual after I have worked on anything, I am wondering if you will like the outfit. Thought perhaps you would like a little lid to wear with it. It fits Lorene so I thought it would fit you. If you do not care for it, send it right back, for they will take it back. We cannot seem to get any cash in. The group, instead of paying $1000, paid only $100, so we get nothing until the first of the month. We have no plans about a house yet. I am getting a bit uneasy.

The dark blue iris is out. I am so fond of it. Just got the washing and some naphtha, so will send along the rest of your clothes as fast as I can.

Well it has poured all evening. Billy was over and we played games with them and now for bed. I had such a lovely time while I was with you.
Lovingly,
Mother

June 1, 1929

Dear Dorothy,

Was so glad to get your letter. I was thinking maybe the dress did not fit or that you did not care for it and I put so much work in it, I was going to be disappointed, but from your letter, it seems to have gone over big. I am so pleased. I am afraid I cannot get anything more made for you before you come home, for I have not been able to buy the material.

It was so nice that Fleming could come. These lovely times are something you will always have to remember although I hope you will have lots more of them.

Daddy and I have a perfectly wonderful invitation, but I am afraid we cannot accept. Mr. Spencer invited us to go with him and Mrs. Spencer to New York in their Packard to a convention about July 9. He is going to try to get the company to pay the hotel bills. If they do it would only mean a few clothes, but I am not going to think about it too much.

I hope to know by Saturday what we are going to do about moving. Last night I went to Eastern High with Mrs. Dunseith. They organized a PTA. Yours truly was made treasurer, but I may move and fool them. They had stunts from each department and they were all exceptionally good, but it was very warm and lasted three hours. I was nearly exhausted.

Have been fussing around and washed the cover on the old chair, the upholstered chairs, and the small rugs. Just trying to have things a little bit ready for moving. I am so anxious to get it over.

Tomorrow is Decoration Day. J.M. has to march in the parade. We may take a lunch somewhere with the Smiths. John M sang in the glee club last night and wore his long white trousers and looked so well. He is at HiY tonight. Daddy went to Detroit again today, so I am alone as usual.

Friday eve—my letter did not get off this morning so will write some more. At six we had a lunch ready, picked up Smiths and went out to the picnic grove at Silver Lake where they have a lot. It was lovely there. The birds were all singing their little bedtime songs and we saw two orioles. It is a beautiful place. Then we drove around to Sylvan Lake, but Silver Lake had spoiled it for us. I do not seem to care about it as I did. Then I did not go to sleep until 5:00 this morning.

Wasn't it nice Lydian could come back? Will she be able to finish her work? Remember me to her. I cannot see any practical way for you to go East. Your transportation would eat up all you saved and it is hard to save money away from home.

Daddy is sending you a little check and we will send enough more to finish you up in a few days.
Lovingly,
Mother

June 4, 1929

Dear Dorothy,

Will write a note for Daddy to mail. Lorene is coming over to Albion Saturday afternoon and wanted me to go over with her, but I do not believe I can make it. However, she has also offered to bring you and all your luggage home and while we had planned to come after you, it will save a day's work for Daddy and he sure needs to work every day. So if it is all right with you, we will do it that way. I told Lorene I was sure you would be glad to find a bed for her. I will come if I can, but I think from Saturday until Monday will be too long for me.

Daddy hopes to be able to send you a check to pay up every-thing about tomorrow or next day. He has not had his check from the big case yet and we need it. Uncle George may have a job at the Wilson Foundry if you do not find something better or do not work with Daddy.
Lovingly,
Mother

Dear Dorothy,

Looks as if the big case will go through after all. Daddy was in Detroit today and Uncle George has asked him to get the insurance for them so I really do not see how it can slip now. Daddy said it would amount to about $200.00 a month for a year and then some renewal for 3 years. I do not know whether he will think he has to hand Uncle George something or not.

I think likely I will come Saturday since the case is looking so good. Daddy is tickled to pieces and I did not feel like leaving him while he was so discouraged.

I am a tired lady, so will not try to write more, for if I come I can really accomplish more talking than writing.
Heaps of love,
Mother

Dorothy and her family moved that June, to Avondale Avenue, Sylvan Lake. She went to work at the Oakland County Treasurer's Office as a clerk, checking property descriptions and collecting delinquent taxes.

That fall the family finances were worse than usual and she was not able to go to school during the 1929-30 school year. That was the time of the disastrous stock market crash and selling insurance was difficult with the Great Depression underway.

The family moved again in April of 1930—this time to Glendale Ave. in Sylvan Lake, where they stayed a mere four months before moving to 226 Longwood in Detroit. These moves were certainly hard on the family and were made due to financial necessity. But Blanche never failed to fix up each new place to make it homey. She took her prized antiques with her each time. Not only were they functional furnishings, but they gave her a sense of security.

Dorothy had an offer for financial help from Blanche's half-sister Katherine, but refused it since Katherine wanted her to major in business and to pursue a more "practical" course of study. Dorothy and her family were proud and independent people and would not accept this offer. (Ironically, 40 years later, Katherine died and left Dorothy over $15,000.)

Wanting to resume her education, Dorothy wrote to Albion College's President and received this response:

Albion College
Office of the President
July 10, 1930

My dear Dorothy:

I was much surprised and more pleased to receive your letter of July 5. Of course, I am gratified to know that you think of Albion College with an increased fondness and find in its associations some fine values that cannot be forgotten.

I do recommend that you return to Albion and complete your course. I think it's the best thing for you. In fact, I thought at the time you decided not to return that your plan was of doubtful wisdom. You have had some valuable experience while you have been out of college, but it certainly is time for you to complete your course.

There is another reason why I am especially happy to have you come back. You are the kind of girl that Albion College, and indeed every college, needs. Much is being said in these days about a lowering of ideals among college students and about an increase of disregard for the Church. Many of the things that are said are plainly exaggeration but there is an element of truth in them. How could it be otherwise? For we are only eleven years away from the War, when for a period of more than five years, all of the ugliest passions of human nature had been turned loose. The effect upon home was immediate and is now being seen in high school and college. It will be at least another ten years before a normal condition is reached and normality then will not be the old normality that existed before the war. In colleges like Albion with church connections, we need girls like you and young men of similar quality to help in creating a new order that will conserve the best of the old order.

I will arrange to provide some scholarship help for you. I cannot, at this moment, state just how much because the final approval of the awards is made by our Committee here and by a gentleman who controls the majority of our scholarships. You may depend, however, upon some help.

You know, of course, about the loan fund of the Methodist Episcopal Church. In an emergency you could obtain help from that source. The loans are made without interest for the time the student is in college and are payable on easy installments after graduation.
With kindest regards, I am
Cordially yours,
John L. Seaton

Fall of 1930 finds Dorothy back on campus at Albion College. We can only imagine how much saving and sacrifice this required on the family's part to send her back. Their correspondence resumed:

Susanna Wesley Hall
Albion College
Sept. 19, 1930

Dear People,

Arrived OK at 9:15 last night and found my roommate and her mother already installed. From all indications I think Joyce is planning to buckle down and study hard this year as this is her senior year.

Spent the night with Dot Malmborg last night as Joyce and her mother used our room. This morning I got my unpacking done and straightened the room, took a shower, did my pressing and am all dressed for lunch. Saw Miss Gray about working and am to see Miss Dean this noon right after lunch—I hope it will be all right. There are loads of old girls here and it seems just like home and more of them will be coming today. After I get my schedule arranged and find out about working, the worst will be over—and then will come the fun.

I already have a job making invitations for one of our rushing parties. I think they're going to be real clever—in the form of a movie contract with a gold seal and ribbons.

Of course I'm wearing my new dress and it looks fine, I think. We have a beautiful view from our window and get a nice breeze. Must go to lunch now.

Later: I got a job serving nights. It was a tough pull—there were about twelve ahead of me, but I did it. Don't have to start till tomorrow. Will go downtown now, then come back to campus to arrange program, then press serving smocks and have dinner. Did you find one of my brass candlesticks at home?

Heaps of love to you all,

Dorothy

Wednesday night

Dear Mother,

Just a little night letter to tell you that I'm still here—but how!

Tonight we gave our sailor party and it was very clever, I think, but my hand is so tired from making invitations that I can hardly tell you all about the decorations.

The fudge came this noon and I was real tickled to get it. J.M.'s making, I immediately surmised. Tell him he's a peach and I'll write him extra special soon.

Tomorrow we are having personal dates and Friday is our last party and after that the tension is over. I don't know how things are coming out for us—we haven't much idea.

I am sending my schedule. P.S. 111 means Public Speech, P.S. 121 means Interpretative Reading and P.S. 261 means Play Production. (Two of the courses from Miss Champ), Eng. Lit from Battenhouse, and he's marvelous. He's one of those cultured people who see nothing but the best in everything. It's a joy to be in his class. Ed 221 is Principles of Education from Carter and it's the sort of course that demands a bucket of cold water every five minutes to keep one awake (nuff said)!

Wish I knew how everything is at home. I'm just a bit homesick and letters don't come fast enough it seems. Wish I could see you all. Wish I could write more, but you'd be shocked at the time now!!
Love to Daddy, J.M. and yourself,
Dorothy

Sunday morning

Dear Mother,

I have lots of news—some is very good. I have changed from night work to noon. Some girl had a change in schedule and offered to trade so now I won't have those birthday dinners to serve. Although I don't mind working at night, now that I have started. I really don't mind the kitchen work, it's a healthy change, and I eat everything in sight and really think I am gaining. Had my physical exam and found I weighed 127 1/4 and got a B+ on posture. (Imagine that!)

I simply eat up this interpretative reading and play production is fun. Of course they will require plenty of time and debate will be stiff I know. However, they aren't like Greek. My English Lit will be work but I'll love it. So you see there are only Education and Biology which don't thrill me.

Next Saturday will be the tryouts for Dramatic Club and I'm going out for it. I have my doubts about making it, but anyhow, here goes.

Wish I could get home soon, but don't see much hope. We are only allowed three subs in the kitchen during the semester. I don't know how strictly that will be enforced.

I found my candlestick in a tennis shoe! We are pretty well settled in our room now, but haven't any pictures hung as yet. When I come home I'd like to bring back a little lamp of some description.

Yesterday we washed all our clothes and cleaned the room, ironed and mended. So today I'm resting for the first time. Am going to wash my hair, clean out my top drawer and write a bushel of letters and serve tonight. Then study and go to bed very early. We bought ourselves an alarm clock at the dollar store and it has the loudest alarm in the dorm. We love it—one of those big nickel ones, you know, very decorative to say the least!!

Did I tell you I earned $2 registration day working over at the gym? Besides seeing all the upperclassmen register and spotting all the tall men, it was a snap job. Four Kappa Deltas worked and we had a real good time. It's nice in many ways to have the sorority behind you. It certainly helps you on this campus. We're all rather disgusted about rushing, but thank goodness the worst is over.

You don't know how glad I am about Mr. Spencer and the whole deal. It takes a big load off my mind and I have one of those feelings that we're due for a "lucky break."

I'm sitting looking out on the tall swaying trees and the front lawn. You will love our room. It's such a pretty view and not dark. It's not under the porch, but is the first room this side of the porch. They are widening the street in front here and I hope they'll soon be done. Several streets in Albion are newly paved. I fear it's becoming a city.

Now that I've sort of caught up on my news, I'll be able to write you every night, I hope. Next week will begin to be regular in its schedule. And remember that I like letters too. I'm inclined to be homesick.

Love to all of you, from all of me,
Dorothy

Monday night

Dear Mother,

Just got home from a sorority meeting and potluck. I haven't been so sleepy since I've been here. I think it's a good sign. Am going to take a shower and do a little studying and then to bed. I really want to go!

I had a call from Miss Champ this morning about Dramatic Club. At 5:00 p.m. I went over and, with eight others, had another tryout. I guess they have too many and are trying to eliminate a few. Time will tell how it comes out. I doubt whether I will be lucky enough to be chosen.

We have done nothing but eat all day, and it surely tasted good. I feel very happy—the very best since—oh—ages ago.

I suppose you were tired after the trip but it was a tonic to see you. Don't any of you get all worn out—for someday soon I'll come home and inspect you all.

Love,

Dorothy

October 1, 1930

Dear Mother,

Haven't heard from the family all week—I think maybe they're all lost, strayed and stolen. I got a package from Lorene today with three caramel-covered apples in it. We immediately consumed them, and my, but they were good.

I don't feel at all like writing tonight. I hope you will forgive me. I have a fierce cold and am feeling like nothing human. Everyone here has them—a regular epidemic.

I waited table tonight for one of the girls and then later went to formal pledging at the lodge. Nothing very exciting has happened except that I feel like going to bed. A good night's sleep is what I need. Don't work too hard.

Love to you all,

Dorothy

October 12, 1930

Dear Mother,

The weekend is almost over and we've laughed till our sides ache tonight. This afternoon Fran, Joyce and I went to Olivet just for a ride and looked over the college. It certainly isn't much of a place beside Albion. It was simply desolate and depressing and reminded me strongly of Ypsilanti—that same homesick feeling. It was gorgeous driving—as warm as summer and the leaves all beautiful shades of red and brown. It couldn't be any more beautiful here.

Friday night we went to the game and beat Hope College. It was quite exciting—my first night football game. Terribly foggy though. I was so glad you could come over Wednesday and I did want you to really see one of our formal occasions. I wish sometime you could come to a formal KD party. Then you'd see the most thrilling thing of all. Sometimes I think that I'm made funny—I love color and the glamour of it all. I guess I'm all glamour—those are the things I love and yet I love the very simple things too, like the falling of red leaves by my window and the tall stateliness of a black tree trunk. (But that doesn't buy the baby shoes! I wish I liked anything practical!) Oh well. Do you love me? Say you do or I'll crush you like a grape.
Heaps of love from your crazy daughter,
Dorothy

October 12, 1930

Dear Dorothy,

Should have written before, but have been busy of course. Had a lovely ride home in the moonlight—thought we would not buy gas in Jackson, but would wait until we got in the section of reduced prices—so we ran out a little beyond Chelsea. I drove and Aunt Nellie pushed. Then we finally both pushed into a gas station where gas was reduced three cents— never laughed so much in my life. We enjoyed our time with you so much. They are surely a darling bunch of girls. They were so friendly and nice to us.

I was all in the next day—the woman came to demonstrate the ironer, but I did not do much. I was all right Friday. Just so you might have something to rave about, I must tell you I did three washings, ironing, cleaned the house, and made two trips to Albion beside the regular work.

Did all the ironing on the ironer and think it pretty fine. Last night the family went to the show. There is the nicest movie just a little walk on Woodward. We saw *Little Accident* and it was quite cute.

Aunt Ada, Uncle George, and Lorene were here about an hour yesterday afternoon. Lorene hopes she can come to Homecoming and wants to stay with you. She wanted to know if you could use her pink beaded formal by adding tulle or a net flounce and her tomato colored one—she said she would not get a chance to wear them.

Yesterday a man came to the door about noon, asked for Daddy, then asked if I was Mrs. Hill, and did I have a daughter, Dorothy. His name was Dr. Brooks and I couldn't think what he wanted, but it was about your loan. He said they had the money all right, but wanted to know about the case. So I told him everything he wanted to know and more. Finally tumbled that he was the famous Dr. Brooks, surgeon. His daughter is attending Ypsilanti and wondered why you didn't go to there when it was cheaper. I told him you had been unable to get the course you wanted. He was very nice and said you would get the loan all right.

John M. had croup Thursday night, so was out of school Friday, but is OK again. Daddy went to Pontiac and is not back yet. I wanted to get out, so I called Aunt Minnie and she came for lunch, then this afternoon we went antiquing on the street car, but did not find anything thrilling.

Would like to have gone to Vassar, but I guess we couldn't. Anyway we are invited to the Gasses' home for dinner at three, so I won't have to work tomorrow, I am glad to say, for I am really fed up on work for this week. All the curtains are down and clean. Next week they will be ironed and up, I hope.

Had your key made tonight. We made a new rule—I hope it works—that Daddy lays off Friday night and Saturday and Sunday from now on. It would be very sensible I think.

Tonight J.M. & I had a fish and chips dinner. I didn't feel like getting supper. They have a special for 25 cents so J.M. went over and got two specials. It was easier than cooking.

Hope everything is fine with you. I expect you have had to study to make up for the company you have had. I had a letter from the Dean asking me to send in my permission, which I will do at once. Remember me to the girls.
Lovingly,
Mother

October 14, 1930

Dear Mother,

"Each day will bring some lovely thing—some gay adventurous lovely thing." Today has been full of many things. Classes almost all day, play practice, and then histrionic club meeting at KD lodge. This noon I had a big surprise—a lovely letter from D.J. I expect you knew he was going to write me, didn't you? I was so surprised and elated. Then this afternoon play production—another joy—and finally histrionic club, which turned out to be dinner. Geraldine G., the little freshman you met at the birthday dinner was there. She was the only freshman voted in. She's awfully sweet and I found out that she taught expression last year—quite a coincidence! I am anticipating a real good time in the club. There is a nice spirit and for once, a good bunch of men. We'll have a good job selling tickets for the season (four plays) and ushering at the plays—for this time anyway. The first play is being practiced now for homecoming.

Then to cap the climax and give me another surprise—I found a whole box of Hershey bars from Aunt Minnie lying on my bed. (I can hear J.M. groan at that!)

Did you know your daughter had a dramatic instinct? I walked over to the club with Peg Monroe and she informed me that Miss Champ considered that G. Goddard and I and one other girl were the prize people of this new bunch—and that we had the dramatic instinct. When I come home please note the dramatic twist of my new key in the lock. Don't know when I'll be home. We have to stay here October 25 for homecoming. Your future Maud Adams. Love to you all,
Dorothy

October 17, 1930

Dear Dorothy,

I am sitting up with Teddy. It rained and thundered tonight and he will not go to bed—disturbed me so I could not sleep, so I am up.

Sunday we went to church and Sunday school, then Auntie Gass cooked for us. She had some dinner—chicken, potatoes, cauliflower, celery, etc., pineapple pie, and frozen cream cheese salad.

Monday I washed twice again. Tuesday I cleaned house and ironed some. It was a beautiful day and Aunt Carrie came over and brought her mending. We sat on the porch and it was so nice. Florence was over Tuesday night. She brought over a washing and I washed again, which was a mistake. Wednesday evening I went to class at church and enjoyed it very much.

Today I expected Aunt Nellie, so did some baking and got things ready for dinner. She came and we decided to go to Pontiac, called Aunt Ada and went there for lunch. Packed your laundry case and mailed it on the way at Birmingham.

I received your letter. So glad you are happy and able to do the things you enjoy. Doesn't D.J. write the nicest letter? He sent me a snap of himself and four sisters and I wanted to save his letter, but I can't find it. He asked for your address and if I cared if he wrote to you. I like him a lot.

I was quite attracted to Geraldine. Glad she got in and hurrah for good men! Aunt Minnie didn't tell me she sent the candy. She doesn't let her left hand know what her right hand does. She is so good to me.

I am glad to know there is "instinct" in the family—something new for us to appreciate. John M. cleaned the living room ceiling. I think he used a dramatic swing—anyway the result was very pleasing—you cannot imagine how dirty it was. I am still hoping I can get the curtains up and the house in order by the time you come home. I am afraid it won't look too good until we get a dining room rug. When, oh when—but I'm happy!

Last night Dr. Phelps brought *Fear* and *Victor & Victim* to loan. Also *Nerves and Personal Power*—it is very good, wish I might have read it twenty-five years ago—perhaps I could have managed better.

I'll say I love you—don't you dare to crush me!!! Sorry I didn't get this letter written sooner but you will get it before Sunday. We want you to come home soon as you can, but I realize it is hard for you to get away and perhaps someone may take us over—you never can tell. I just must trot off to bed even if Teddy does howl.

J.M. has had croup and a bad cold. I guess I'm getting it—not the croup. I have the vestibule paper cleaned and the closet, so you see I'm started. Remember me to Joyce and the other girls.
Heaps of love to my little girl,
Mother

October 24, 1930

Dear Mother,

Arrived OK but haven't written a line all week—it's seemed so short, getting back late the way I did. Our little lamp looks adorable. I made the shade Monday morning and pinned it together for lack of paste.

Last night D. King and I waxed ambitious and, in spite of the fact that we have no classes today, we went to the library. I got some good stuff for my oration. Am hoping I can work it out. Today is clean-up day and we upperclassmen are being righteously lazy—freshmen work! Am going downstairs to wash, then will serve and this afternoon go downtown to reserve play tickets and buy cord to hang our "cats" by.

Saturday night I'm ushering at the play—in formal dress! It will be lots of fun, I think. No dates for this weekend, but I should worry! Everybody will be going somewhere—I don't know what I'll do tonight. It seemed so good to be home last week—a real event. Must go and wash my many clothes.
Love,
Dorothy

Tuesday afternoon

Dear Mother,

Laundry just arrived and I was so pleased because I was desperate for hankies and even thought of going to the length of washing some. (I've had another cold for nearly a week now.) I'll send my case and clothes home in a day or so, so we can make connections—that is if you're still trying out washing machines.

Well Homecoming is over. It was rather hectic although I enjoyed the play and it was lots of fun to usher, in my roommate's green formal. Am enclosing the program and will you save it for me please? Our pictures are hung and the lamp enthroned on our dresser. We look quite spiffy. Thanks for the nuts. Joyce just came in with a starved look and I told her I had my laundry and she said "anything else" in breathless tones! The poor girl gets so hungry between meals.

I went out for debate yesterday and started reading material. I don't anticipate it much, but it is sort of interesting—it's about medical practice and clinic care in the U.S. I don't know any details so far.

171

One thing made my heart glad today. I got a bluebook back in Eng. Lit. on which I expected a D and got instead a B+— hooray! I think I'll work the prof. for an A by writing a paper on some obscure subject. I would like all the good marks I can get.

How is everything in that dull town of yours? I expect you do seventeen times as many things as I do in a day.
Love to you all,
Dorothy

October 24, 1930

Dear Dorothy,

Tuesday night I was all in with my cold, also Wednesday, but the demonstrator came and we washed. Minnie brought me some cold capsules. I'm feeling better tonight so I used the new ironer today and like it very much.

Had a letter from Clara saying she would be in for teachers' convention next Thursday and Friday and could she stay here. She would be here for dinner Thursday. It is convention time now for Detroit teachers, so I thought she meant today and scratched around and got up a nice meal and waited until 7:00, when my mind clicked that it must be next week that she meant.

The antique lady came tonight and I traded the Bohemian glass vase, wee walnut chest and the despised whatnot for a big brass basin. I think it will be lovely for apples and popcorn. Anyway, I did it. The men of the house like it and think I did well. She doesn't pay as much as Mr. Harding. I'll get around to some more places and maybe I can trade some more of the old things we do not value.

It is late and this child must get to bed. It sure did seem good to have our little girl home. I was sorry we had a cold epidemic just when you were here. I forgot to pay you for the lemons. There is no school tomorrow and J.M. and I are going antiquing for a change.
Lovingly,
Mother

October 29, 1930

My dear little girl,

It is one o'clock, I have just had my lunch and as I have been working like a billy goat all morning, I'll take a few minutes off and

172

write to you. We have been neglecting each other this week, but I expect you have been busy like I am.

Sunday we went to church and Sunday school. Dr. Rice preached such a good sermon. Daddy and I walked over to Palmer Park. He was so tired he went to bed at seven, so J.M. and I got Auntie Steed and Minnie and went to church again. He talked on the joy of work and when I got home I wished it was Monday morning so I could get at the washing—he is so helpful.

Monday I cleaned the house, shopped and washed, then met Aunt Lottie. Tuesday a.m. I took Aunt Lottie down to Metropolitan, coming back alone. I got led off into an antique hunt and in a district where the transportation was not so good—I don't know just how many miles I walked (a plenty). Then went downtown to look at washing machines and back to the church at four. Went to the station with Aunt Lottie and reached home again at six. J.M. came in, raring to go—had been invited to join the HiY—he was so tickled and so was I.

This morning I have put kitchen, cupboard, icebox, and whole house in order. Have to clean the bathroom yet, go downstairs to do the ironing, and then to the store for eats.

Hope comes tonight for teachers' institute. I think she plans to stay over Sunday. Clara Smith comes Thursday. I am not exactly bored!

Think I will go downtown tomorrow and look around for some Christmas ideas unless I can get some ideas to make something out of nothing. I'm afraid we won't be able to do much. Still spending my spare time answering ads for a roomer, but haven't landed one yet—maybe soon. Guess I'll go iron now. Then maybe I will think up some more news.

I don't know whether I should even write this, it is so terrible, but I learned what the trouble was about Mr. Reynolds. He has been going around with another woman for two years. Her husband is getting a divorce. Bessie is staying on account of the money. Gordon just entered the University this fall. I can't believe it, but it is so.

Sorry you had another cold. Glad for your B+. J.M.'s marks come next Monday and I am anxious to see what he gets. He says he is at the head of his department at work now—Spuds—works so hard, but seems to enjoy it.

Have changed my mind about ironers and decided I want a different kind, but Daddy thinks I should only get the washing machine, so it may be that way, but it is the ironer I am thrilled about. I'll try to look around at clothes before Thanksgiving and I have an idea for cut velvet. If I get the mending done perhaps I can sew. You ought to see the window seat—it is loaded with jobs that I should do and I'll get most of them done this week.

Wish I could see you, but if you are all right why I'll keep busy and get along. If you don't like my brass pan, you will be in Dutch because it is really very good—so there.

The house looks pretty well and washing and ironing are all done. I will be getting a washer right away, so send your duds. Teddy is a bad dog—he dug the bathroom rug because I went downtown. Daddy works day and night—he ought to get $10,000 per—maybe he will someday, who knows? His new men are doing pretty well. He has nine of his own agents now that he makes over-writing on, so he is coming along.
Heaps of love,
Mother

Tuesday 8:15 a.m.

Dear Mother,

This is a perfectly stupid class—I can hardly stand the lecture—it's so monotonous. Last night we had a feed in D. King's room—it was her birthday and D. Malmborg gave the party as a surprise for her. We had fun, but as usual ate too much. Also had a sorority meeting and Joyce and I almost forgot to go—we were so busy sorting over my clothes. Joyce put on my old jersey dress and planned it so it will be quite presentable, also my orange wool one. We'll have about one more session and get them all planned. She's awfully good at it and you know how famously I sew. If I can get my things that I have here all fixed up, or thrown away, I'll be through fussing with them.

I'm going to the first debate meeting this afternoon (am scared pink), besides three classes, then tonight Histrionic Club meeting. Tomorrow debate squad meets again. I would like to make the squad but there isn't a chance with no experience at all.

It looks like a busy week, but I'm rather glad—I don't seem to have gotten really going at my usual rate this year.

I had word from the loan fund saying that my loan had been approved and wanted to know where to send the check. I said here. I wonder if I'd better transfer my account to this bank. It's costing me a dollar a month in Pontiac. If Daddy could find out what my balance is before long, I could draw a check for the balance and deposit it here.

The sorority is having an informal November twenty-first and I've a good notion to go. I haven't the slightest idea who to take or what to wear, but I hate to have them think I can't go, so I guess I'll take my life in my hands and ask somebody strange (and tall!).

I expect you're so busy you won't even have time to read such an epistle as this. Lorene brought me her beaded formal. It's awfully short, but Joyce suggested a way to fix it that I think will make it very pretty. I'll bring it Thanksgiving. I don't know yet how I'll get home but I hope to have good luck.

I wonder if we could manage to entertain Joyce a part of Thanksgiving vacation. She has friends in Detroit, but I haven't heard her say that she was invited anywhere for Thanksgiving and she can't go home until Christmas.

Later—we've been cutting up a frog last hour. Would you think it possible for me to do such a thing? I'm getting hard boiled!!

Had both my smocks stolen from the laundry, so I'm wearing Joyce's for the present. Don't know whether to buy new ones or not.

Battenhouse is lecturing at a great rate and thinks I'm taking down all his "jewels" of thought. He's fooled. I'm creating a masterpiece of my own. (Preserve this as great literature.)

Sometimes I think I'd like to write more than any one thing—but I'm afraid that's one of those impecunious things to steer clear of. (Don't worry! Yours truly is as practical as the most practical!!) Write me, my dear people, you're very bad! Almost as bad as your daughter!

Love to you all,

Dorothy

November 6, 1930

Dear Dorothy,

Eight bells and I think I have done a day's work, anyway I am going to stop and write to my little girl. I was getting desperate to-day when your letter came. Monday a.m. I washed and your laundry came at 11:00, after I was all through. I should have waited. Cleaned the house and did some mending. Tuesday Edith came after me and we went down to the library. I found some books on antiques—all new to me. She went with me to do my grocery shopping. I like her very much—she is a little younger than you are. I like her the most, I think, of the relatives here—she certainly has all the in-laws beaten.

Guess I told you Lester was starting in the insurance business. Last night he went alone and closed $3000 and was real tickled. I hope he will be able to leave the awful shop where he works by spring anyway. He has always wanted to be a salesman and is so excited about it.

This morning I thought I would wash your clothes and J.M.'s bedding—in my haste, I let the hose slip and the boiling water was turned on me—just below the waistline. Maybe I am not blistered, but I guess if I am careful it will be all right.

Why don't you bring your dresses home that you have planned and let me fix them? I don't see where you have time to do any more. Hope you make the debate squad. Perhaps you will be surprised. I'm so glad you have the loan fund approved. I would surely transfer the checking account if you don't have to pay any-thing there, or even if you do—it would be more convenient.

Wish I could send you a new dress for the informal, but I guess I'm not much of a manager. Anytime I am too busy to read your letters, I'll tell you not to bother writing!

I think you can have Joyce come all right if she wants to. You know her better than I do, but I feel perfectly comfortable with her and will be glad to have her if you think she will be happy without being entertained and with us just as we are. I like her very much. Do you want me to write to her especially or will you just ask her?

I am so sorry about your smocks. I suppose you will just have to get more—if so you had better send them home to be laundered. I wouldn't mind them with the ironer. Could we get them here cheaper, do you think?

Sometimes I think writing is your forte too, so you aren't the only one who has thought of it. I am entertaining washer salesmen every day. It is very thrilling. I do not know yet which machine I will keep.

Don't see Daddy at all—he just works, works. Mr. Spencer gave him the leading featurization at their last meeting. That doesn't cost him anything. I am mean, but I am anxious to have our drawing account increased—for various reasons.

Auntie Gass is starting to work now—Daddy soon ought to have quite a big overwriting from his agents. I'll try to write oftener. I'll have to plan a certain time for writing, then other things won't be allowed to crowd in.

You must come home Thanksgiving. If you can't get a ride your mother will have to come across and pay your railroad fare—for we need to see our little girl or maybe she will forget all about us.

This is Wednesday—class night, but I couldn't go out with my burned front. Clothing irritates it, so I'm only wearing loose things.

J.M. is having trouble with his Latin—do not know if he is going to make it or not. He doesn't have much time with his job. Be careful of the frogs—don't get the habit. I will be so glad when you come home and glad to hear all the doings.
Heaps of love,
Mother

Tuesday night

Dear Mother,

So sorry to be such a poke about writing—mid-semesters are this week and we're just tearing. I have decided to go to our party Friday and have a date with a Delt whom I don't know. Haven't any conception of how or why I'm going, but it's arranged anyway.

We debated today and the prof. was very nice, even complimented me on my material. It's more fun than I had thought. Marks are coming out soon and everyone is hectic with studying.

Forgive me if I don't write more now—will write again tomorrow. My mind is blank and it's midnight. Your letters are lovely—don't pretend they're dumb. How's the burn?
Love,
Dorothy

Thursday afternoon

Dear Mother,

You surely should have more letters than I've been writing lately. I wish I could come home and visit you (with your bandages) or send you something very splendiferous! But I guess I'd better save my millions for the cold winter.

Don't worry about me and my clothes. I get along beautifully and when I want to, I can always wear something of Joyce's. We get along very well, using each other's things.

We gave our play in class and it was pretty good, I guess. Anyway, Miss Champ seemed to think so. Last night I went to the debate meeting where Dr. Hall spoke. He is a darling! This afternoon will be full up with debate meeting again at 5 p.m., then I must dig in and finish my oration.

The days are beautiful lately—so shiny and not at all cold. I had a letter from Fleming—very casual. I guess I'll wait quite a while before I answer it. Also had another letter from Dudley.

It seems to me you're just doing the little entertaining act most of the time. I think you'd better go slow for a little while—at least till you get feeling better. Must run to class.
Heaps of love,
Dorothy

Thursday night

Dearest Mother,

Tonight I have again caught that glimpse of something that makes me go on. Oh, I was so lonely, so forlorn. I wanted to run home—run away and hide from living. It's been an effort to smile and I haven't written often, nor much, because nothing mattered.

Isn't it funny that everything comes in flashes—like a sudden light—an answer to an impossible question? I was reading and my eye caught this poem by Matthew Arnold:

> "Weary of myself and sick of asking
> What I am and what I ought to be,
> At this vessel's prow I stand, which bears me
> Forwards, forwards, o'er the starlit sea.

And a look of passionate desire
O'er the sea and to the stars I send;
Ye who from my childhood up have calmed me,
Calm me, ah compose me to the end!

Ah, once more, I cried, Ye stars, ye waters,
On my heart your mighty charm renew;
Still, still let me, as I gaze upon you,
Feel my soul becoming vast like you!

From the intense, clear, star-sown vault of heaven,
Over the lit sea's unquiet way,
In the rustling night air came the answer —
Wouldst thou be as these are? Live as they.

Unaffrighted by the silence round them
Undistracted by the sights they see,
These demand not that the things without them
Yield them love, amusement, sympathy.

And with joy the stars perform their shining,
And the sea its long moon-silvered roll;
For self-poised they live, nor pine with noting
All the fever of some differing soul.

Bounded by themselves and unregardful
In what state God's other works may be,
In their own tasks all their powers pouring,
These attain the mighty life you see.

O airborn voice! Long since severely clear,
A cry like thine in mine own heart I hear,
Resolve to be thyself; and know, that he
Who finds himself loses his misery."

Perhaps this doesn't appeal to you, but it was like a gift out of the blue. Tomorrow I shall be happy! I wish I might squeeze you all right now and sit by the fire at our home. It seems as if I would go

179

crazy this last week—such a myriad of thoughts and contradictions kept fighting for supremacy within me.

Tonight all is calm (time out—temporarily) and after all what does it matter? Our little opinions—human foibles—laughable and lovable. If we put the emphasis on the last, everything will work out better perhaps.

Your crazy little girl who loves you all and wishes she might not be so dumb—that she might make her dear family proud of her. Dorothy

Hi there, John Merritt! How's the good old job? Don't work too hard.

November 10, 1930

Dear Dorothy,

J.M. and I went to church and SS this morning. Daddy was too pokey. We heard a marvelous sermon. I always wish you could hear them as they are so helpful. "I will be with you always" was his text and you can imagine what it would be—he said he had come to believe religion was only this—to experience the companionship of Christ and said he could not meet life without it.

We have been alone all afternoon. It has been such a gorgeous day I did so wish we had a big car so we could make Albion and see our little girl. Ann Arbor would be so much easier.

Aunt Minnie came over yesterday afternoon and went to John R. with me to shop, then she stayed to dinner. Friday Auntie Steed and Carrie came over and brought their sewing, had lunch and stayed till five. The box of dates was a treat Aunt Lottie bought for us—so we saved most of it for you. We don't forget you, ever.

J.M. painted the fenders, etc. of his bosses' car yesterday and made $3.50 this week, so with a little help was able to buy gloves and a hat. If you could see him with his first hat! He came home and put on a style show like you used to when you had something new. He was afraid to wear it to church but wanted to and, of course, did. He was so happy over it—about the only good thing I see about not having much money—you do appreciate things so much when you get them.

I am so sorry you have been so unhappy. I finally sensed it in your last letter, but thought it was probably because you wanted clothes and there is so little I can do to help you. When these times come and overwhelm you—probably you are overtired and have not had enough change. I am glad you found the beautiful poem that gave you a lift.

I wished this morning that you might have a faith as great as Dr. Rice—it would help us to a clear vision.

The family is looking forward to your coming. J.M. is so excited. Seems to me he has grown a foot this fall. We are going to church tonight. I wish you were here.

Is Joyce coming home with you? Forgive the scrawl—J.M. is using my pen.

Lovingly,
Mother

Home again—Dr. Rice talked on the worth of character—if I was clever like you I could tell you all about it.

I have been down to put the clothes to soak and in the morning I will wash. I think I am going to take the "Easy" machine, as it has had a ten-dollar drop that interests me. Now for bed. I hope my little girl is feeling on top of the world. It isn't hard for you to make us proud of you, but it is hard for you to live up to your own ideals, but you can do it. Night night.

November 11, 1930

Dear Dorothy,

This is one of my nights sitting up with myself—nothing wrong—so will write you a note before I go to bed again.

Aunt Nellie came this a.m. so I ironed your few things and some of ours—packed your laundry case and mailed it in Birmingham again. Sent you all I had in the house. I am going to try to get myself on a schedule, if I can, so my work will be done and I will have eats on hand, you know.

Bought some eats on the way home—hurried home and got dinner. We played bridge a while and Aunt Nellie left at 11. Now I must go to bed—hope you are not worrying about anything. Everything is okay here. I expect you need clothes most of anything. That is the case here—but things are so much better with us that I don't seem to mind what I can't have so much, for I think we will soon be able to have things.

181

Night, night, be happy all the time. You can if you think so. You should write to me real often, for I really have a bad burn—I'm bandaged in front!
Heaps of love,
Mother

                                          Sunday afternoon
Dear Mother,
    It's one of those gorgeous days—all sunshine and freshness. We have our window open and it's all blowy and shiny. Couples keep going up and down the walk leisurely—it's all very peaceful. Joyce and I have felt quite "purry" the last few days—getting content in our old age I guess.
    She has been invited to a friend's in Detroit for Thanksgiving, but I expect she'll want to divide up her time between us and them. We're going to try to get a ride home because we're counting our ducats.
    Don't scold when I tell you that I slept right through my 8:00 o'clock Saturday morning. It filled me first with horror, and then with fiendish glee! I can see where I'll have to buckle down on that biology course or I'll never get through—it bores me so.
    We are practicing for our play to be given in class Tuesday. Then next week I have the lead as a dumb Swedish maid. Quite in the limelight!
    Received a letter from Dudley today and I guess he's planning on coming to Albion next year. Says he's very busy and should work harder, but doesn't.
    I'm anxious about your blistered self. Don't do anything to irritate it. For goodness sakes be careful. I'm so sorry my old clothes made all that trouble. The dates and apples were delicious and eaten with much satisfaction as usual.
    Am getting cold feet about asking anyone to our party. Probably I won't go after all. Well anyway it's just about two more weekends until I come home.
    Do be good and let your front get healed up well. Daddy seems to be hitting the line hard. My only advice to you children in anything is: "For the love of Mike, use discretion." Yours truly, one more college sap.
Love, loads of it
Dorothy

Wednesday eve.

Dear Mother,

Without doubt you'll note the high falutin' stationery. Don't worry—I haven't gone wrong—just giving you a break.

The hectic exams have sort of let up and I guess I'll manage to pull through till time to go home. Joyce and I think maybe we'll bum home. Won't that be cute!

I fixed my jersey dress over and it looks pretty good. Will bring home most of my stuff and get it in order if possible.

Please don't work too hard. It's quite important that you get feeling good, you know. J.M. is just more than working, isn't he? Tell Daddy not to monkey around with that ulcerated tooth business. I must see that you all behave.

Marks will be out right after Thanksgiving—and then we can be thankful for small favors. I am getting a real kick out of my courses and even liking debate.

Haven't heard from Hope at all. Is she still alive after teaching at Yale? Had a crazy letter from some boy at Schreiner Institute the other day. It was funny—evidently Dudley's been over-estimating my charms. (ha ha!)

Love to my dear family,
Dorothy

December 2, 1930

Dearest Mother,

A glorious winter afternoon with the sunlight and shadows across the snow. Today has been nice in many ways. I got two letters this morning.

Our bus got here Sunday night at 8:30—it was packed with Albion people. Joyce got the wrong suitcase and then excitement reigned. However she got her own back yesterday and we heaved a sigh of relief.

It was so good to be home and I really do appreciate my dear family, even if you'd sometimes never guess it. I think somebody went putting things in my purse. (You are an incorrigible bunch!) I don't know what to do with you but love you all, and wish that every girl had the sympathy and support behind her that I am always certain of.

I had a letter from Lucille at Ann Arbor. She gave me all the information she could and said she'd sent application blanks, but the more I figure the more I decide that for next semester the cost would be greater at the U, everything considered. She said work was hard to get this year and probably I couldn't get steady work. An interview with the social director is necessary also and Lucille said I might stay with her while over there to see about it. I guess I won't try to make the U this next semester, but do think it would be well to have my application in for next year. I also had a letter from Fleming.
Love,
Dorothy

Sunday eve.

Dear Dorothy,

All ready for bed, but will write a note, then the postie will take it. Fussed around Saurday a.m.—it was rainy and nasty, but I went out and shopped. Then thought it would be clever to do next week's washing, so I did, then Aunt Minnie came over and stayed to dinner and till 10:00, then J.M. & I walked home with her.

Came home, had a bath, crawled in my nice clean bed and thought I was going to have a wonderful sleep. Teddy decided to cry all night for J.M. so I was up with him six times. Hope tonight will be different.

Steeds called for J.M. and me this morning for church. Daddy worked most of the day—me mad!

This afternoon J.M. and I worked on the nativity. Am anxious for you to get home. I expect you will think of a lot of new ideas. J.M. is so happy with it.

Think I will go downtown in the morning and see if I can get Aunt Lucy something and I have some ideas simmering for Daddy, but they may not work out. Forgive the scrawl, I am sleepy.
Heaps of love,
Mother

December 5, 1930

Dear Dorothy,

I am sure in disgrace, but I'll hurry to the corner, then you will sure get it tomorrow. Was so glad to get your letter, for I felt as if you hadn't had a very good time and that your family didn't rate much—when they have cars that won't go, etc. However, if you still like us, we are happy.

Monday morning I washed and in the afternoon I went out in the "boo" cold to the library. Didn't have long to stay, but had such a nice time and found out where our sampler came from—isn't that thrilling? Petrockstone parish, Devonshire Co, England.

Tuesday I ironed, shopped, got meals, cleaned, etc. Wednesday the same and mended. All the time in between worked on the oval table. It is a lot of work but is going to be very lovely, I think.

On Wednesday Daddy was in session with Mr. S. most of the day and was fagged and wanted to go to the show, so I left my class at church. We three met and went to see *The Spoilers* and it was very good.

They were trying to work things out so Daddy would have more time for personal production. Got our checks but will have to go slow for we have just a certain line of credit. It is that and no more. However, I think things will eventually work out all right.

Thursday Aunt Ada came and stayed all night. We went downtown this morning and spent most of our time looking around. Found sets of the Nativity but think ours will be lovelier when we get it ready.

Haven't talked with Daddy about the car, but if it is not repaired, we cannot go to Vassar. Just had a letter from Aunt Lottie asking what to do about gifts. She has written to her sisters here, planning just to remember the children and only practical things for them. They wanted to know what our two families had better do. She says, "Shall we just have funny gifts or little gifts? I want to do the thing that will make us all the happiest. The fact that we could be together would make it Christmas for me."

I had planned to buy their gifts today, but after her letter came I didn't know just what to do. So I am waiting until I can decide.

Now I must run mail this. Tell Joyce I enjoyed her nice letter so much. She was a very charming guest. You will be home again before you know it.
Heaps of love,
Mother

Wednesday morn.

Dear Mother,

More and more hectic are the days and still less do I study. Today I must really get down to business and in the short, short while before Christmas, finish my work. I am feeling real peppy anyway. I fooled away last weekend and Sunday night dated my little Delt boyfriend, Norman. He's all right and a peach, but rivals the best in indifference. Anyway, I had fun. Joyce dated once this weekend too, so on that score we're even.

Perhaps you won't know your child when she blows in. However, look hard, before you reject me as an impostor!

I think Aunt Lottie is really sensible about Christmas. I think it would be nice to give each one a little gift and go to Vassar if we can. However, whatever we do will be OK with me. I shall buy Joyce something and not send any cards or other gifts to people here.

Had a long, long letter from D.J. Real sweet it was. He said he liked my style of writing, so I wouldn't be surprised if he might get on my regular mailing list. He's enjoying Yale very much, I take it.

Just got application blanks from Martha Cook. Perhaps on my way back from Christmas vacation I can stop in Ann Arbor for an interview although I don't intend to go there this year. Time to serve now. Will try to get another letter off soon. Rah for Petrockstone! Love,
Dorothy

December 11, 1930

Dear Dorothy,

Hope I'll get a letter this morning. I was wakened from a sound sleep about 4:00 by a dream that my little girl was dead. A few startlers like that make you feel that nothing matters if we are just all here and well. However, no more sleep for me. A letter did come, so I feel better.

I don't understand why the days are so hectic when you aren't studying or doing any Christmas things. I'll have to get over there and see that you study. J.M. got a real good card, and wasn't he proud?

Bet you have cut your hair or traded your coat—you can't bother me if you are alive and well and good—so there.

Spent another day downtown yesterday—I am all through except you and J.M. and Aunt Nellie. I thought maybe she would be here today and I would find out something she wants. Did I write you I bought material for making Daddy a housecoat? It was a marvelous sale—54" wool tweed for $1 a yard. J.M. likes it. I do not know whether you will or not, but think Daddy will. Now the next job is to get it made.

Bought material like the enclosed bit for Aunt Lucy. I'll make her a bed jacket, trimming it with the green. Will probably have to send it before you come. I won't wrap the other little gifts, for I thought you would like to be in on that. You can be thankful you did not have to shop—the crowds were terrible Monday.

Tuesday I did the ironing, then went to Royal Oak to see the Dunhams and had a nice little visit. Now I can get busy and clean the dirtiest house imaginable and get the jackets made. Expect we will sew during your vacation.

Glad you had the date, even if he didn't realize who he was dating. I think D.J. is a peach.
Heaps of love,
Mother

December 16, 1930

Dear Dorothy,

Bedtime. I am sitting by the fire. J.M. is in bed and Daddy is not home yet. I had a wild spell today—visited two antique shops and an old bookshop. The blasts were wintry. When I got home I decided I was a goop, but I went to the basement and did a big washing, so don't feel quite so guilty now.

The enclosed bulletin gives you the church Christmas program. We would like to go and hope that you would be interested too. If you come in on the same train as before perhaps Daddy can meet you (if he does not have to work) and bring you to the church on your way home.

Iron and clean tomorrow and then sewing the rest of the week. I will try to finish Aunt Lucy's jacket tomorrow, then get at Daddy's coat. Expect you are stepping lively this week. It won't be long now.
Heaps of love,
Mother

Tuesday night

Dearest Mother,

Am still alive and howling—but not writing many letters it seems. Today has been so full—classes all day, debate, play practice and we also gave a play in class. I did my dumb Swedish maid part and Miss Champ said she didn't know I could be so dumb. (Aha! She little knows me!)

I think with good luck I'll be able to get most of my work off my chest before Christmas. Just three more days—a terrible lit. blue book, one bum oration, a semester project in both speech and interpretation, a Christmas breakfast to serve at 6 a.m. Thursday and finally work Friday noon—after lunch we are through for the year.

I will take the 2:11 train from Albion Friday which gets into Detroit about 4:30. Everything is swimming along beautifully. I always feel better when the work's all piled up ahead you know. Debate is getting to be the real thing and it's such fun to see things develop. Last night we had dinner at the Lodge, and invited our patronesses and also some prospective rushees. Will be seeing you very soon and talking all your heads completely off.

Love,

Dorothy

Sunday Evening

Dearest Mother,

Arrived O.K.—puffing like a beaver with my many possessions. I had a merry time with the girls. Dinner was served at 6:00 (regular dinner in my full condition). Found a box of homemade candy from Margaret, which has been here since before Christmas.

Am all unpacked and have washed my hair, taken a shower and talked my fool head off and it is now eleven o'clock.

Joyce has not come in—I don't know what to think, but I guess she's all right. It seems good to have everything clean to start out the year. We ate the food, or part of it, and now I guess I'll make a beeline for bed.

That extensive studying session didn't materialize, you will be interested to know. However, there awaits me a busy tomorrow. Don't work too hard and take care of yourself, Mrs. Ritz!

I found out that exams are from January 26-30. Next semester

starts February 2. Nobody seems to have any new clothes, so I guess we'll all be in the same boat. Well, now to bed.
All my love to you all,
Dorothy

January 12, 1931
Dear Dorothy,

J.M. has my pen so I'll have to pencil it. This has been a dark, sleepy day. J.M. got up early and got breakfast—bacon, pancakes and syrup, if you please—they were good too. Then we went to church. Came home and no one was hungry, so we did not get dinner until after 5:00 o'clock. It is just 8:00—I have the dishes done, the clothes put to soak and have written to Aunt Lucy and now you.

Yesterday I worked at J.M.'s room, getting it ready to clean— it looks some different and when I get the woodwork cleaned and fresh curtains, it will be a change.

I took my coat over on John R. It is going to cost $14.00 to have it repaired—wow—but he says then it will be just like new—it had rotted where the stitches pulled out.

Wasn't Franklin Dunn nice? Mrs. Dunn came to the door and said that Franklin was going to Albion and thought perhaps I might have something to send to you, but I guess he was too scared to come to the door himself. They have a new radio upstairs, I think, by the sound—we hear it very plainly.

J.M. got $2.50 this week so he felt better.

Did I tell you Norman gave Auntie Steed a little Philco radio like we want— wasn't that nice? Haven't a bit more news to tell this time. Hope I get a letter Monday.
Heaps of love,
Mother

Tuesday a.m.
Dear Mother,

Your good letter came this morning—you will think me an awful poke not to have written before this, but then you know how rapidly everything has to go these days, and I get pretty tired.

Have interviewed Mrs. Wolfe, Miss Hindman, and Miss Gray in turn about a job, and as yet there is nothing definite. Miss Gray said neither yes nor no, and told me she would tell me before registration, which is the 24th. I think she will do the best she can. I am going inactive in Kappa Delta.

The days are real fun in spite of the hectic rush. I am entering an oratory contest, and I need your prayers. I'm afraid it's going to be awful. Today Mr. Hance will tell us who goes to Ypsilanti tomorrow to debate. I really don't want to go, but I would like the satisfaction of knowing that he thinks I'm good enough. Am quite crazy about debate.

Just went down to see the nurse and get something for a beginning cold. I feel sort of rotten, but am trying to ward it off.

I didn't know that the young Mr. Dunn was responsible for my package. It was left at the desk for me. It was awfully nice of him to think of doing it.

Well perhaps soon I'll be able to write a real letter, maybe next week when I'm loafing around with nothing to do but write a term paper, read collateral, and various other little details.
Love always,
Dorothy

Jan. 17, 1931

Dear Dorothy,

I guess I had better write a note while I am still awake—did not sleep much last night—so I have about walked in my sleep today.

Was so glad to get your letter—while I love to get them, if you can't get time to write when you are so busy, I will understand.

Mr. Dunn ran an ad in the paper for a roomer at $2.50 per—and has rented a room, but I do not see how they can make anything at that price—they are making a fight like everyone else, I guess.

I think I will advertise your room. If I could get just a reasonable amount it would tide you over till June—and I hate to have you change in the middle of the year if we can avoid it.

I am anxious to know how you come out in your debate and oratory contest. Do your best and then never mind—however it comes out, you have had the experience. Do hope you have checked your cold—do not like my little girl to have so many colds. Your laundry case came, and I will wash Monday, I expect.

My coat came back tonight—maybe it is a good job, but I have found two or three rips, so am going to take it back—he says I ought to get a couple seasons wear out of it—so that doesn't sound like a lifetime coat for me after all.

John M. is very happy he made his grades in all his subjects, so he does not have to take finals next week— and he will be home most of the week. Next Wednesday J.M. & I are going to Pontiac for the day. Aunt Ada wants Daddy to come if he can—he may have an interview there that night—so if he does, fine.

I have the clock face enameled and ready for decoration. I am anxious to finish it. Don't worry—insist on being happy—cause you have folks and they love you all the time.

Lovingly,

Mother

Susanna Wesley Hall

January 16, 1931

Dear Family,

I thought it might interest you to know that Albion College, in the person of Dr. Seaton, and under the cooperation of Miss Gray, has granted me an additional scholarship of $50 for the next semester, which will enable me to stay in school here.

I never in my wildest thoughts dreamed of such a possibility, but even the wildest thoughts often don't provide for emergencies.

J.M.'s letter came this morning and he is an old dear. It seems that everyone is trying their best to get me through school. I will write him in the near future when I get my oration off my chest.

The contest was postponed until next Thursday at 4:00 p.m. Did you all know that your daughter went on a debate trip to Ypsilanti with eleven others? It was quite thrilling. We left here at 12:30 noon and got home at 1:00 in the morning. We were with Miss Gray's load and certainly had a gay time both coming and going. We stopped to eat outside of Jackson on the way home and had a perfectly gorgeous time. I got to know some of the girls so much better, and it seemed that everything was so worthwhile. Dear old Ypsilanti was just the same. I saw Hope's old roommate. They served us a nice dinner, and yours truly did as well as could be expected in the debate. Further trips are being planned, some out of the state, and

I'm holding my breath and working hard, hoping that I may get a chance to go.

How are you all? I was glad to hear that J.M. is being paid a living wage, or something like it. Just give me a week or so to get my work caught up and I will really write a letter. Don't you think this Albion is pretty wonderful?

All my love,
Dorothy

Sunday p.m.

Dear J.M.,

Dinner has not yet been served in the dining car, and yours truly has been working her fool head off making up lost time and getting a whole semester's work done in a week. I'm glad to hear that you're almost through with your misery. We have this week yet before exams, then a solid week of them, but that won't be so bad because I have a day to study for each one.

Today I've been writing on my worthy oration, which will surely win the first prize, if the judges know their business, and I shall see to that, for I expect to pick them out, or bribe them on the side. The first prize is 25 golden berries and my heart pants for it, but there are a lot of other hearts panting for it too, so farewell money.

I think you're quite a business executive to save so much money for your poverty stricken sister. You shouldn't have sent it, but anyway I do appreciate it a lot. This is just the time when I need it most. I'm going to have to be pretty careful next semester, because I'll be awfully short of cash, but I don't care, for I'm so happy to be able to stay here at all. Don't you think the college was pretty grand to me? Altogether I have $100 scholarship for the year now.

You know college is a pretty good old institution even if it does take some figuring to get there. I hope you'll decide that it's worth something to you, for there's no getting around the fact that you learn a lot in more ways than one, and it gets a person feeling that there are loads of opportunities, and that time spent there is far from wasted. You have heaps of fun and all the while you get more confidence in yourself, besides getting a bigger viewpoint on living in general. Waiting table, slinging the trays, dancing (and you can learn very easily), parties, classes, are all worthwhile.

192

Joyce enjoyed your greeting, and giggled. Last night she went to a formal party and the favors were little banjo clocks. They're just darling. Mother would fall for them.

Well, goodbye, old man, I must browse in the books a little more now, or lose that college education. Write me often and tell me all the scandal, and if you ever need my humble assistance let me know, and maybe we can figure things out. I am anxious to see that new sweater.

Love to you all,

Dorothy

January 21, 1931

Dear Dorothy,

You surely have had a break. Seems if we just hold steady and do our best, things work out for us. I was surely surprised. I am so glad to think Albion has stood by you. I think you owe Miss Gray a great deal even if she is sometimes temperamental—perhaps you may be able to do a good turn for Albion someday.

I don't quite understand, when you first went, they gave you $25 and then the $50. In J.M.'s letter you said you had $100 in scholarships—when did you get the other $25?

Saturday night I couldn't sleep so I was reading in the living room—when just after 1:00 a.m. the doorbell rang. I snapped off the light and called Daddy—we waited awhile—couldn't see or hear anyone so finally went back to bed.

We slept in so late that we did not get up in time for church. About 1:00 o'clock. Daddy walked out on the porch and there was a letter in the mailbox, so the mystery of the night bell was discovered and we had a special delivery from our little girl. I am so glad, for I couldn't see anyway to help you unless I could rent the room. I am going to try advertising the room for I ought to rent it—would be quite a help.

J.M. and I were over to Steed's about an hour Sunday afternoon. Mr. & Mrs. Dunn finally called on us a few minutes Sunday night. They are very pleasant and the boy, Franklin, seems nice when you get to know him a little. He is twenty-three and doing some kind of work with his camera now—has a darkroom arranged in the basement. He washes dishes and scrubs for his mother and seems to try to be a good scout.

Did the washing this morning and will have a big ironing for tomorrow and may go to Pontiac on Wednesday.

J.M. has the cot pad on the floor and is doing gym stunts and trying to egg Daddy to do what a fat man can. Daddy is playing the mouth organ.

There, have the clothes dampened and my howling hyenas put to bed—they have sung and played until I'm all awhirl, but isn't it nice they enjoyed it? And now for bed. I'll be glad for a long letter in full detail when you get through the rush. My thoughts will be with you Thursday, hope you will be so good you surprise yourself. Heaps of love—so glad about everything
Mother

Dear Dorothy,

I am sure lonesome to see you today— have been wishing all day someone with a big car would like to go to Albion, but I don't seem to know the right people.

It is a good thing you called us up for I have literally worn the papers out looking for the write up of the oratory contest and not a word have I found. I was so surprised when you called, I couldn't think, but afterward thought of a dozen questions to ask you.

We were all thrilled—it was funny to see J.M.'s face and you know how the money part of it would get him. $25 bucks now he says what does that mean—well, I said that means you working ten weeks. It was a good point for him—for education, and he wasn't slow to get it.

Little Dorothy has been having some breaks all right, hasn't she? I dreamed last night that the back door opened and in you came wearing your winter sport coat. I worked hard Thursday cleaning. J.M. washed windows on the outside—it surely helps. Thursday evening J.M. and I started caning chair seats. He is doing the old maple chair and I am doing one of those old ones of grandpa's. I think we will keep at it and cane everything in sight.

I also want to do Auntie Dee's mirror, rush the two chairs and finish the old clock. J.M. and I are working on our old clock face too. He had a whole week home. He is so proud of his card—one A and the rest Bs. J.M. has been skating this week, but today it is so warm that water is running everywhere. Franklin Dunn is copying the old family pictures for me.

194

I wish you would send your oration home—we are anxious to read it. I do so want to know all about everything. I want to see you so much. Write a lot, tell me everything.

Heaps of Love,

Mother

January 25, 1931

Dear Dorothy,

I am sitting in the old Windsor chair before the fire with Teddy at my feet, while both John Merritt and Mother are reading, writing, and visiting. An easy family party complete except for your own presence, but we are all most happy to know that even if we cannot have you here that we are closely related to one who has the honor of first place in Albion's Oratorical Contest. I should think this may be considered at Albion as one of "the honors" of the whole year.

We are all so pleased and I was glad you called Mother up to let us know the good news. But when I arrived at home that night— she was almost too proud to speak to me and so was J.M. but when they finally came "down to earth" and told me of my daughter's accomplishments, I refused to talk to either one of them. I said "I'm her dad!" and I'm sure that they both know now what it means for a young college girl to have picked the right kind of a dad, especially when she enters oratory.

Well, the big thing to do now around here seems to be to prove which one of the three of us has the honor of the closest relationship to you. J.M. says he'd rather be the brother of a celebrity than her mother or dad. Anyway we are all very proud of you and we always have been and I know that we always will be. I sincerely hope that joy of accomplishment will at least partially pay you for the splendid work you have done!

With heaps of love,

Daddy

Monday morning

Dear Ones,

Here it is the beginning of the week and also the beginning of exams. It is a lovely morning with the sun shining on the bare lawn, while the trees cast black shadows across the sunny yard. I just finished studying for my first exam, which comes this afternoon. Am all registered and everything. I have a course that I just love and am carrying sixteen hours besides oratory, for which I get one hour's credit, and debate. All my courses are two hour courses, except one, and I expect they'll be a lot of work, but I will enjoy them.

I will have Extemporaneous Speech, Advanced Composition, Interpretative Reading, Argumentation and Debate, English Lit., Educational Psych. Gym, and English Methods.

There's nothing like winning the oratory contest to make one a celebrity around here. I was one surprised mortal when the results came out. In the first place, I had worried and worked over the old oration till I thought it was no good at all, and at the last minute was beginning to get it learned, when Elta suddenly popped in with the idea of entering the contest, and I could tell by her tone of voice that she thought she would surely win it. It seems Prof. Hance urged her on, with the idea she would win, and it was two days before the contest, so she simply took her debate material on state medicine, borrowed a story which I had used in debating at Ypsilanti, and went out for the contest. Confidentially she told me that Prof. Hance thought it was nice I was a junior, for I would surely win next year.

In the meantime Prof. Weiss, to cheer me up, I guess, informed me that I was to be the winner, for from what he had heard of my oration, it was the most likely material of any in the group. So there we were, and I was simply swamped with work and worry, term papers and sundry things.

Well, to make a long story short, there were seven entries in the contest, but no one that the judges thought would stand out. The judges were Prof. Hance, Halstead, and Miss Champ. Prof. Weiss had to be out of town that day. We drew for places, and I drew last place, so when everyone had given theirs I got up, with a feeling closely akin to cold feet, for I didn't know mine very well.

Joyce went to the contest to pray for me, she said. Well, it was soon all over, and Prof. McCulloch stepped up to me and said, if I were judging the contest here's the young lady who would get first place, where have they been keeping you all thru college? So then we waited, and joked with DeVinney, who won the men's contest and Bob Cullum said, well I'll call you up and congratulate you when I hear the decision. So we went home. Nothing was decided that night, and everyone said the judges were in a deadlock, because all the orations were so good. Friday noon when I was serving I had a phone call and it was Bob calling to congratulate me. I thought he was joking, but he said not.

When I went to Miss Champ's class Friday morning to give my project I was all tired out and afraid I couldn't give it, but I managed to get through it, and after class she handed me a wonderful criticism, and said she didn't know I had it in me. She said, "Young lady, you took me off my feet in the contest yesterday, and this morning you did it again, I haven't any criticism to offer on your project, it was fine." I found out afterward that the judges have unanimously given me first place, and that the big deadlock was over second and third places. Miss Champ was just bursting to tell me, but couldn't.

So I will be $25 richer in June when the prizes are awarded, but that is only a part of the good fortune. Prof. Hance is helping me to revise my oration for the state contest at Hillsdale, March 6, in which DeVinney and I will represent the college, and if we place there, will later go to Kalamazoo for further elimination contest.

So you see it has elements of thrill all the way along, and I'm going to dig just awfully hard to make it good. I hope to be able to make some of the long debating trips if I have good luck.

I think I have talked long enough about myself. Wish I could see you all. Don't work too hard, or worry too much. For from now on, we're the lucky Hills!
Love to you all always,
Dorothy Hill, B.O. (Bachelor of Oratory!)

January 30, 1931
Dear Dorothy,

Expect you are busy with exams—cramming, etc. I was glad to get your letter and hear some of the details. I should think Elta would feel a little flat—so sure of herself— and then not make a place at all. I hope you will keep on winning, but any way you have had one real thrill—I do so wish I could have heard you.

Monday, I washed as usual. Tuesday I ironed, and between times have been working on my clock face, chairs, mirror & etc. Will be glad when I get through with this stuff, but as Aunt Ada once said, I never will—I'll always be seeing something I want to do—but I'm not so sure. Went out long enough to get my hair cut yesterday— think he saved it for a baby mattress. Today I walked as far as Steeds', then got groceries and home again.

Hope you will get a chance to come home, although I worry about your riding with folks. Write soon as you can.
Heaps of love,
Mother

Tuesday Evening
Dearest Mother,

Your good letter came today. You almost make me want to chuck my work and come home to see you all. But I'm afraid the middle of the week isn't a very good time to throw up my hands and run home.

It has been simply glorious outdoors the last two days. Just like spring—with all the attendant spring fever. Classes are such fun, they're nearly all new ones for me. I've dropped argumentation and am taking public speaking methods in place of it. So now I have 8 o'clocks five mornings of the week, but only one Saturday class at 10:00.

Advanced comp. is such fun—all creative writing in the section I've chosen. And extemporaneous speaking from Prof. Weiss promises to be good.

Wednesday night the men have a debate and dinner over at Robinson Hall, to which the women's squad is invited. Friday M. Nixon and I debate again. Meanwhile every day this week will be rehearsals for histrionic play that I'm directing and then February thirteenth, Nixon and I are debating here with Adrian, in a decision debate (my first decision debate!) and the same night are the Histrionic plays. February fourteenth Kappa Delta is giving a Valentine party (informal house dance) at the lodge. By the fifteenth I must have my oration all rewritten and ready to send in to the contest judges. Also I will have to give it at Chapel later and at the High School—and finally March sixth at Hillsdale. If I should place there, then I will go on to Kalamazoo. (Meanwhile I'm supposed to be studying and attending college!)

Aunt Minnie sent me a whole box of chocolate bars and her congratulations so the whole corridor is feeling congratulated too. It sure was a nice surprise.

Joyce and I have cleaned the room at last—after all the exam mess—and it looks quite nice. Saturday and Sunday we didn't have a bit of studying and it was gorgeous. Saturday we washed and cleaned and Sunday, D. Malmborg and I hiked five miles in the morning with high topped boots and everything. Then came home and had my hair waved by Joyce and served dinner. Fussed around in the afternoon, poured tea at our Sunday night tea and went to Epworth League, and then church to hear Howard McCluskey from Ann Arbor. And so to bed!

Tonight I think I'll clean out notebook and drawers, make out my new schedule and clean shoes, gloves, and comb—write several letters and well, you wouldn't believe any more if I did tell you.

I wish you might be here the weekend of the thirteenth, but I expect you can't. I hardly know how things are at home—you're so close-mouthed about everything. Here's for all the good things anyway.

The longer I go to college and learn about the desirable background and equipment necessary for living, I find myself constantly measuring the things I've been given—and find that if everyone had had as much, there would be few problems for psychologists and other doctors of mental and physical health.

It's pretty fine to be able to look at your home life in perspective and find that in quality and relationships it verges on the ideal. Meeting problems and facing reality through a period of years, seeking and finding for your children the very best at your command, seems to me to be a fulfillment of purposes and ideals in right living, that few parents can equal and none surpass.

You can't imagine how often in the life of any student, he looks back, and in the light of new knowledge, evaluates things—home and parents particularly. And too, he looks ahead down the years, seeing with new clarity this perplexing thing we call living. And it is then that the realization, at least in part, comes, of what living involves. He sees his parents—not alone as parents—but as individuals. That is the real test—and when I think how gloriously mine have passed it, I wish that someday, perhaps, someone may think me half as worthy of recognition.

With all my love,
Dorothy

P.S. Enjoying Mr. Hill's letter immensely—though it was a shock! Do it again!

> February 6, 1931
> Memphis, Tennessee

My dear Dorothy:

I want to tell you that I am simply crazy over my bread plate and Staffordshire plate, as well as the two Graham prints. Nothing pleases me like an antique and these are so charming.

I am glad you are finishing university. You surely know, dear, that I am keen enough to have sized up that impossible home situation of yours long ago. When I was more prosperous I considered very seriously helping you through college, but I was not quite satisfied that you were going to do something that I should consider practical and worthwhile with it. In short, you seemed to vacillate so badly for a time that I was just a little out of sympathy. However, I heartily approve now and just wish I could help you today, but Dorothy, we have been badly cramped this year like most other folks in this old world.

You know your Auntie Dee and I were very successful women and we too, when we were young, found out how necessary it was sometimes to put aside our impossible dreams and come down to earth. I wanted with all my heart and soul to be an artist—but I couldn't afford to indulge in so great a luxury—now I have the leisure and can do so. Your time for frills will come later—if you keep your head now and I feel sure you will. Red and I were very proud over your oratorical victory—we hope you will win out in the finals. Lots of love and write me,
Aunt Katherine

> February 9, 1931

Dear Dorothy,

Your letter was a real thrill—when you only get one in about ten days—it is some event—it has been read over and over. Guess you had best write a bit oftener even if it is only a note—it is strange how much your family needs to hear from you.

We do realize how busy you are, and I am glad you are busy for I think everyone is so much happier and more interested when they are going full speed and feel they are really accomplishing something. Isn't it just great to have courses that you enjoy?

This week has been just the regular routine. Spent most of the day with Florence on Wednesday. She has had a cold and is not feeling too good and then Earl was laid off Wednesday, but he hopes it is not permanent. They have insisted on a reduction of rent and may possibly have to move.

Friday—busy all day, working on that old family history. I have the pictures now. Sim's came over in the evening to get their pictures and to plan a way to get it typed. While they were here Charles and Clara walked in—we were so glad to see them, as we haven't had any Pontiac company in a long time. J.M. went to the kitchen and served us with cinnamon toast and tea. He seems so grown up and is so good about trying to help in every way. He is writing to you this afternoon so I am not supposed to write about him.

I didn't tell you our car had been stolen. Daddy managed to get the brakes relined and got the car out of the garage a week ago. Thursday he picked up the Gasses to go to a meeting at the office and when they came out, our car was gone. We felt pretty bad—Daddy needs the car, for he is out trying to write personal business—but the next Monday, the police called and had found our car. It was not hurt at all, so we were very thankful to see the old bus again.

Yesterday morning Daddy cleaned the living room rug for me. I cleaned the small ones. They look so nice. I thought they were worn out, but it was dirt. Shame on me!

It is a wonderful provision that love blinds, for your mother wouldn't stand your tests of thought very well if you did not have a very loving heart. If one only had the strength of character or something to make themselves what they would like to be. I do not like to look backward, for I am not in any way satisfied with my life. If it were not for you and J.M. I would feel it had been a complete failure, but I try to feel I have had a little part in you. If J.M. will give us the satisfaction you have, we ought not to mind other things, for you have never given us an hour's worry or trouble—except the hurt we have had to bear because we could not do the things for you that we have longed to do.

201

I am so glad that we did give you expression lessons, for with your natural timidity you would not have done the work you are doing along that line now. I want it for John M. so much, if he will only take public speech the next two years, I think you can persuade him to. I was so happy about him sending you the little money—for I had not mentioned such a thing—he is proud of you—says he can't go to Albion after your record there.

I was hunting for some dates yesterday and found some scraps of things I must have saved for your baby book and one notation read "Well you made your own bed, what did you do that for?" You said: "Oh to help my mother and make her happy." And it just seemed to me those few words were a description of you. You have always been so dear to me. How you will love your baby book if you are given the joy of having a little child of your very own.

Sometimes I look and think of people and at first glance they seem to have so much—but at second glance they haven't Daddy, Dorothy and J.M. and I don't want what they have without my own riches.

Teddy is slipping every day and is getting to be more trouble, but the worse he is the more J.M. loves him. There seems to be no way out and he never has sick spells any more.

Do not worry about home problems. Everything is all right—only it is very difficult to make collections—that is why I haven't been able to send your money yet—will put one dollar of it in this letter, but there is nothing wrong—conditions in the auto centers are still bad.

I don't think they are going to raise our rent—we would move if they did—I'm very anxious to rent your room—someday I will find someone who wants it.

I am so interested in your oration and debates and would so like to come over, but I don't see any chance at present. Any time there is, you may be sure I'll be there.

Don't understand why you have so many colds, unless you are overdoing—take care of your health, first, or home for you. Hope to hear good news of the play and debates soon.
Bushels of love,
Mother

February 11, 1931

Dear Dorothy,

I'm home today because I didn't feel very well. I had a miserable cold and a headache. We get the breaks I guess. The boss thinks I can count now, so I clerk on Saturdays and do spuds during the week and I got $3.00 last week, but I'll probably get docked this week.

I got through last semester and got out of all my exams, but this semester is fierce. I got Miner for Latin. She is eighty-three years old and has been offered a pension three times but won't take it. She teaches Greek and Latin and she talks in a real low monotone and hardly opens her mouth and never moves her head. I sit in the back row by the streetcar and try to guess what she says. I got Tuomey for American Lit and like it immensely. She is a good three inches taller than you are and an old maid and you would think we were in kindergarten. I call her "tummy." I got Toddy again for History and got 100 on the first exam. Mr. Severn is my Geometry teacher and I can't make him out. All he does is crack jokes, though yesterday he cracked a mean test on us.

Mother and I are sending you a little box but it may be late. Wish you could come home so that I could spank you. Mother went to a banquet and found out what an adult was: "It is a person who has stopped growing at both ends and just started to grow in the middle." So now we are going to call Daddy an adult.

I've got piles of studying to do this afternoon, mostly Latin. Happy Birthday to you,
John Merritt

P.S. Tell Joyce to spank you for me good. I got my Hi-Y pin. Mother is quite an aristocrat, having shaken hands with Governor Brucker, his wife, the Attorney General and others, to say nothing of Bishop Nicholson.

February 12, 1931

Dear Dorothy,

Mailed a package to you this morning from your Mother and maybe you can use this money to help buy a pink something to go underneath. I am putting it all in money this time instead of part in candy. I wish you many, many happy birthdays.
Love,
Aunt Minnie

Enclosed in this box with the new formal: A note reading: For our darling Dorothy—we do hope you can wear it.

And a letter:

I do hope the dress will be all right. You will see the material does not match, but when a pink slip is under, it does. I did not get tulle because I went to French rooms and high grade departments and they were not showing tulle at all. Beads are good, and the style of your dress is splendid. It is prettier than anything I saw. I hope it fits and you like it. I sent scraps and thread if you wanted any little changes. I don't know just when you will need it, but you can dip your white slip in Rit dye if you need to wear it before I can get you a slip. We did so want to get you hose, shoes and slip, but we couldn't.

J.M. saved his money and bought the material for the dress. I thought that was dear of him. He is still waiting to get his sweater. I didn't suggest it at all, so whether the dress is a success or not, write to him—he did his part. Of course I don't feel sure of it, not being able to try it on or have you see it. I was so glad Aunt Lottie wrote me she was sending you a cake, for I had planned to do that but I couldn't get it done.
Lovingly,
Mother

Dear John Merritt,

You are a peach and I mean that literally. You shouldn't have bought me such a lovely gift, but I hope that you know how much I love it. I'm pretty proud of my big brother—in fact as my roommate says "he's quite the nuts" (and I'm a squirrel—so that's why I keep away!)

You're a real grown up man (but not an adult, I hope!) I'm glad you're taking such good care of the family—I appreciate it a lot. Cause between you and me it's up to us to see that they go straight.

I wish you would save your money for your sweater, and if you get in a hole, write me and we'll see what can be done about it.

You'd laugh to see the hall tonight—all the girls in the West wing have their beds lined up out in the corridor and are sleeping out there tonight because the Dean is away. It looks awfully funny—just like the Army bunkhouse.

We had a mock trial in Hillie's room tonight because two of the girls opened a box of her chocolates that she had hidden, so they had to come to trial. They came all wrapped up in sheets and we had a skull and crossbones draped over the lamp. It was awfully ridiculous and Hillie had a black coat on backwards and addressed them as scorpions.

It's four bells now and I still must write another letter, so adieu—in fact good night.

Love,

Dorothy

Monday

Dearest Mother,

Haven't done much this last weekend except sleep. I can't seem to get rested. Didn't even write letters. I kept wishing that you'd come over and sort of half expected you all day Sunday, although I didn't really think you'd get here.

Our February birthday dinner is Wednesday night, couldn't you and Aunt Nellie come over?

Am sending you a *Pleiad*—the game is to find your child's name—(twice on the front page). Also have another pleasant surprise for you. Semester marks came out last week. I got seven hours of A, seven hours of B+ and three hours of B-. Here they are: Biology B+, Eng. Lit B+, Education B-, Speech 111 A, Play Prod. A, Interpretation A. That means unlimited cuts and if I had three hours more of A, I'd be on the honor roll.

The sun has been shining and it's almost warm out. I know you're feeling good if it's shiny in Detroit now.

205

Tomorrow I have to have my oration completely rewritten and ready for final criticism from Prof. Hance. Today we are debating and then Friday comes our real debate. The plays will be given then too.

Prof. Carter is lecturing and he talks so loudly, I can't think. (The old bird is beginning to like me better, because I wrote an oration on education so I guess he thinks maybe I have a brain after all.)

I've invited Fleming over for our party Saturday night, but don't know yet whether he's coming or not (I rather hope not.) I just invited him on impulse, when he wrote rather a desperate blue letter. My laundry came OK. Write me sometime, won't you?

Love,
Dorothy

February 12, 1931

Dear Dorothy,

Well it is almost midnight and I have finally greased my two boys and gotten them to bed. J.M. has been home two days with a cold and Daddy came home early tonight all in and I have doctored him. They are sleeping now and fine and I am just plum tired.

I talked to my little girl tonight, but a phone call is unsatisfactory in a way. There is so much you want to say, that you can hardly say anything, but I thought it would seem a little more like home to talk to us a minute and I love to even hear your voice.

Monday night I went to the banquet with Aunt Minnie and it was the best I have ever attended. The reception was in the parlor and I shook hands with the Governor and his wife—poor dears all of them—1000 people to shake hands with. Dinner was delicious.

Your letter and the *Pleiad* came today. Your name is sure in the headlines. Your marks are great—we are mighty proud of all you are doing—but please don't overdo, for if you get sick your good times will be spoiled.

I am so sorry we can't come over, but I just try to be thankful you can stay. So many people are hungry and going thru desperate times and we are a lot better off than we were last winter.

Well my dear, I hope you have a happy birthday. I know the birthday dinner was nice and you had your cake. You are having so

much more than last year and I am so glad even if I do miss you.
With heaps of love from us all,
Mother

Monday, February 16, 1931

Dear Aunt Minnie,

You are so sweet to me! First a box of candy and congratulations, then a lovely birthday card and that ever useable money. I don't believe you ever forget, do you?

Every year I have a happy birthday, but this year seems to crown them all— although I did want to come home—there is so much to be done here that I hardly have time to think.

Not for a long time have so many lovely things happened to me. My oration is all in written form at last and when I can get an extra copy I'll send one home. I'm practicing and hoping—but after all—I don't expect to win again—but will do my best.

Wasn't it darling of my family to send me my dress—and I'm just going to use my money for a slip. It will be such fun!

I wish I could see you and squeeze you tonight. Maybe we could put on a little "act" all our own. Anyway, I love you a lot,
Dorothy

Tuesday night

Dearest Mother,

Another nice something! To-night Miss Champ called me in to ask me if I could possibly take a part in a three-act play to be given March thirteenth, Barrie's *You and I.* I have the mother's part, Nancy—and I am simply in love with it! Thrilled is no word for it. Really it seems that good things will never stop coming my way. Dwight Large plays opposite me and he is lots of fun—and so nice. We start working on it tomorrow night.

Yesterday I said my oration over the Dictaphone and then listened to the record. It was highly interesting.

I think I'll wear my new formal in the play. It calls for one. Now that I've told the latest, I'd like to ramble on, but it's so late (or early) now that I must go to bed. But remember, I love you all, more than "tongue can tell."
Love,
Dorothy

February 17, 1931

Dear Dorothy,

Here it is Tuesday and your letter came this morning and I was so glad to get it. I was so anxious about the dress. I was so worried for fear you might not like it and I did not know whether the neck would be right or not. Have quite a little news, but it isn't nice and thrilly like your wonderful letter.

J.M. was sick with croupy cold and I guess, flu all the week, then when I was just finishing your dress Wednesday, Daddy came home sick. He had a light case of flu—normal temp. Friday, but he was not up. At 2:00 o'clock Friday morning I was taken sick and Daddy had to get up and take care of me, until yesterday. My temp. was 103 and that frightened him so he got a doctor and then we got Mildred to come and take care of me. Carrie came over yesterday and worked all day, of course we did not allow her in the room. Sunday she sent over the dinner. They are real friends.

I am very much better and out of all danger, so you do not need to worry a minute. J.M. is back in school, got 100% on his Latin test, and they put him in a speech class with three other boys, for which he gets credit. I was so pleased about it. I think it is some school.

I want you to write to Hope and Aunt Lottie right away, Hope called Friday a.m. for me to come as her father had had a stroke. Ruth went right away and I am so anxious to go, but of course I'll have to wait. Maybe I can go by Sunday.

I loved your letter, will write again soon.
Lovingly,
Mother

Wednesday morning

Dear Mother,

Your letter just came and with it such bad news. Why don't you tell me when you're sick? I can always get away when it's necessary. Please, please do be good now and don't try to dig in and work. Give yourself a little rest. Perhaps some way I can manage to come home this weekend. I'll see.

I'm so sorry about Uncle Doctor. I just had a letter from Fleming telling me the same thing. He said paralysis had affected his face

and voice, but that Brad says he can eat and talk now. I shall write
to Aunt Lottie right away.

And don't hesitate if you need me, I'm always right here.
All my love,
Dorothy

Friday night
Dearest Mother,

It was so good to talk to you and know that you're all right. I
feel awfully selfish not to be home helping, but I don't know of any
way to get there and then this Sunday night debate is coming on.

I am so tired tonight that I wish I could stop breathing for a
while and rest myself. "I wish I was a little stone a-sitting on a hill.
I'd sit and sit and rest myself, by gosh!"

Later—Well my phone just rang and I have a date! Will my
tired carcass navigate? Who knows? I'm dating George Hill, Albion
alum from Northwestern, who is working on his Ph.D. there. He's
the one who once remarked several years ago that I was one girl on
campus he'd like to date. We're going over to the Delt Sig house.
I've never been there and I shall have to mind my Ps and Qs.
Love,
Dorothy

Wednesday Morn.
Dearest Mother,

Haven't heard from you, but am hoping everything is O.K.
It might amuse you to know that Monday night was Albion College Night on the radio, all over the country. Our deans departed
to speak over the radio and meanwhile—mischief was afoot in the
dorm. The frats decided we needed a big "bust out" and dance at
Moose Hall. The plan was not very well supported but some of our
girls got ready about nine and went. There weren't enough, however, and the boys came back to the dorm to see if the girls wouldn't
come out. Bedlam reigned supreme, and everyone expected the
doors to open any minute and that the boys would rush the dorm.

Finally poor Mrs. Wolfe got the whole dorm-full down in the
parlors (for safety I suppose!) and just as Governor Brucker was em-

phasizing the character building that Albion College was noted for—
the chain on the front door was broken thru and a few girls burst out.
Then the crowd shifted to the back of the dorm and there opened the
back doors. It was an exciting evening and when finally everyone did
get to bed, we discovered that two stalwart watchmen were on guard
in the drawing room, where they slept till the next morning.

Our play is to be given Wednesday night, March eighteenth.
To-night I am chairman at a house debate with Hope College at a
debate and dinner at Rob Hall. Then after that, play practice. We will
begin working on the second act.

Between times I am practicing the good old oration at the
chapel, where I can shout. They haven't yet decided whether I have
too much facial expression or not. I may have a chance to give my
oration at Marshall for *money*. Be good to yourselves.
Love,
Dorothy

February 24, 1931

Dear Dorothy,

Daddy went after Mildred Friday morning and she ironed,
cleaned the bathroom, did a washing, and everything she could to
make me comfortable.

Aunt Nellie walked in, all dolled up for the day. Carrie came
over and got the lunch. Then Mildred said I would have to go to
bed for a while, so Aunt Nellie went downtown to see some of her
friends and said she would be back for the evening, but she didn't
come. I was provoked at her sitting and letting Carrie get lunch. I
got along alone Saturday. Sunday the men were home. J.M. did the
cooking and Daddy the dishes. I didn't do anything. We were all
lonesome to see you.

Today I cleaned the kitchen floor, got the dinner and helped Daddy
with the dishes. Did quite a little picking up. So you see I'm coming back.

Uncle Doctor will not be able to work for six or eight months
and must rest. I am so anxious to get up there and really know. Ruth
is still there so he can't be very well.

You didn't say how you liked Mr. Hill on your date? I am going to get Barrie's play so I will know the play you are working on.

Well Florence and Earle came in and stayed till midnight,

when I needed my rest so much. Maurice did the same thing Sunday night. Will have to ring the curfew, I guess.

Take good care of my little girl, she is the only one I have and I don't like her to get so tired. Write to me.
Lovingly,
Mother

Thursday Night

Dearest Mother,

How are all the "flu" victims? The one educational victim is OK and slightly hoarse (or horsey) from orating.

Today has been the most delightful of blue-skied and fluffy-clouded ones! The days are just like spring—radiant, crisp and cool!

Then too, something exciting happened. I discovered I had more money in the bank than I thought I had, my idea of a great thrill! Here I thought I was down to my last two dollars and now find myself comparatively rich. Now I know how it feels to receive a legacy.

Went downtown, attended class this afternoon and finally finished up by giving my oration in the chapel in the presence of Miss Champ and Mr. Hance—for expert criticism. They have decided to let me keep my natural spontaneity in speaking, in spite of the fact that it is quite informal. The last few polishings now, then I'll work in the church for volume, and a week from tomorrow—with fear & trembling, I'll represent the good old Alma Mater.

Tomorrow we have a debate with Kalamazoo, and I am going along and driving Weisses' car part of the way. Expect we'll have a real good time. This is our hardest debate of the season and we do want to win. Saturday we practice hard, most all day. Wish I could get home. I worry about your overworking.

Must get that beauty sleep, cause Joyce's boyfriend said I was a "keen looking girl, but too tall!" Too bad I'm not made of shrinkable fabric—I stretch!

Do you know of any possibilities for teaching positions, for Joyce wants one? Is there anywhere a little pull would get her a job? She is a history major, English minor and can teach art and coach basketball.
With many hugs and kisses,
Dorothy

March 2, 1931

Dear Dorothy,

Another Sunday gone. I will write a note before I go to bed. This morning Aunt Nellie stopped on her way to Pontiac—it was a gorgeous day—so I went with her.

Uncle Doctor is very much better. I am so glad—if he continues all right I think I will not try to go, for things get in such a mess here and it costs so much more when I am away. It is hard for J.M. to do the cooking with everything else too.

Why not write to Uncle George about Joyce? He is on the school board and she is a friend of Lorene's, or maybe writing Lorene would be more effective.

Glad you had such a thrill with your bank account—hope we will have more coming in soon so we can help you when you get down to the "lastest."

I am glad they let you keep your facial expression and spontaneity. I think they will spoil you if they cause you to be in anyway unnatural, for I think you would lose most of your charm and appeal. We'll all hope you win and I expect you will—but if you shouldn't you will have done your best anyway—so why worry—but it would be mighty fine to win. Let us know just when and where it is so we can be thinking hard for you.

Expect you had a good time debating at Kalamazoo. Your debating and oration have brought you a lot of pleasure. We always get more out of things than we put in, if we work.
Lovingly,
Mother

Monday night

Dearest People,

So long it has been since I've heard a word that I'm beginning to wonder what your trouble is. If I don't hear by tomorrow, I shall get desperate and call you up.

Events are rolling around very fast here and I keep wondering if I hadn't better keep a record of all the things that happen. The latest is a party to be given for us by the pledges at the lodge. It sounds quite nice and will come off March fourteenth. I am going to get pink crepe for a slip and make it like one of D. King's, very long, to wear with my formal. In Jackson I can get slippers and have them dyed pink to match, for very little expense. It certainly will be lovely to have my formal then. I think I'll wear it in the play March eighteenth too.

I do wish you could come up for the play. It is on Wednesday night—also a birthday dinner night and quite a festive occasion.

Wednesday and Thursday of this week, I have to give my oration in chapel and at last the final test—Friday at Hillsdale. I am shaking in my boots because I do so want to place in the contest. Well, here's hoping you are all feeling good.

Love,
Dorothy

Tuesday Night

Dearest Mother,

Your letter came today, just wish you could come up, but anyway we'll see. Thanks just heaps for the cookies. I came in after that busy day of the contest and found my laundry and food. I was just starved and sat right down and ate.

I won't be sending laundry for a while so don't plan on it. Have I any hankies at home? I believe there are a few Christmas ones in my drawer. Could you slip them in a letter?

About my slip—I was going to buy material and make it myself but I've been so rushed that I didn't see how I could do it, so providentially, Thelma Cooper offered to loan me hers. It's real long and pink. My formal looks very lovely and sparkling. And I'm quite thrilled about the party.

Tomorrow morning I give my oration to Weiss's high school class—to practice on them—then I'm going to let it rest till Friday. The latest news is that we leave here Friday morning at 7:30. The contest is at 3:00 p.m. and we'll come home Saturday morning, because the men's contest is at night. Then the party Saturday night will either be a consolation or victory event.

If I should win???—I'll wire you as soon as possible. If you don't hear very soon, you'll know it's all off. I'm awfully tired to-night and am going to bed right away and try to rest up for coming events.

All my love,
Dorothy

March 4, 1931

Dear Dorothy,

Expect you are a busy girl, putting your last touches on your oration. I am a busy girl too. I finally washed yesterday, not from choice, but need. Stood it pretty well—had some wash with fifteen shirts and so on.

Today I cleaned the house so it looks very restful. Tomorrow I start the ironing, but will not be able to do it all in one day, so will do yours for I know you will need it. Ruth, Florence, and a friend walked in on me yesterday, just as I came up from the basement. I was so ashamed of the house! Today, with perfect order, not a soul comes in, it's exasperating! J.M. bought himself a sweater yesterday, plain dark blue.

Wish I could be a fairy on Thursday. I would come over and go to Hillsdale, but I'm not a fairy, so I'll have to content myself sending you "mentals." I'll sure be sending them all day and will be so anxious to hear the good news. Don't worry about it, for you know you have two chances, either you win or you don't, but of course, I think you will.

Heaps of love and good wishes and good luck for Thursday. You know you are the lucky Hill and can't help winning. Wish I knew who goes and all about it. I don't even know where Hillsdale is.
Lovingly,
Mother

March 7, 1931
Saturday night

Dearest Mother,

At last I am settled down once more in my room—with the tension at least partly out of my knees. And on the table is a lovely basket of pinky-red tulips and large luscious snapdragons, with the congratulations of Kappa Delta!

I've just finished cleaning the room and myself and we both feel better and look slightly more presentable. It is beautiful out my window now—all snowy, drifted and white. It's the end of the week and my legs ache, but I am very happy.

To-night we had a little party in the dining room for debaters from Ohio Northern. I sat by my dear Mr. Hance—and basked in happiness. He is such a dear—and so thoughtful. He and Prof. Weiss and I went together to Hillsdale. They got me a room at the hotel and "carried me around on a chip"—even supervised my food, so I'm doubly glad I got first place because it made them feel good— and didn't break Albion's enviable record of the last three years.

The Hillsdale people were charming hostesses, and I had a wonderfully happy day. I saw their new dorm and went to the Kappa Delta house, was entertained at a little tea dance in the after-noon, and at night we had dinner—the whole crowd—at East Hall. The women's contest started at 2:30 and about 3:00, Prof. Weiss and I came in—and he told me not to stay for all the orations, but to keep in the fresh air and not worry. The rest of the contestants were sitting up in the front row—looking eager. I sauntered in and sat down in the very back seat and listened for a few minutes, then went out and came back in time to walk down the aisle for my turn. I was fourth on the program and had a slight advantage as mine was the first oration to be given on education.

The decisions were not given until after the men's contest at night, but Prof. Hance held the scores of all the afternoon judges as he is chairman of the organization, so after we left the church at 4:00 p.m., he looked to see if I had gotten it and sure enough! He was pleased as punch and simply beamed. I had to keep the secret till 10:00 p.m. that night and even then the relative placing of the three contestants wasn't made known. They simply announced the three colleges which had placed and were entitled to go to Mt. Pleasant.

Our pledges are giving us a formal Saturday, March four-teenth and have even invited our guests for us. We're not supposed to know who we're going with, but I found out I am going with Wesley and he's lots of fun and just the most comfortable, nicest per-son that ever happened. I think it will be loads of fun.

I am hoping that I'll be able to enjoy the party, when it fol-lows so closely on the heels of the final contest. It's too wonderful to hope that I can celebrate winning first place—but oh how I wish it might be!

Well it's far past bedtime and I'm very tired and very happy. My washing is done and the room clean—there are flowers and a victory. God bless you and keep you safe always,
Dorothy

March 10, 1931

Dear Dorothy,

I was so glad to get your letter and clippings. It seems as if we know so little about everything. Saturday night's paper had notices that really told us something and now those you sent make it quite plain what you are doing.

J.M. got your play, *You and I,* from the library for me today and I have just read it, so now I know just what you are doing when you are practicing. I don't know how you possibly manage to do so much, but of course you are always at your best when you are just loaded. I am glad they take good care of you on your "days" at least. You will feel "let down" I am afraid when the finals and your play is over—but then there will be other things come along. The party sounds good too.

Mr. Dunn was telling Daddy tonight that they read about the play in the paper and he suggested driving over with their car. I do not know whether it really means anything or not but wouldn't it be fun, though?

I am so glad the Kappa Deltas sent you flowers. We are proud too, but we can't do the things we would like to do. I was just thinking today how much you are accomplishing and wondered what you could do if we could help you as we would like to do. I know it would make things easier for you.

J.M. sends the clippings. He wants me to help him with his studies—his card was not so good today, so I expect I must.

Don't worry about the finals, you will probably win, at least I am expecting you will—but if you shouldn't, you have done your best. I don't think there is much chance of your not placing if you are careful about not getting too tired this week—you know what that does to your voice. I am wondering who will be the judges over there.

You have pretty hard times getting to school, but you do have real lovely thrills when you get there: your life is somewhat like that all thru—lots of sunshine in with the shady places.

We will be shouting for you all day Friday. Last Friday night every time the phone rang, I jumped and said, that's Dorothy, for I felt sure you would win and you did.

It is reported that Mary Thompson's father lost most of his property in stocks and that her grandmother is sending her to school.

We will be waiting for the good news. All kinds of luck and bushels of love,
Mother

Monday afternoon
Dearest Mother,

So many things to tell. I am hoping that you aren't too much disappointed. Miss Champ, Prof. Hance, and I went to Mt. Pleasant early Friday morning. We had a pleasant trip and got there about noon.

The contest at 2:30 was disappointing in more ways than one. A mistake had been made in the printed program and I was put first instead of fifth, as the constitution provided. However we thought it best to avoid unpleasantness and take the arrangement as it was.

It was sad because as it happened, the doors were not closed during the first oration and the elevator outside added to the confusion. One judge graded me way down, last, because he didn't hear it all. It was very unfair everyone thought, because two judges gave me first and two others, third, and then this other judge graded me fifth. Result was I won third instead of first or second as we had hoped.

So I don't feel that I did poorly. It was a combination of circumstances and a new judge. The Detroit girl only received one first place, but enough second and third places to make up for it. I have a little bronze medal which is to have my name, college and date engraved on the back. It is very unusual looking and rather pretty.

I hope you won't feel too badly about the result. If you had attended a couple of these contests you would understand upon what a slim thread of chance or whim the decision rests.

Miss Champ felt so sorry about it for she thought I really should have received more. Saturday afternoon we got back and I went straight to play practice and got back just in time for dinner at the dorm and to find a lovely corsage at the desk from Miss Champ. She knew about our party, but how she knew I was wearing pale pink, I don't know. It looked lovely on my dress.

I wish you could have seen how nice I looked, with my pink slippers and hankie and everything. I was so tired and worn out that I doubted whether I'd have a good time, but I got all excited and when I was finally ready, was all pepped up for it.

Wesley was darling to me. He's such a peach anyway, and

217

I feel perfectly comfortable with him. He was heaps of fun and we laughed all evening. It almost seems that people like you better when you don't win. The boys in the kitchen were adorable. I think sometimes it's better to be unsuccessful if you wish to be popular.

I teased Wes about taking anyone who only got third place, but he didn't seem to care if I was dumb. He has a happy faculty of doing the right thing at the right time.

This afternoon I have to get my clothes together for the play. I cleaned the room this morning and now I'll go home and finish things up and then at 5:00 p.m. the histrionic club has its picture taken. To-night at 7:00 p.m. is our final practice before the dress rehearsal.

All my love,
Dorothy

Dearest Dorothy,

Have been thinking of my little girl all day, but this is the first free time I have had. We are hoping you are not worrying about the results of the finals. We found it in the paper, but could not understand how one could place third on one day, then first, but I expect you understand it is all right—it seemed unreasonable to us. We will be waiting to hear the details.

I do hope you won't worry, for you have done all that you could and I am sure your professors feel that you have.

Daddy wrote some business last week, which made us feel encouraged, for he hadn't been doing much, but you know it goes in streaks. Here is hoping we will have a wide fat streak.

Don't do any washing that you can send home, because I have so much more time than you do. Do not look for me Wednesday. If anything works so I can possibly come I will, but I do not want you to plan on my coming, for it is uncertain. One consolation is that it is nearly time for your vacation—two weeks from yesterday—hope we will have nice weather while you are home.

I hope you had a wonderful time at the party and were not too tired after your trip to Mt. Pleasant. We can't see you, but we are loving you all the time.

Heaps of love to our little girl,
Mother

Friday afternoon

Dearest Mother,

I suppose you might be interested to know how Wednesday night came out. I've had a horrible cold or I would have written you sooner. The day of the play I woke up with no voice at all, and was so worried about it—but by cutting all classes Tuesday and Wednesday and doctoring, gargling and cold compresses, I managed to have a voice for the big event.

I did so want you to be there, and all day kept unconsciously looking out the window in hopes that you'd be walking up the front walk. Miss Champ was so darling to me—pampered me like an infant.

I'll have a picture from the play as soon as the photographer gets it developed. The stage looked lovely and you should have seen my costumes. I had five changes, all pretty. At the beginning I wore a deep rose red crepe de chine that came right to the floor, with a cowl neck, gold belt and shoes and and fur trimmed short sleeves. It was a knockout—for once at least your child looked gorgeous! I wore a little knot of hair on my neck and had the sides of my hair just touched with white.

Dwight was an old peach and said I looked lovely. Miss Champ told me he came to her and apologized for not having his tux—said he thought maybe when he wore that, he'd come up to something near as nice as I looked! Imagine that.

The play went over very well, I think. Everyone seemed to enjoy it a lot. Some people said it was the best we'd ever had at Albion. Yours truly has to get down to work now and study for mid-semester exams. I had one yesterday and there are more to follow!

Prof. Weiss was kidding me this morning—said he didn't suppose Albion could keep me next year; I'd probably go on Broadway.

Well, it won't be long now, will it? I'm anxious to see you all and hear everything new. I guess I can stick it out another week or so.

It is a gorgeous afternoon and I'm going downtown and mail this now.

Love,
Dorothy

March 18, 1931

Dear Dorothy,

Your play is over and I know it was wonderful. I did want to be there so much, but couldn't swing it. If we had planned to go, probably the weather would have kept us home. You will surely have to talk all the time you are home to tell us all the things you have done. I just know you were thrilled over it. I hope Miss Champ was pleased. She was a dear to send you the corsage. I was so glad that you did not let the contest make you sick.

Have been cleaning house—closets, linen closet, dresser drawers, dining room window box, etc. It makes the cleaning so much easier when those places are done first. Have the ironing and mending done. Aunt Nellie is coming out to-morrow. She always wants to play Honeymoon Bridge.

I had my clothes and myself all cleaned so if things had worked out right, I could have gone to Albion. Daddy has one of his spells on, working day and night. Mr. Spencer is going to make him a new proposition—we are anxious to hear what it will be. Of course, we are always looking for the joker in his offers. Perhaps we misjudge him.

Peoples State Bank in Pontiac closed its door this week—things are not very good there.

You have been away so long maybe it won't seem like home anymore, but you will look good to us. Lorene sent some things for you the other day—dresses and a new pair of shoes, which are too short for her—but I think everything is too small for you. I am afraid you cannot wear the shoes. I would send them but it is so near time for you to come.

Didn't Wesley used to date Dorothy K.? I remember hearing his name, but don't remember the connection. Glad he made the party a happy evening for you.

J.M. is busy studying as usual and Daddy isn't home yet. Have you enough money to get home?
Bushels of love,
Mother

Monday Night Late!

Dear Mother,

Your letter arrived today. It will be only a few days now till I can talk without ink! Plug your ears or you may get a headache.

I don't know yet whether I can come Friday or Saturday. If I can get someone to serve, I'll come Friday afternoon—probably get in to Detroit around dinnertime.

This weekend, just for a change, I went to Battle Creek on the deputation team to the Methodist Church there. Had a real good time and it was a change after Albion atmosphere and dorm fare. I gave a couple of readings Sunday night in church. They were a real live crowd and entertained us beautifully.

To-night I'm supposedly studying for a blue book and writing my speech for extemp class, this is time out!. I am beginning to weaken and talk myself into going to bed instead. Sleep is a great thing and you must have more of it, young lady!

This is a tame letter—no major events, no clippings, nor excitement. Just four days till vacation anyhow. Do you suppose I can get a job for that week? I surely would like one.

I think I hear a solitary frog singing. I'll bet Daddy's jealous of that. Detroit hasn't a frog song, has it?

Love to you all,

Dorothy

Monday morn.

Dear Mother,

It is a lovely windy, warm day. Just like summer, and it hardly seems worthwhile to study. I'd like to go riding and swimming instead. However, the gods judge otherwise and here I am in education class, being bored to death.

Yesterday I wore my brown chiffon. I took the belt off the neck and wore my long wooden beads and everyone was crazy about the dress. I went to league with the Luthers last night. We saw a large framed picture of me in the photographer's window. It's that one I had taken for the annual this year. It's better than I thought it was—very serious looking.

I've decided to go to our party April twenty-fourth, though heaven knows who I'll take. I found out that Juliette is taking Ernie to the party, so I'm going to be on deck, if it's the last thing I ever do. So here goes!

I may surprise you and do something else exciting soon, but I shan't tell you what it is, till I see how it works out.

You might be interested to know that I got three A's for mid semesters and four B's. (making eight hours of A and eight hours of B) for a 2.5 average.

This morning I saw Prof. Hance and he almost apologized for giving me a B in Advanced Composition. He said I'd done better work than that. Ha Ha! I told him that the mark mattered little.

You are certainly having beautiful weather for Aunt Lottie's visit. Give my love to them both and lots for yourself.
Dorothy

April 18, 1931

Dear Dorothy,

Tuesday I got busy on the telephone and found that we could go to Mr. Ford's Village of Greenfield (the antique village) by appointment.

Wednesday morning, the four of us went; the guide met us at 10 o'clock and took us all through. Of course it is only started, but we saw a lot and got the idea of just what they are doing. We will go again when you are home and J.M. can go. I was so glad we could go—we had taken Doctor and Lottie every place he wanted to go except there. He was so pleased. Then we went to Ruth's for lunch and Pete sent up a driver to take them to the train. I think they really had a lovely time and seemed to enjoy everything so much.

A letter from Auntie Dee explains why I have more than cleaned today. I do hope she comes—I will get ready for her anyway.

What would it cost to have a small picture of the one you had taken this year? I would like to have one if I can. Now you have me all curious to know what surprise stunt you are getting ready to pull—be careful—don't do anything I wouldn't do.

I am surely proud of your marks. I consider that good work at any time, but with all the extras you have been doing it is extra good work. J.M. was "regusted." His marks came up this time, but of course, there is plenty of room at the top. Wish I could see you—but if you are just happy.
Lovingly,
Mother

Wednesday a.m.

Dear J.M.,

I dreamed about you last night and it wasn't a good dream, so I wondered if you are all right. I'm sitting in my high school methods class, listening to the Albion High School class recite. It's lots of fun. Tomorrow I'm going to teach the class about writing

orations. Here's hoping they don't cut up too much. I'll have to take them over my checkered apron, and I'm afraid they'll be a little big to handle.

It's just like summer up here and almost too nice to go to classes or study. Our next play comes off the twenty-second and I have charge of all properties and the privilege of selling tickets. A week from Sunday night, I'm debating at South Haven. Next week Friday is our big formal, so I guess things won't be too dull for a little while. It's a great life and heaps of fun.

Don't miss going to college—it's great sport and gives you a big start in knowing what living is all about. After next

Dorothy

year when I start bringing in the filthy lucre (or ducats) and you are a worthy senior in high school, we'll begin planning things for you? How's that?

Write me a letter and tell me all the gore.

Love,
Dorothy

Saturday night

Dear Mother,

A rush order! At the last desperate minute, I'm remembering a picture in my scrap book which I need for English methods on Tuesday. It's a long colored panel of Cordelia leaving her father's house. If you see any other pictures in the book or anywhere that might have a historical background will you send them along too?

I am going to the formal next Friday with Lucille's brother from Ann Arbor. I expect to have a peach of a time and he seems to want to come.

We went shopping today and tonight I'm going to Eaton Rapids with the Y.M. bunch to hear Bill Simpson speak. I'll write you all about it. Our room is cleaned and all changed around. We should have company now while we're immaculate. Must go wash socks and iron and get ready for tonight.

Love,

Dorothy

Sunday

Dear Mother,

The day's work is most all done—of course there are heaps of things I could do—but I think I shall go to league to-night—walk down and mail your letter and type awhile on my term paper.

Last night was a wonderful experience. At the Y.M. retreat we met Bill Simpson—and of all the interesting, dynamic personalities, he is the finest I have ever met. He has a simply staggering philosophy of life—one that cuts deep and shows our civilization and us up in too clear colors!

When I have hours to talk, I'll tell you what he believes. He is absolutely essentially honest, has no use for sham or superficial institutions. He lives without owning any property or worldly goods except the corduroy trousers he wears. He looks like those mining pictures of Uncle Roy—and yet he has a spiritual light and a dazzling smile which seems to come from his whole being.

He does not even work for money—but only for food and shelter. He has a fine education, has been a successful minister and knows the Bible better than anyone usually does. He is married to a Vassar graduate who has her master's degree and she lives in New Jersey, where she has a vegetable farm.

Dr. Hall approves heartily of his thesis—and one of the most interesting parts of the whole evening was to sit in that rude little cottage on makeshift chairs, grouped about a stove and listen to two men who both have found a way of vital, exultant living.

We rode home with Dr. Hall and I shall never forget the many things he told us—and the insight, which it gave me into the mind of a *real man*.

Bill Simpson said he never wanted to convert people to his way—he is "singing his song" (his way of life) and if others wish to sing it too, all right. Someone asked him if, in spite of the fact that he did not wish to convert people, wouldn't he like them to follow his way. His face lighted up and he said very softly. "Of course, it's such a wonderful song." I looked at him and wondered if perhaps the Christ didn't look like him when he was here.

Lovingly,
Dorothy

April 23, 1931

Dear Dorothy,

It is really my bedtime, but I feel like a visit with my child. Daddy went downtown at 9:00 o'clock on a collection and J.M. has just gone to bed.

While I was getting dinner Monday, Auntie Dee called from Battle Creek, saying she would be in at 10:30. I scurried around and finished by train time. J.M. and I went to meet her, and we talked late. In the morning we went downtown. She bought two lovely dresses. Then she felt J.M. did not have a fair deal at Christmas, but she had not known what to get him, so she bought him a pair of socks, two pairs of shorts, shirt, tie and sleeveless sweater. She also bought two pairs of hose for me, which I needed desperately, but which did not thrill her, a tie for Daddy ($3.50—wicked), and a little parcel for Dorothy which I will mail. Then she insisted on taking me to Hudson's for dinner. We ate in the Early American dining room, where the furniture was all maple.

It rained and sort of spoiled the afternoon. When we came home, Auntie Dee saw the restaurant on the corner and we had to go there so I wouldn't have to get dinner. J.M. had a HiY banquet, so the three of us went over to the corner to eat.

It's still raining this morning, so we loafed and talked till train time. Dee is not very well. She expects to have her tonsils out next week and some x-rays. Her stomach has been bothering her.

When you get your parcel, try to write her a nice long letter if you can possibly find the time. They feel very bad about Uncle Dan's sister. There seems to be no hope for her—she is a very charming woman.

She brought me a brown velvet dress that is too short for her, but just right in length for me if I can alter it in other ways.

It seems strange, but I do not remember ever hearing of Bill Simpson. Wish I might have been there and will so enjoy hearing all about the evening. A spiritual uplift would be a very good thing for this person. Hope the party will be a success and that you will enjoy the Ann Arbor man.

Aunt Nellie may be here tomorrow. We have had quite a spell of company, haven't we? I have to iron in the morning. I didn't do a thing the two days Auntie Dee was here—she is very sweet. She liked some of my old things—was really excited over the little oval brass frames, would like me to find her one and would like a pair of the little lamps. She likes Grahams' prints, our Westward Ho glass bread plate, old gray sugar bowls, luster pitchers, little tables and spindle chair. Our stuff rated pretty well, with her. She also liked our flat and thought our rent very reasonable.

Will be anxious to hear about the party. Write to your mother soon.
Lovingly,
Me

                                                      Tuesday night

Dearest Mother,

It is just growing dusk outside. Such a gorgeous spring night, and yet cold too. Everything went off according to schedule—so Miss Handyman remains serene. Joyce got in at 7:30 this morning after riding all night. We are all unpacked and are rejoicing in our spotless purity. Every rag either of us owns is clean.

I found a bumpy bag of mints in my case—and am wondering just who is responsible. They're awfully good—we've been eating them this afternoon.

Albion looks so spring-like—with gay colors flashing out. I'm going to be very lazy and not study hard to-night, but take a walk, a shower and then to bed. I feel all set to begin the fray tomorrow, but will need to use discipline to get that term paper written with this glorious weather.

Tell J.M. I wore the sweater and everyone liked it. If he wants it any time, just write and I'll send it. Joyce went riding this afternoon and brought home some cattails.

I have to arise in the morning at the early hour of 7:30! Just think of it!
With heaps of love,
Dorothy

April 28, 1931

Dear Dorothy,

Daddy and I went to church Sunday, then were quietly at home all afternoon. Went over to the park for a walk in the eve, but we about froze.

Yesterday I washed as usual, then went downtown to change J.M.'s shirt for him and to change the $3.50 tie Auntie Dee bought for Daddy. I got him a shirt and tie for it and he was delighted. Gave myself a thrill by going up on the tenth floor and looking at all the lovely dishes, model kitchens and everything, then I did the art department. I also went over to Mac's Book Shop. I was interested as the proprietor was in and visited with me about *Grahams'*, *Godeys'*, etc. He has thousands of prints and sells them for $1.50 per or $1.00 in quantities. He has a man at every big paper mill in the country and when the bales of old paper come in, that man picks out the old stuff. Clever idea, clever chap. I tried to sell him one of my *Grahams'* but we couldn't deal. He pays nothing and asks a heap—good business.

J.M. is missing some school—having trouble with his eyes—Daddy is trying to get in touch with someone today to send him to. Daddy is working hard and has some cases he expects to close soon—he is feeling good. Spencer has held on to the men Daddy was hoping he would get. We think he has offered them wonderful things and in about six months when he doesn't come thru, they may feel differently. As far as I see it, I am glad they didn't come. Daddy was giving them too much. I hope I hear from you this afternoon. Auntie Dee's little gift will be in your laundry case.
Heaps of love,
Mother

April 28, 1931

Dearest Mother,

First one thing, and then two. I hardly know how to begin—or where I left off. Our play went off very well last Wednesday night

227

and I was the tired property man in the case. I had barely gotten up stairs to a badly messed room, when my phone rang and I discovered that my name had been petitioned for candidate for house president to run against the two other nominees. Miss Gray also asked me if I'd like to go to Ann Arbor at 8:00 the next morn to a National Women's Self Government Association Convention in Ann Arbor. Needless to say, I packed up, cut my Thursday classes and went on the train (expenses paid)—met the other candidates and Miss Gray when I got there. We had a lovely day, met new girls from all over—Carleton, etc. and went thru the dorms and came back here for dinner.

Friday was our party and I wasn't at all sure I was going because I hadn't heard from Lucille, but everything turned out OK and I went. At the last minute J. Moore wanted me to wear that taffeta formal of hers that I wore in the play, so I did. I wore my pink slippers and long white gloves, my bracelet, and blue earrings. I wore a dark blue velvet wrap and looked very nice.

"Oke", my Ann Arbor boyfriend, was a little shorter than I, but very nice looking, and just heaps of fun. He's the easiest, most comfortable person and just will have a good time. We had Tommy Towners' orchestra and it was keen. It was a lovely party all around. Oke said he hadn't seen so many pretty girls at one time, ever. I danced with Ernie and was very gay, in fact so much so, that he kept watching me. He couldn't quite figure out why I was having such a good time all evening. We have a picture of it which I'll buy if I can collect the funds someway.

Saturday I was simply dead and tried to recuperate. Sunday Prof. & Mrs. Hance and three of us went to South Haven to debate (90 miles) and didn't get back until 2:30 Mon. morning. It's lovely over there—right on the big lake, Michigan. We enjoyed it a lot, were entertained at an Albion girl's home. It seemed such a nice change. I guess I'm pretty tired lately and nearly swamped with things I must do.

Another Kappa Delta has announced her engagement to a Sigma Nu—Louise Shumaker. I'm about the only single soul left unattached. (The one independent woman on campus.)

We just had a nice little scandal here—three freshmen girls expelled yesterday—and three fellows who ought to be. One of the

girls was a Kappa Delta. All the good sororities were represented. It was one of these dubious weekend parties discovered. We were just going to initiate this girl and now are glad we hadn't.
Love,
Dorothy

May 1, 1931

Dearest Mother,

A marvelous shiny day and today is class scraps and the end of freshman week. We've been treated to all sorts of sights around the dorm. And this morning the fellows announced we'd have no classes— and guarded the whole campus, padlocked the door and forbade anyone to go to classes. So today has been one mess of excitement. This afternoon will be the scraps. I think I'll go to the library instead. Term papers weigh upon my soul.

Wish you were here and we'd do big things. We could go riding, it's so gorgeous out. Just four or five weeks and it will be all over. It hardly seems possible. I'm getting spring fever badly these days. I tremble to think of the wild things I might do.

I was glad to hear that Auntie Dee finally came. J.M. must have new glasses and Daddy ought to have his fixed. Please go ahead and have it done and we'll use that $25 oration prize of mine to apply on it. Remember what I say and do it, for eyes are a bad proposition to monkey with, and J.M. mustn't spoil his at this early date.

I wish I were there and could give you all a squeeze—you're such a dear family.
Love,
Dorothy

Excerpts from the 1929 Susanna Wesley Annual
Reprinted with permission of Albion College

DOWN SOPHS!
"Take the bitter with the sweet!"

This was the only consolation that the freshmen had on parading to and from the campus decked in their heavy slickers, clumsy rubbers, and raised umbrellas, carrying their books in baskets which gave them the appearance of little housewives on shopping tours. Added to the freshmen insignia during the momentous period of frosh week were the girlish green hair-ribbons which made the wearers realize that they had only started to climb the steps of college life.

Lo, and behold! There stood a sophomore ring-leader barring the front entrance from freshmen feet. Blood curdling shrieks rent the air as the first burst of spirit escaped from the meek green-ribboned students when they audaciously burned the soph flag at the stake in front of the Chapel, having replaced it in front of the dormitory by the green '32. However, the sophomores forfeited the flag battle in that they admitted that they used unfair tactics.

Wearing dresses backwards was another feature of the week. The disobeyance of this and several other senior rules were brought up before the sophomore court, held in a very solemn atmosphere, where such penalties were placed upon the accused as wearing their hair in seven braids and carrying French dolls the following day. The failure of a certain frosh to appear before court brought forth much excitement when she was ducked in the cool water of Susanna Wesley.

Two serenades were enjoyed by the upper-classmen—one at 11:00 putting them to sleep with the music of alarm clocks and tin pans; another at 4:00, waking them with the sweet voices ringing through the corridors.

Several freshmen faces were washed on the campus since they had disobeyed the rule of no cosmetics. Also several sophomore faces were washed during the night with flaxseed water with the hopes of bestowing upon them better complexions.

Alas! The end had come! The sweet had arrived to sugar the bitter, when the seniors presented the freshmen with a very delightful dinner at which the sophomores graciously furnished the entertainment to repay for all that the frosh had given to them on previous evenings. This final evening was completed when through the archway formed by the upraised hands of the upper-classmen; the freshmen ceremoniously marched from the dining room to the flames of the fireplace in which the green ribbons were forever tossed.

Freshmen, rest! thy warfare o'er.
Sleep the sleep that knows not breaking;
Dream of campus scraps no more,
Days of danger, nights of waking.
(With apologies to Walter Scott)

Dear Dorothy,

Four o'clock Sunday afternoon and the sunshine is glorious. We would like to be in Albion. Daddy and I went to church this morning. They had a wonderful sermon. Home again, dinner is over and the dishes done. J.M. is out with Chuck. Daddy is having a nap— Mother is sitting in the sunny dining room, with her feet high on the window seat. We will go over to the park for a walk if no one comes, and I guess they won't.

Yesterday I cleaned and fussed till about four o'clock. Minnie came over and we went for a walk on Six Mile and back around and through the park, then for the groceries. Then dinner, dishes, a hand of cards, and we went back to the grocery to see if we would be the lucky winner of a basket of groceries, but we weren't. The John R. merchants are making an effort for business alright.

I have been mending clothes, bedding, etc., also making some aprons, which we really needed. Pulled out the rag bag to make a dress and planned three, but I don't know whether I'll get them finished without you to egg me on or not. I seem to want to do other things. Also want to make some more rugs soon as I can get to it.

J.M. thinks he has a job next week to paint and clean for Chuck's mother. She wants most of her walls cleaned, I guess. He is planning to work after school and nights. Hope he pleases her. He has his glasses, so is feeling better. He went to a specialist Daddy knew years ago in Otisville. We will not plan on your $25 for that. That will be very helpful next year for you

You are surely a busy girl. I am glad you can do so many lovely things—take time to realize how many lovely hours you are having. I am anxious for you to be home, but am afraid you will not be too happy, for we cannot seem to do the lovely things for you that we would like to, or that are possible at school.

Hope you are doing some resting this weekend. I don't want you to come home looking like a shadow.
Your own mother

Dorothy's oration "Our Finishing Schools" was accepted for publication, a happy milestone in her life, with the prospect of a small royalty, much needed considering the family finances.

The Artcraft Shop
Detroit, Michigan
May 1, 1931

Dear Miss Hill:
We have submitted your selection, "Our Finishing Schools," to our editorial department and they have reported it very satisfactory for our use.
We are, therefore, submitting to you copies of our agreement in duplicate for your signature. Will you kindly keep one copy, sign and return the other to us. These selections will go on sale in our fall catalogue and you may expect your first royalty January first.
Very truly yours,
A.S. Cantlebury

May 4, 1931

Dear Dorothy,
Monday a.m. your letter came early, early. Daddy went out to view the weather about 6:00 o'clock and it was there. It has made him so happy he is just stepping high this morning.
We are so proud of having an author in the family, even if it should not bring in a heavy income. How did you know about trying it?
Dr. Hall hasn't anything on us—we have a rattly old car and we can have a good time in it too. In fact, I'm seriously thinking of living in a tent this summer—it would save a lot of dusting.
Daddy is going to the office—he says he feels like a million dollars this morning—as soon as we get another collection in we will divvy with you.
Bye Bye,
Me

May 5, 1931

Dear Mother,

Was so glad to get your letter this morning, as I had been feeling pretty blue and thought you'd forgotten me. I'm all for living in a tent this summer too. You asked how I got to be an author—my dear, I was urged! They wrote me saying that they had heard I had an oration in the state contest and asked me to send it and see if it suited their needs.

I think we get out about June eighth. I wish you could come over then, if not before. (I rate my $25 at the Commencement exercises.)

You'd better get busy making those dresses, because I'll expect you to be wearing them when I get home.

Have you any envelopes you don't need? I'm absolutely out. If I had a bar of Ivory, or any white soap, and some envelopes, I'd be all set. I probably won't be sending my laundry case very soon, so don't expect it.

The dance set Auntie Dee sent is certainly sweet. I feel like wearing it on the outside, but can't get anyone to dare me to.

Have to go to class now. I am doing a forty page term paper this week for Prof. Carter (ugh!). Then I have a thirty minute speech to give, an interpretation project from *As You Like It* and then a speech methods notebook, a short story, and at last finals!
Love,
Dorothy

Dear Dorothy,

Didn't get your letter written last night, cause I was bad and sat up and made a wastebasket, which I guess we needed, out of that fiber Mrs. Reynolds gave me years ago. It looks keen.

Yesterday I went with Daddy to Hazel Park and stopped to see the Lofts—my he has changed—he had accumulated property to the tune of about $100,000 since we saw them. Now the depression has hit them and I am really afraid he will lose his mind. Two years ago he started drinking, but stopped that. I just felt terribly about it—why he might better lose it all—he can't take it with him.

It has helped me so to hear about Mr. Simpson and Dr. Hall. This week I have shed my worries. I seem to have a feeling that everything is going to come out alright and if not the worrying that

I have done so consistently has never helped—but only hindered. Daddy is going to try to get Mr. Dunn to lower the rent to $40. If he won't we can move and I guess I can stand that if my family is alright.

I think we may get some cash in tomorrow. Anyway, I'll try to send you bits and always let us know what you need—because you know you are our child and we love you a heap. It is funny—J.M. is proud of you and just a bit jealous. I do want you to get close to him this summer for he is at such a critical age. I think you can do more for him than we can.

Well Daddy is leaving so I will have to send this along.
We never forget you,
Mother

May 7, 1931

Dear Dorothy,

I will enclose a little money for soap—this is John Merritt's donation. I patched awhile on the old dresses—it's great sport, but I expect anything I get out of them will be good for a vaudeville stunt, however, my daughter insists that I do it.

I'm afraid I won't get all the house cleaning done before you get home. I can't sew and clean too and I almost think I'd rather have the sewing done than the cleaning.

John M. wants my pen and I guess I am about thru anyway. I'm not an author, so I can't think up lovely and wise things to write. Find out the date and hour of commencement so we will know when—if we can come.

I am sorry my little girl had to get out of soap, cause I wouldn't want you sent out of class with a dirty neck. About how much do you need before you come home? We will try to see that you have it, for we want you to finish your year all happy.
Bushels of love to the only author in the family,
Mother

May 7, 1931

Dear Mother,

Events are swinging along as usual. Nothing exciting except house elections yesterday. My name being petitioned in for house president made three nominees and necessitated a two-thirds vote for anyone to win. We anticipated a second election because there were three sororities represented and the resulting vote was split. The question was which two of us would win out. Last night Evelyn came in about 11:00 and told me that Frances S. and I were the two. So today will settle things, a new vote taken and I am very doubtful as to whether I'll have a chance or not. Will let you know how it works out.

Last night it just poured and Ann Nash and I went out for a long walk in the rain and then came in and I took a hot shower. Today is rather cold and dark outside—a good day for me to finish my term paper, I expect.

I am trying to wangle a full time breakfast job next year, but don't know whether I'll have any luck.

Wish I might be home today, we could stay inside and have fun. I'll let you know whether your daughter is influential enough to be elected. Cheerio—don't worry—"You still have two chances."
Love,
Dorothy

May 11, 1931

Dear Dorothy,

Guess I'll rest my weary bones a few minutes. It is just noon, but I have cleaned hall, hearthstone, bathroom, and kitchen on my knee bones. Have dusted and the whole house is at least in order and the bird cared for. Now it is time to have my lunch, go to the store for eats, and prepare dinner. Just when do I sew, and that is the way it goes every day. I think when I used to sew so much, I just let the housework go, but I can't seem to stand the house in disorder any more—old age creeping on.

Aunt Nellie came yesterday and we went to Pontiac. I went into Uncle Dalton's as I wanted to see him and he was just leaving for home and insisted I go with him. He was so dear to me, he is sure grand. Beatrice has been very miserable all winter, she looks just wretched. Dudley will be home for three weeks, then go to camp, where J.M. was, as assistant leader. He has finished high school and three college subjects and will go to Albion next year.

Tonight I am going to the YW missionary banquet at the church with Aunt Minnie. Do not want to go for I like to know where J.M. is evenings, but Aunt Minnie tries so hard to do nice things for me that I did not like to refuse. J.M. is still working. I think he will work all day tomorrow.

I am anxiously waiting to see who wins out in the election. You do have such exciting times and lots of honors, I think. Even if you don't make it you were in the running.

With all my love,

Mother

May 11, 1931

Dearest Mother,

Just got home from sorority meeting and haven't yet settled down to studying. It's all April showers here, sunshine one minute and then rain, but lovely and green and springy.

The banquet went off very nicely Friday night. I wore my formal and no jewelry except a bracelet. I was seated between Dr. Carter and a Teke boy who is in my interpretation class. We didn't lack for conversation, and I surely played up to Carter. I have to get an A in that education course somehow. He remarked about how pretty my formal was, and entertained me with funny stories. In the meantime my little Teke boyfriend was growing restless, so I spent the remainder of the time entertaining him. I've had a feeling for some time that he was on the verge of asking for a date, and sure enough, he took the opportunity to ask me up to the Teke house to dance. I stalled him off until I decided it would be better than going home and doing nothing, so I went.

Dorothy K. was at the house with Mark, and when she came in and saw me in a formal, dancing, she just about popped! Everybody looked surprised. On further acquaintance, I decided my date wasn't so bad, so I took another date for Saturday night, and had a good time. He was quite surprised that I would take the date. (I being one of the nicest girls on campus and miles above him, he informed me.) From now on I make a mental note that being the nicest girl on campus is bad business. I am taking all dates, regardless!

These frat men seem to think I'm the high-up, untouchable orator! Harry says his roommate wouldn't believe he had a date with me. He doesn't know just what to make of me. He had me all labeled with the conventional stickers of "niceness and ability and oratory."

I think he was honestly surprised to find that I was a girl who was easy to talk to and quite ordinary. I laugh every time I think of it. What funny reputations you can get by merely going your way and letting people surmise about you! At any rate it made a pleasant weekend and I think every Teke has talked me over by now and are all scratching their heads over a new phenomenon.

I have finished my term paper and done some typing for Marian E. Thanks so much for the money. I hated to have you send it, but it tided me over very nicely, so don't worry about my not having enough. J.M. is such a brick. I wonder if I can pay him back for his part before long. He has so little and shares everything so willingly. If I can make next year, I'll be able to help him a good deal, later.

I'm fixing over my blue dress and I think maybe I can make it really up-to-date and clever. If it turns out well, perhaps I can send it to the cleaners.
I love you,
Dorothy

Tuesday night
Dearest Dorothy,

Guess I'll rest a few minutes before I do the dishes. In the meantime, I'll write to my nice child. Didn't earn my salt yesterday, but have made up for it today.

Saturday afternoon I met Aunt Minnie downtown in spite of the rain. We paddled out to the Goodwill right through the foreign district. I would not like to go there alone. We found they were closed on Saturday afternoon. We had lunch at the YWCA, then went thru the building across the street for a peek in the antique shop. Then we went on to the Detroit Historical Museum, which we enjoyed.

Sunday we went to church and heard the usual splendid service. Dr. Rice just never disappoints us. Went for a walk in the afternoon, then Auntie Steed wanted us for lunch. We came home, and my nice child called me, and that completed the day.

It is also green, springy and lovely here. Our back yard is quite nice and the park is so pretty now. We have been digging around some in our yard. I would like to get a few plants and seeds to put in.

237

I thought the Tekes were the outcasts, or am I mistaken? Perhaps it will be good advertising for a nice girl, an orator and person of ability to be also human and a good one. They probably didn't know it could all come in one package. I surely wouldn't want them to take off the nice label just because they knew you. Glad you had the date and good time anyway, even though he is "miles below you."

You needn't worry about the little J.M. does for you. He is not even with what you have done for him yet. We will be getting something in soon I expect. Then we will send you some more for we don't want you to be out of soap. I surely hate to have you typing. You have enough to do.

I "born children" (Blanche's term for new ideas) every day, but most of them are no good, "born" another today, don't know whether it is good or not. Miss Aull, who rooms upstairs, is selling something (not in Detroit). She turned down a job at $25 per week and said she couldn't afford to take it. She told Mrs. Dunn she thought she would make $50 at this sales job—sometimes they work in crews and maybe you and I could do the stunt too, come home weekends, maybe J.M. too. Or maybe he will go to Vassar and Lapeer. I wouldn't like to do it alone, but with the two of us, it wouldn't be so bad. Anyway I am going to find out what she is selling and all about it. If she makes good I'm for it, cause I could use some cash and that would be a way for you to earn something this summer and be doing something different. I'd keep it quiet because maybe just everyone will want to do it. Don't you laugh! I think it's a good idea. Maybe I would find an antique too. Well it won't be long now till you will be home and we can scheme to our hearts' content.
I love you too,
Mother

May 16, 1931, Saturday morning
Dearest Mother,

Thursday afternoon our English methods class went to Jackson High School to observe. I went with Marian to a show and ate there. We were home by 7:30 and little Harry called me up and I went for a walk with him.

I am going to write letters, work on my blue dress, and write a theme. Tonight I am going over to the Teke house. I think I'll wear my little chiffon number, it's such nice weather today.

I am trying to arrange to room with Eunice Mary next year. She's a freshman, and perfectly lovely. She goes in for the same type of activities as I do, has very little money and the highest intelligence rating in the freshman class. Besides all that she is as natural and sweet as she can be. She asked if I wouldn't please room with her. She is an independent, but so popular that she could go any sorority if she could afford it, or wanted to.

I think your job idea is a good one. I have been trying out another project, but I don't think it's going to materialize, so we may as well have something on the string.

Oh yes, I have more good news. Ann, who works in Hindman's office, told me that I am slated for full time breakfast work next year. I went to Mr. Cochrane yesterday to let him know I needed the work. The list hasn't been approved yet, but there is at least the possibility that I can get free board by working only in the morning.

I want to write Aunt Carrie about a P.E.O. loan for next year. I think I can get it if I apply soon enough.

Dorothy K. had very bad news from home about her father being in the hospital. We persuaded her to take Mary's car and Mark drove her home. They don't expect him to live more than a few hours. Poor Dotty, I don't know what she'll do. In case he doesn't pull thru we thought it might be advisable for several of us to go from here for the funeral. I must get busy now. The spring is so lovely here. I just wish someone didn't always have to be heartbroken, no matter how beautiful it is.
Love,
Dorothy

Sunday afternoon
Dearest Mother,

The day is perfectly beautiful and my Sunday duties are done. Joyce has cleaned the room up and gone out. From my window I get a wonderful view and breeze. Our books are nicely arranged on the table and there are two glasses full of luscious red strawberries just waiting to be eaten. I have my washing and ironing done, now I just need to write letters and study.

My little boyfriend informs me that I dress well, so I laugh up my sleeve and make a mental note to keep him believing that. It seems nice to have a date during the weekend. It's just enough frivolity to keep me going. I have fun with Harry because I can be just perfectly natural—even wisecrack if I feel like it. And in case you didn't know, I found out that he dates me because I'm intelligent, dress well, and don't use excessive make-up, and above all because there's nothing artificial about me. (I'm the most natural girl on the campus, I'll have you know!) So you see my hidden worth has at last been discovered.

And while I'm on the subject, perhaps you'd like to know that the honorable Harry is to be editor-in-chief of the *Albionian* (yearbook) next year. He has just been elected. I don't know whether I'll rate the Teke informal at the Marshall Country Club next Saturday or not. I'm not planning on it. Maybe he's sick of intelligent girls already.

Perhaps you've already heard that Dottie's father died Saturday in the hospital. Poor Dottie, I don't know what she'll do—there are sure to be complications of all kinds, and the financial situation will be far from good, I'm afraid. We'd all like to be of some help to her now, but there seems little any one can do. I shall write her a note and special it today.

Love,

Dorothy

Dearest Dorothy,

Have had two letters from you today. I am so sorry for the Kings. I will write to them if I can. It just seems as if there is nothing I can say to help them.

I have been downtown this afternoon and interviewed the people Miss Aul (the lady upstairs) is working for. Think I will try and see if I can do anything with it. I don't feel at all sure whether I can swing it or not. I will have to work in Detroit on account of J.M., when I would so much rather go to small towns, as Miss Aul is doing. She doesn't like to do it, but is sure she can make money at it, for she already has. I think you can make enough for college doing it, so if my grit holds out, I'll be going downtown Wednesday a.m. and trying to see what I can do.

Lorene is going over to Albion to visit Miss Gray soon. Try to be a little extra nice to Miss Gray if you can. You know what someone said—you were too independent for your own good.

Well, Harry rates with your mother for he proves her theory that there are boys who like nice, natural girls. I have heard so many things about the girls the last month that I have just been so depressed. I look at J.M. and feel I just can't have him go out to meet what he is going to be up against. So glad you are having some good times with Harry.

Your Eunice Mary sounds very attractive. I think I would prefer the intelligence and lack of luxury. It is easier for me to do without things when they are not facing me every minute.

Fine if you get the breakfast job, and when you know about this job I have for you, you could handle the article at school too. Wish we could make so much that you wouldn't need to borrow.

The Crawfords are losing their home and everything, I guess. That's about all one hears from Pontiac.

Bushels of love,

Mother

May 15, 1931

Dear Dorothy,

Have pudged around most of the morning, but haven't done much. I had a sick headache Wednesday and can't seem to get over it—nothing serious at all. I'm trying not to eat and I get hungry.

I walked by the park and it was gorgeous. The apple and other fruit trees are in bloom and fragrant. Maybe I'll get around to it and walk over again today, for they will soon be gone.

Hope you are not needing things too badly. Daddy was disappointed and did not get some money he was expecting. I think we are going to move. I was talking to an old friend of mine, Mrs. Bender, and she said there was a flat next to them for $30, so we intend to look at it. I am trying to get a job for you and J.M. at General Motors at the Blvd. Her son is the one who has such a fine position in the advertising department. She's going to speak to him about J.M. I am so in hopes J.M. gets in and I really think he will. She is also going to speak for you. I will find out if making application will be any help.

Last night Daddy wrote $10,000, I do so hope it goes thru alright for we need it. However it has already given Daddy a good bracer, a little business makes him feel like a million.

Washed and ironed the dining room curtains and put them up—even if we do move—I can't bear those windows bare—would rather not wash them again.

The porch looks good these days and the back yard is getting so pretty. I shall hate to leave it, but have no idea if he will come down on the rent enough to suit us. You will soon be home and I hope I have a job lined up. It won't be much to start with, but every bit helps.

Oh, I most forgot to tell you—I called up Ford's Village to ask about a position there and I think I would have gotten one—but Daddy spoiled it—absolutely no married women with husbands. I was so disappointed—they are training people now for the work.

Bushels of love to my child, the author.

Lovingly,
Mother

Monday afternoon

Dearest Mother,

Good news today! I have the proctorship on second floor next year, and also got first choice of proctor rooms and took 236, on second floor east. Am planning on rooming with Eunice Mary, and we're quite excited about it. I haven't found out about my scholarship yet for next year, but am hoping to get one. Getting full board will be one big help.

I also have something else up my sleeve for next year, which I will find out about tomorrow. I am quite hopeful, but don't dare tell you yet for fear it's too good to be true.

If this last business works out and I can earn any money this summer, it won't be necessary to borrow.

Just two more weeks remain, but a lot of work to finish. My exams will be over Friday, but I expect I'll have to stay over till Monday or Tuesday to work.

Theta Alpha Phi and the histrionic club are having a banquet Thursday night and I have to speak for the Histrionic Club—give a toast called "Props." I would so like to make a good impression because Weiss and Hance and a lot of clever people will be there. I think I'll wear my little chiffon number.

I have an appointment with Dr. Brown for tomorrow. Three guesses, what that means? Tomorrow morning is our May breakfast on the court.

All this while, I've been writing with one hand, and listening to Education Class lecture with one ear. No wonder this letter is such a mess. The boy who is giving a report now, is red headed and darling looking and terribly intelligent! Nobody on campus has ever been able to date him. He isn't interested in anything except books and athletics. Too bad!

It's so lovely out today that I would like to get up and shout. It seems like a good old world somehow. It must be, when a chronic old cynic like me falls for such a belief.

Write to me once in a while, or are you out of stamps? I have four, so you may expect to receive letters— that is if you'll write once in a while.

All my love,
Dorothy

May 25, 1931

Dear Dorothy,

Saturday afternoon again and J.M. has gone for a drive with the Franks. Daddy has gone to Dearborn, so Cheerie and I are alone.

I have been trying out the sales idea—have not made anything yet, although I have gathered some experience and have an appointment with the principal of the school over here Monday.

Going to write to Aunt Lottie and see if there is any chance for J.M. up there. Maybe he could get on the farm with Leland or Elmer. I don't think he is going to get in at General Motors, but of course if he does, that's different.

If neither of you get anything good here and he can get something at Vassar, I would like to find someone with a car and then have you, Marion Wilner, and myself make the little towns with this article. I sure think we could make good, so get your thinking cap on.

Daddy has written $22,500 this month so far, which is fine, but of course, no money yet, so we are having a cramped time.

But we know he has finally got himself started. If he can keep this up and I see no reason why he shouldn't, we will by alright before long. If you and I could do the other stunt, fall would see us quite comfortable for a change.

Daddy has come to earth and forgotten agents, etc. Mr. Hands advised him that way, so if he keeps on he will soon have a stand in with the company, so he could get a little help if necessary.

I keep up a long train of thoughts, wondering if the things I have been thinking about are the best—there are so many sales ideas and I feel that probably a sales line is my stunt as long as I couldn't get in at Ford's Village. It is less confining than anything else and you make just what you put into it—but how to know the best article to handle.

I hope conditions will be such next year that we won't have to get along without seeing you for such long periods, but I'm still glad you can be there.

J.M. ushered at Chuck's recital this afternoon at McGregor library. He was quite thrilled. He couldn't go to church this morning because he would wrinkle his suit where he sat!
Night, night, would like to hug you,
Mother

Dear Dorothy,

I was so delighted with my birthday letter from you and expected to have time to reply long ago, but have been so busy trying to collect some of the money which we have outstanding—and made a few sales too. I drove 120 miles recently on collections and received $2 so I'm dividing with you. Hope we have more soon. We are all so happy to know that things are opening up for you for next year.

It seems now that your final year at college is assured, regardless of the Depression in business, and I cannot tell you how relieved I am and how proud I am of my daughter's ability to do things when her Dad seems powerless to do what he should do for her. We are counting the days till we shall see you.
With much Love,
Daddy

Saturday morning

Dearest Mother,

The busy week is about over, and even more things have happened since I talked to you. I have planned a beautiful schedule for next year, and only have to take fifteen hours and debate all my last year. Isn't that a break? I won't know how to act, but I guess the various activities will keep me busy.

My little Teke boyfriend called me up to go to the show Wednesday night, which I did. I never miss an opportunity to get something for nothing, and besides he's quite entertaining and not at all dumb, and for some unknown reason, seems to like me. I wore my roommate's swanky knitted suit, and does it ever look stunning. I think he got the benefit of the whole effect. He never misses anything like that. I catch him looking things over every once in a while. He approves of my clothes, though, for he thinks I'm very well dressed!! He's quite the artist when it comes to dressing himself. Always manages to look exceptionally nice.

The next new item was a great surprise. I was invited to go to the Sigma Chi Formal. Did that ever make a hit with Lorene, she couldn't quite get over my going out Wednesday night, and then when I calmly informed her that I was going to the Sig party, it was the last straw. She was so thrilled that she loaned me her mitts to wear. The party was last night, a dinner dance, with a one o'clock permission attached for good measure. I went with a worthy senior who is *six feet four inches tall.* (Believe it or not.) We had a darling time, double dated with Betty and Tom. Tom had his car here so we were very high hat. I wore Louise's pink lace formal, and my pink slippers with buckles on them, a big black ribbon sash, black earrings, pink mitts, and a black velvet wrap with a soft white fur border. It was a keen looking outfit.

Before we went, in the afternoon, I had the unique satisfaction of having Harry call for a date, and telling him how sorry I was I couldn't take one. (I guess he'll begin to realize just how popular I am!) The party was a huge success. The boys were heaps of fun and kept us laughing until we were weak. The favors were little link bracelets with the Sig Chi crest on them, so I'll have something to show you. We also had white roses and a scrumptious dinner. Then imagine dancing with six feet four. Finally we went to Parma and ate about twelve o'clock and then came back in time to get in by one o'clock. Loads of fun and I didn't even get tight. In fact our crowd was an exceedingly dry one.

There's nothing like dates to get dates on this campus. It's almost funny how it works. If you date, people will break their necks to get you another, but if you don't, you're not even considered. (Him that hath, gets.)

Today is a holiday for us too and I'm really going to try to get caught up and ready for exams next week. I'll walk downtown for my health and mail this. I had a lovely letter from Daddy yesterday. He's a man after my own heart.
Love,
Dorothy

May 27, 1931

Dear Dorothy,

Such a lovely day, getting warm again, and the trees and everything are so pretty. Best of all I had a letter from my child and I was so lonesome for her.

Your letter was a thriller. Proctor means honor and a nice room, doesn't it? I am so happy for you. You are certainly coming along in leaps. Yes I can guess what an appointment with Dr. Brown means—religious dramatics or work with the young people or both. I think it would be grand and do hope it works out for you. Carrie was here a few minutes yesterday. She was anxious for you to borrow from P.E.O, but it would be wonderful if you do not need to.

Well I have changed my plans. I was not satisfied with the article I was trying to sell and am thru with it, but have other plans. I am going into the insurance business for women and children, also accident insurance with Daddy's company. It is not his idea—it is mine and I am real excited about it. They have no women with the company so it is up to me to do anything I am willing to work for. Of course it is not quite as thrilling as antiques, but I can't seem to find a way of making money thru them, so here goes.

When Auntie Dee was here she said she would go in the business with Daddy if she were in my place, but I didn't see it that way then. I will have been out trying it out before you get home and unless you get a real job, I think you can make the money you need doing the same thing. I am determined to do something so I don't have to be cramped all the time. I think when I get used to it, that I will enjoy it. Yes, we just about have stamps, haven't missed any meals yet, although there have been some narrow escapes. J.M. did not work much last week, but is working again and made ninety cents last night.

Daddy has gone to Pontiac again today, trying to get some collections in. If he can keep his production up, it won't be long until he will have an income, but being behind as we are, there are no clothes or extras in sight unless I get out and earn them. Here is hoping I keep my grit. It will be easier when you come—we can do up our work together and then go out and see what we can do with sales. I have done some reading along sales lines and there is surely a field for women.

Expect little redhead does not like flappers and is just letting them all alone for fear he gets in wrong. He is the kind you should go after.

If I'm working next year there will be some weekends with you—I am sure of that. Must clean up the house and expect I must get right at my rate book. Wish me luck, for I am desperately in earnest. I just must make at least a hundred a month and of course being at home will save so much expense. Hope you will be interested too, then we could boost each other.

Being hard up is somewhat annoying, but I think being bored would be worse, and we are surely never that.

I am just counting the days till you come—while I expect we will work hard this summer, I think we will enjoy it here. The porch and back yard are so pleasant and we are all well. Will send a dime soon. Heaps of love,
Mother

Summer of 1931 found Dorothy at home, but still thinking about her oratorical experiences. She wrote this entertaining piece:

I maintain that the best time for living is at night. Then if ever, they come tumbling out—those helter-skelter thoughts of the day. My tired head, like a worn and bulging suitcase, bursts its straps and there before me is the ill-packed baggage of the day.

I find a cheese sandwich a suitable companion for my labors. There is something soothing and reminiscent about bread and cheese. To get the best benefit, try sitting on a tabletop near the window, where you can stare out into space; then swing your feet and at intervals of five minutes, take a bite.

The combination of the munching motion and the rhythmic swaying of the legs heighten the quality of the reverie.

Last night, thus established, I had engineered the sandwich to my mouth for the fifth time before anything happened. (I forgot to mention that you must give the process time to work.)

It was a badly crumpled mass of fact and fiction to be straightened. There were riddles still unanswered, such as "when is an orator not an orator?" The answer might be, "when he's asleep."

I chuckled to myself as I recalled the story Charles Lamb tells of Coleridge pulling his friend from the street into a convenient doorway to talk to him, all the while holding on to his friend's coat button. The listener finally cut the button from his coat and slipped away. After three hours he returned to find Coleridge still discoursing to the button. Alas! Orators need not even a button for an excuse. All afternoon they had roared, ranted, raved, (according to their several choices) and of much speaking there was no end.

Taking the part of the humble button, five judges sat back and with all the different degrees of blackness, gloom, and despair, registered facially at least, the results of the contest. Analysis of the bodily attitudes of our reputable judges, had I had the time and inclination to note completely, would have made our present library on the seven branches of Psychology look infinitesimal. Lassitude in the extreme—suddenly frenzy—and then a climax of despair were the three acts in the simpler tragedies of the afternoon.

Yes, as I smoothed the frayed edges of those criticism cards given us by our honorable judges—I felt in the black and white of them the heat of a living drama.

Night and cheese sandwiches added sharpness to the recollection. I felt it happen all over again—from the beginning of that fatal walk to the platform, I had wished for the felt hat of old Fortunatus, which when clapped upon your head, suddenly transported you far away. (No doubt all this, while the judges were wishing for this same hat.)

I stopped swinging my feet—the idea came to me! Why not turn from oratory, (that uncertain profession) to the manufacture of space annihilating hats. Surely there would be market enough among the judges of oratorical contests.

It has been decided. Who can say, in the years to come, that this night and this bread and cheese were of no benefit to mankind!

Lest you, kind reader, think me too critical of contests, bear in mind that I have colored them with but one of their many shades.

When I am of more mature years, I shall prove my lack of bias by attending one occasionally. (But I shall put my felt hat under my arm—and in case it is necessary, it shall be to me as a parachute to an aviator.)

Dorothy was also busy raising money to return to Albion for her senior year. One of her class schedules shows fees for the semester totaling $276, which included $75 for tuition, $178 for room and board, as well as a general fee of $20, library deposit of $1, and a $2 fee for math or Psychology. Dorothy was appreciative of the help Albion College provided in the way of scholarships and campus jobs. In response to her thank you letter for her scholarship, Albion College President John Seaton wrote:

July 28, 1931

Dear Dorothy:

On this hot and rather depressing morning I very much appreciate your charming letter. Indeed, I should find a stimulus in it at almost any time. There is a surprising difference in the way in which people acknowledge a scholarship award. Perhaps there really is not so much difference in their feeling about the consideration that the College gives them but certainly some are much more gifted than others in expressing appreciation.

How nice that you are a big business woman, with a paycheck and everything. I suppose that the emphasis should be put on the paycheck in these difficult times. No, I hardly think that is true of you. The emphasis in your mind would be on the service that you were giving.

"No one shall work for money
And no one shall work for fame,
But each for the joy of working."

That may be somewhat more idealistic than is often found in our modern world, but after all, there is a profound truth in it.

I shall be happy to see you in the fall and we shall all hope that the next time you will take first place for Albion in oratory.
Sincerely yours,
John L. Seaton
President

Fall 1931—Sadly Blanche's letters are missing for this period, possibly lost in one of the family's many moves. Dorothy continues her letters, which hint at things back home.

Dearest Mother,

Arrived OK—had a lovely trip. It was almost hot at times. Bob and Marian are heaps of fun. We ate luncheon at Parker Inn, where we were sufficiently exclusive to have the whole dining room to ourselves and a private waitress to boot. Then I went to a waitress meeting and came back to find my luggage all unpacked and carried upstairs.

Then we explored our huge campus—saw the rest of the dorm and about 4:30, they left for home. We then went downtown—Eunice Mary and a couple of others—and spent all our money. We came home just in time for dinner. It was awfully hot. We barely made dinner. Oh so many changes—and some new people in the working class. After dinner a walk to campus, then a YW meeting. Tomorrow I meet freshmen arriving all morning and serve at noon. I meet with Dr. Brown in the afternoon. In the evening YM & YW Cabinets meet at Delta Gamma Lodge.

I finally unpacked and found my dresses in pretty good condition, so I am practically settled here with the exception of curtains. Pictures are all hung and everything is ship shape.

A lot of marriages and engagements come as surprises. My feet and legs are pretty tired, but aside from that I'm quite all right. We had a board meeting at 10:00 o'clock with refreshments and everything and I have taken proctor roll. I am already fed up on meetings, but alas there are more to follow.

Everybody is hard up and the stories are amazing. Will write better soon.
Love,
Dorothy

Monday morn

Dearest Mother,

By now you must have completely disinherited me—or forgotten that you have a daughter. I'm still here, but never has time evaporated as quickly as this week. It has been unusually warm and I've messed up most of my clothes. I've attended meetings till I'm blue in the face. I've planned parties, met new people and entertained the freshmen at a picnic Friday afternoon and evening. Finally, I registered, then worked awhile for Dean Gray in the library Friday morning. Also got half of my church scholarship and finished paying my fees.

Incidentally I've been doing the social stunt too. My old friend Harry called me Wednesday and made a date for Thursday (the night of the frosh reception, at which I was a hostess). So I skipped out early and went for a walk.

Saturday was registration and I met Dudley over there. He is trying to decide if he should join a fraternity. I gave him some good old advice. (Oh, I forgot to tell you—he took me to Parker Inn for dinner Tuesday night.) Then Saturday he asked if I would like to go to the show and I didn't know for sure just how my dates were working out, so he called me later. By that time I was mad at Harry for not calling, so I took a date with Dudley for dinner and the show. Five minutes later, Harry called, saying he'd been trying to get me all day to ask me to go to dinner with him. (Well I was flabbergasted to say the least!) Two dinner invitations the same night—it was too much even for your distinctly popular daughter. I compromised by going to dinner with Dudley and discussing all his difficulties and then later had a date with Harry.

Sunday morn I worked at the lodge for a while, went to church, came home and served dinner and had barely gotten upstairs when Harry called. I showered and dressed and went for a walk with him, after which we took one of his friends' cars and were going for a drive when we had a flat tire! Came back to the dorm—rushed up to get my little sister for the Big Sister Tea. Then got talking and forgot the time and was late for league. Met Dud down at league and he wanted me to go out with him, but I had already made a date with Harry. Finale for the evening was a lateness of ten minutes.

Perhaps by now you have a very faint idea of why I haven't written. Eunice Mary has been as busy as I have, and our room looks it! I'm pretty tired, but very happy and above all busy. Louise told me this morning the Pan Hel council has decided to put me up for Vice-President of the Senior Class. They have a new system this year which automatically elects fraternity and sorority students to all the class offices—so I guess I'm all settled. Much more to tell you soon.
Love,
Dorothy

Saturday night

Dearest Mother,

I've worn out everything except stationery during the last week! Oh, what a busy, tired, lovely time we have had.

Last night ended rushing, with our garden party "Lavender and Old Lace," at which we wore old-fashioned dresses and decorated the lodge with deep blue sky paper and silver stars, as well as white lattices and climbing roses. It looked lovely. The favors were little old-fashioned kerosene lamps. I wore Louise's pink lace dress and my new long slip, pink shoes, and long earrings. Tonight is the final decision night and in an hour or so, we expect to know just who pledged Kappa Delta. We have been rushing a darling bunch. Marjorie Harger from Pontiac is one of them. She is certainly sweet and lovely. She is 5 ft. 11 inches, incidentally, has curly hair and a neck as long as mine, but nevertheless we're all crazy about her. We took her to dinner at the Green Shoppe last night and had a wonderful time. This is the first year I've really been in the midst of rushing. Our group is so small we have to rush pretty hard. But everybody seems to work together so beautifully, and know each other so well. Classes have been merely a side issue this week. Every night I've either been to a party at the lodge, on a personal rushing date, or had a date with Harry. Dudley called me for a date Sunday night and tonight I'm going out with Harry.

Eunice Mary has gone home and to Ann Arbor for examination of her leg. She has inflammatory rheumatism so badly, poor child. She is a dear.
Love,
Dorothy

Wednesday night

Dearest Ones,

Not forgotten, but neglected! I'm sorry I've been such a poke about writing. Events just seem to happen too rapidly and often. I need a secretary to keep the news up to date.

Sunday was a busy day—church—dinner to serve—date with Harry till 6 p.m.—league and church at night. It just left me time enough to get into the proper clothes at the right time. Monday classes—helped Dud with his French and went out to dinner with him in the evening. Then sorority meeting till 9, board meeting at 10 p.m.—no studying! Tuesday—Art and studying. I was a good girl for an hour or so in the library. Costume design is getting better and better. I'll be at the head of the class soon. (there are two in the class—see how I rate!) Then Tuesday night fulfilled my social obligations by going to the show with Harry. (One has to give up one's studying once in a while for the good of the hard-working men on campus!) It was a good show—even if it was a gangster picture. But the best of it all was the satisfaction of having "his highness" ask for three dates ahead. (I really believe he's beginning to appreciate my popularity) At any rate, he never has given me the satisfaction of dating me up ahead like that.

Oh well, strange paradoxes occur even in this enlightened age. Picture me if you can with the record of having dated or been out every single night since I've been here, with the exception of one night! But alas! To him who expects nothing—who is a confirmed cynic, come the breaks, after he has ceased to care anymore. I never thought I'd be so practical before I finished college. Dating is a business to be managed like any other.

Eunice Mary and I have been reading a darling book called *Larry*, filled with letters written by a college boy who was an idealist. It made me think back to the time when I had the very same thoughts and feelings. It made us both wonder about sophistication and its attending evils. There are a lot of phases of it—in fact there are so many problems presented to us to be solved that it makes your head whirl just to try thinking out a few of them! Oh well, what is living if it isn't a struggle to solve something, we don't any of us know just what. And college is a good place, if it is doubted occasionally. I'd never give it up for all the money or pleasure anybody could offer me. It's the fine lasting things that stick in your memory of it all. I thought last year was gorgeous, but this year offers more and more. Good night.

I love you, every one,

Dorothy

P.S. I am tutoring Dud in his French. He certainly is a slow pupil. I'm pretty much afraid for him, but am determined he will get thru the course creditably!

Dear Mother,

I am enjoying a class in Psychology by thinking how wonderful I'd feel if I could just sleep right thru without being disturbed. It's a great life and about the only thing I need right now is sleep. Last night Dud invited me to go to the show and we sat there and ate candy and had a good time. He also asked me to the Sigma Nu Melon Feed Friday night, so I guess I'll manage to be gay. Wait till Harry hears about Friday night. He probably won't date me anymore after that. Maybe I'll start staying home for the rest of the year. You never can tell!

This lecture is most interesting. At least Dr. Marshall doesn't shout and disturb me like Dr. Carter used to.

Eunice Mary isn't back yet, so I'm beginning to feel kind of lonesome. Next week I'm really going to dig in and study.

Monday night after pledging I took a late permission and went riding in an open air collegiate Ford with Harry. I forgot about board meeting and had to give a good story for not being there, but fortunately the Dean was feeling in a very fine state of mind and just laughed about it.

We're having fun in costume design drawing heads and laces and furs. Miss Swanson said my heads were very good, so I felt quite flattered, for I feel rather amateurish over at the art room. You'll have to see it when you're here again. It's a real joy to work in.

Tell J.M. I'm sending him something, for growing up. Love to you all and more later.

Dorothy

October 28, 1931 – Thursday night

Dearest Mother,

At last, a little lull before Homecoming. No classes tomorrow! Today I have just more than straightened and cleaned—then this afternoon my laundry came—so I'm totally pure. I have yet to iron and finish fixing a costume for my old maid part in the play.

Then I decided that having so much time—and so few clothes that I would fix over my green dress. I think it's going to be a pippin! Dr. Seaton has given us a sewing machine, so here goes. I want to wear it tomorrow night on a date. Do you suppose I'll get it done? I'll just have to! I have a date after play practice with Harry.

Dudley is beginning to be a personal problem—he comes over all the time, until it's both annoying and embarrassing. Harry doesn't like it so well! But it does him good. Dud sure pulled a good one, when he gave Harry the keys to the car the other night when I went out with Harry instead of Dud. Harry hasn't gotten over the shock. His code doesn't include giving his rival a car to take the girl in question out.

Joyce and Dottie King are both coming for homecoming, so I guess we'll have a room full. Eunice Mary has a bum leg again today, poor kid.

Debate practice began last night and I am also (I think) elected (or appointed) Associate Editor of the *Albionian*. It's all a big joke or a big pull, whichever you call it. Will tell you more later.

Well my little boy friend hasn't called me—so I'll spite him and stay in tonight. I guess he thinks I have practice as usual.

Here goes for bigger and better dressmaking.

Love,
Dorothy

Wednesday 2 p.m.

Dear Mother,

I still don't know where you are—but expect you must be home by now. I have just turned over a new leaf and decided to settle right down and study. My roommate says I can't do it—but I'll show the lady! This week has been hectic with play practice and everything, but I'm getting control of the situation.

255

Had a nice weekend with Harry feeling so amiable that it was funny. He even offered to do my Soc. lesson last night because I was tired! He'll take wings and fly away soon at this rate.

Dudley has certainly been worrying me with this quitting school business. I've interviewed the whole college faculty, almost, and have done and said everything to him that I can think of. He promised me to come back yesterday, but I didn't see him. I'm about thru now—if he has to go thru this performance all the time, maybe it's just as well to let him leap in the beginning. There won't always be someone to give him backbone every time there is a hard decision to make. He's been pampered to death.

Eunice Mary made the histrionic club and is tickled to death. She says she is famous now too. Had histrionic meeting yesterday, also conference at Dr. Brown's, and between times Harry took me for a short ride. We're both so busy, we're nearly crazy—and decided we'd be late for appointments for a change.

Friday morning I'm going to teach two sections of Prof. Weiss' college freshman speech classes. I think it quite an honor. He will be away, and wants me to mark them and everything.

I have resigned my job on YW cabinet, as it's just one thing too much. I'm going to try to steer clear of over-activity if possible. Have to tear off to drama class now. Would you send me my sorority pin?
Love to you all,
Dorothy

Thursday night

Dear Ones,

Another hectic week—I can't decide what the big events are, yet. However, I've managed to fill the days. My present schedule allows not even a minute for letters or recreation. I have enough and more to keep me busy fourteen or more hours per day. Anyhow I manage to steal a while off by cutting classes or play practice as the case may be. Tonight it was play practice! Had a date with Harry and suddenly noticed that I was already late so stayed out a while longer—then came in.

Explanations to Miss Champ are going to be new and different to say the least. Harry suggested I say I was out picking huckleberries. Harry sure was griped about that date I broke. It seems that his breaking a date and my doing it are two different things! Tonight he was nice as pie and the most fun yet—he recited poetry and clowned around most of the time. We had lots of fun, if I didn't get to play practice! I have a date with him for Friday night and Dudley wants me to go out to dinner on Saturday.

Did you know your helter-skelter daughter was president of Chevron? (An honorary society for Senior Women.) And I also have a minor part in the homecoming play. Harry says I get "more famouser" all the time.

Am too sleepy to write more.

Love,

Dorothy

Wednesday

Dear Mother,

Just received your card. I can't imagine what's happened to my laundry case. I sent it Thursday and I don't know how to trace it.

Am still trying to get rested up from homecoming. Are you tired too? I had a date with Harry last night—went to the show.

Thursday

This seems to be a "continued in our next" letter, but nevertheless, I stumble on. Tonight I am celebrating with a study sign on the door and everything. A real event—Eunice Mary doesn't know how to take it!

Last night was debate practice and after that, I went walking with Harry. (He said, "here I am wasting my time!") So I just said—"And here *I* am wasting *my* time!" Then we kept on walking—which gives you a faint (very faint) idea of the intelligence of college students! Today he has gone to Detroit on *Albionian* business so I remain quite unmolested and no longer waste his valuable time. Tomorrow a blue book in Sociology (The Family) and I just have to make good. Here's hoping.

I haven't touched my dress yet, but think I can naphtha it myself because I rather want to wear it tomorrow night if everything is OK.

Chevron had a meeting today and we've planned a real big "Bargain Bridge Benefit" at Parker Inn just before Thanksgiving. (It is a thirty-nine cent bargain idea.) We're keeping it dark for a week

257

or so and then will spring it as an all college and faculty affair. I hope it goes over big. We're planning on 200 and hope to clear about $60 if all goes well. (Imagine yours truly planning a benefit bridge!) The height of the ridiculous!!

I can't think of any more scandal right now—so had better study and improve the mind, if any.
Love to you all—wish I could see you,
Dorothy

Friday night

Dear Mother,

It seemed good to get a letter from you for a change. My laundry came OK, but I'm afraid I'm going to be late getting it back. The chocolate bar was oh so good! I like 'em like that!

This week has been more hectic than usual, if possible. Have written to P.E.O., and am trying to catch up a little before next week. Harry and I are having a nice "bust up." I got on my high horse, for a wonder, and turned down a date for tonight, because he didn't ask me till this morning. I thought up a lot of sarcastic things to say when he called, but finally decided against saying them, and contented myself with telling him in a very nice, clear way, just how "dates" as an afterthought affect me. He's rather eating humble pie, and is coming over later this evening to try to make things right. (I sure have got a lot of nerve to high hat him when there are no more possibilities for me in sight.) Hope he likes my crust. But he deserves it—he's getting so he takes me for granted—and that will never do. I am going to sit in the drawing room tonight and let him offer the best story he can.

I'm enclosing our tally and ticket, for Chevron's benefit. We hope it will be a real success. All the businessmen in town have contributed prizes, and we hope to get by with spending next to nothing—and making all profit.

Dean Gray was in to see me last night and found me on the verge of tears. She thinks I'm doing too much—but she didn't realize how much Harry had to do with my mood. Also, I worked as a special waitress for the faculty, at the birthday dinner Wednesday night and it sort of finished me temporarily. I now have $1.75 for extra waitress work. What will I do with all this capital!!

Tomorrow I intend to be very good and study most all day. It will be a real treat—if I know how any more. I am sending your pen in my laundry case. I will fix it up so it won't fall out or get lost, but look for it.

This afternoon there was a game with Hillsdale and no classes. We lost 14-0. But it was a pretty decent game at that. It's been just wonderful for about a week, so shiny and warm part of the time.

You don't tell me much about how you are.

Love to you all,

Dorothy

December 5, 1931

Dearest Mother,

I don't know whether you have read the papers or not, but I wish to inform you officially that your child has a second place prize for the extemporaneous speaking contest. It is a silver medallion, with a figure on it, and on the back it says "Michigan Intercollegiate Extempore Contest." So now you know! I feel pretty good about it, although I did not get first place. However, the woman who did was from Michigan State, and did not deserve it as much as the Hillsdale woman, who didn't get any award. So there you are, the typical contest: there were the three of us in the very close running. There were two contests, one in the afternoon and one in the evening, with an hour's preparation for each one. If you think that wasn't some strain, you're mistaken. It's even more difficult than an oratorical contest, for there's nothing canned about the speaking. It takes pretty quick thinking and a fluent speaker. (Even I was at a loss for words half the time, imagine that for a magpie.)

We had a very enjoyable trip, with Professors Weiss and Hance, Homer Yinger (who got first place in the men's) and Stewart Anderson, Harry's roommate. And if there weren't some clowns in that bunch, then I never saw any. I laughed until I was completely tired out. The afternoon contest was really the worst, for I was nervous and didn't have control of myself at all. It's a wonder I even qualified for the evening. There were six in the afternoon and four in the evening. The first time I spoke on Jane Addams' philosophy of life, and at night, on her chief contributions in the last ten years. We got home at one o'clock the other night, and I was pretty tired.

This morning I got a darling note from Mrs. Seaton congratulating me. Wasn't that sweet? She certainly looks after things when Dr. Seaton is away.

Then last night I had a date with Harry, and he certainly made up for lost time in being nice to me. I've never seen him quite as angelic as he was. He told me about his family, and how good-hearted both his mother and father are, and how he can't explain how he can be the way he is. I suggested that maybe there was an overemphasis on doing things for people, which made him contrary to the existing situation. He certainly is honest. He told me just what his ambitions were, and didn't even try to defend himself. Then he wanted to know what kind of aims I had. They certainly differed, although I was sort of vague about things. Well, to make a long story short, I got in at 12:00 o'clock, after having spent a very pleasant evening.

This morning he called me up to get me out of bed. Incidentally, I had about seven phone calls yesterday, including two from Dud. He called up first, just to talk to me, then again later to see if I would go to the show, but it happened that I was busy. (Harry now calls me for weekend dates on Tuesday—ha, ha.)

Nearly time to go and get lunch. Wish you could see my splendiferous medal. Prof. Hance says all I need now is a gold one, and that I can get that at the next contest. I almost believe I can.
All my love,
Dorothy

December 10, 1931

Dearest Mother,

Another shock—a letter. My laundry came this afternoon and I mailed dirty clothes right back. Discouraging isn't it, to get back dirty clothes every time you send clean ones? But oh, think of the good of the cause. Remember that my standing in the community depends upon the condition of my socks! And many other trifles.

Have had a good week so far—have met with every organization of which I am a member, and attended several classes—also went to the one-act plays *Dust of the Road*, and *The Fool* Wednesday night. That was our birthday dinner night and was it good—turkey, chestnut dressing, tomato canapé, salad, pear, cranberry ice, rolls, and pudding and coffee. Not bad and for the first time in a week I had an enormous appetite. Just ate and ate and loved it.

Next week will be mildly busy—one debate on Tuesday at Ann Arbor, for which I haven't prepared as yet. Thursday we give *The Intimate Strangers* at Lansing for some club. Friday the art club is giving a masquerade, and I haven't yet decided whether to go or not. Then Saturday night is our Kappa Delta informal.

I am sure you would like to inquire about Harry's health, so will say he is being angelic still! It sounds impossible. He called me Monday night, saw me and called me Tuesday night, called twice Wednesday and took me to the plays. (Net gain of fifty cents, economically speaking for Miss Hill, loss of $1 for Mr. R.) Tonight he called me and went to the library with me and then to debate meeting. This is absolutely the latest news— I have dates for the entire weekend (booked up in advance, as is proper for a British subject). There is only one fly—affairs are too placid—this cannot continue— Harry loves fireworks!

Our room is clean and neat tonight for about the first time this year, due to about two hours work this morning. I even washed my pillow tops and ironed them tonight. But oh the studying I should get done and don't! Oh well—live and laugh—if one's face does crack! As Freddie tells me when I'm down, "It's a good old world—snap out of it!! Right now I'm very, very happy—there just isn't time enough to enjoy everything and one girl had the nerve to inform me that this week had "just dragged something awful."

Anyone who can get bored around here needs to be taken out of circulation immediately. Wish I could write more.
Love,
Dorothy

Dear Mother,

I feel sort of like "another day, another dollar." Harry and I are through. Perhaps someday I will take heart and tell you the details. I can't decide whether the British subject's pride is hurt or not. At any rate, I have vim and vigor enough left to plan a very full weekend without him. Eunice Mary's tall blonde brother is coming over for our party I think. And Friday night, I have a little plan cooking up for the masquerade ball, which the Art Club is giving. I will tell you about it when I have the planning done. Somehow Harry doesn't seem to bother me as much as he might. As I have often said he is never boring, and the next few days are going to be mighty interesting, and very full too, so I won't have time to miss him.

Tomorrow we go to Ann Arbor to debate. We start at one o'clock and get back in time for play rehearsal, I hope. We're giving *The Intimate Strangers* in Lansing Thursday, so that fills that day and if I go to parties both Friday and Saturday night, I fear there will be little time left for bemoaning such a small matter as the passing of Harry. He informed me he was going to bury himself in work. (I neglected to apply for position of eulogizer at his funeral.) If you have any thrilling ideas for the arrangement of two hilarious costumes for the Art Club Ball please send them on at once.

I don't know yet just how I'm coming home, but school is out on Tuesday the twenty-second. I'll be seeing you——tra la! I love you a lot. Don't let my little troubles worry you, cause you know I should be the one to worry, and what's my trouble, that I don't seem to?
Love,
Dorothy

Sunday night

Dearest Mother,

A New Year's Resolution scarcely cold—I am writing you even before the New Year. We arrived all safe and warm at about 7:00 o'clock. Eunice Mary was here when I arrived. We have eaten sandwiches and signed off food for the rest of the evening. She has just gone out on a date. I came too late, evidently, for his Majesty— he called me about six and found I wasn't in.

Also found a letter from Fleming awaiting me. He's the same old boy, and says "I value your friendship, and fear it because you always see right thru me." He's feeling quite happy at Ann Arbor now. I guess he's had time to get accustomed to it all.

Now that I have the rest of the evening free—I shall do my duty in various ways. Hope I can get fairly caught up for once.

You are all so dear and good to me, I hate to go away and leave you, but it is nice to be sure that you're always there and just the same. My home's about the nicest place yet—I recommend it!
Love to you all,
Dorothy

January 5, 1932

Dearest Mother,

My weight is now 130 lbs., and Harry has succeeded in scaring me into drinking milk. He informs me that coffee is terrible, and that, by hook or by crook, somehow he is going to see that I gain weight. Now that you are reassured about my physical welfare, I would like to state that I am seated before the typewriter with the beginnings of an oration in hand. The contest is a week from Monday. I plan to work on the oration this afternoon, and finish a term paper late tonight. Then there will be time for oration and more oration. I guess maybe I'll survive.

As to my social status, it varies, and varies, and how! Every night last week Harry and I managed to miss connections, and either he was mad, or I was, but now everything is rosy. Went to the game Friday night with Harry and took a late permission at the house. He gave me four apples (my value goes up you see). Then last night we had a short date and I came home with a can of chocolate cookies (he believes in feeding me). Today I plan to really work. For the first time today I began to feel as if I could come out of the woods, and get thru the semester, and the extra work. My formal came, and looks grand. Thanks for the soap—it works fine.

Eunice Mary and I have decided we are a degrading influence on each other. We would rather talk than work—we're beginning to be in the fix you and I were during vacation. But it's great sport.

You must be very high-hat by now, with a brass pan worth goodness knows how much. Better start chaining it up at night. I told Harry about your liking his silhouette and he said "for two cents I'd send her one." (Are you supposed to furnish the two cents?) It seems to me that he would be very susceptible to your wiles. I don't doubt but that you could get around him in no time at all. Right now he is all steamed up about editing a campus ballyhoo.
Love,
Dorothy

Tues. night—the night before the slaughter

Dearest Mother,

Have been thinking about you all and wishing for a breathing spell to write just a few of the things which have been going on.

263

But nevertheless, I will steal a little time from my famous oration. It is now the night before the battle and the oration is still far from finished. But I am rather hopeful, for I think it's going to be pretty good stuff. The contest is at three tomorrow. Harry says if I win it we will go out and get most awfully drunk. (What do you think about that? I knew you would approve.) Anyway I'm just hoping, cause it would be rather thrilling to win. Harry won the election at the frat house last night and is now president of his fraternity, so I hate to see him get ahead of me like that. It would be pretty swell if I could win.

Everything is going along far too swiftly for the things I have to do, but I'm not worrying a bit, but just buckling down and getting as much done as I can and still have some good times in between. Yesterday and today I've felt most ambitious, for some unknown reason, and it certainly is lucky for I've written practically the whole of my oration just lately. I now have my term paper left to finish before Friday. Then I will register Saturday, and work on my speech seminar over the weekend.

You heard about our theatre rush. That night I went to the game and came right home, and Harry went on downtown. The riot wasn't nearly as bad as it was painted in the Detroit paper. Bohm, the manager, is just mean, and says he doesn't even want any student patronage. So Thursday night the Marshall theatre invited the whole college to come over there for a free show at nine o'clock. We had special permission that night till twelve, and Harry called me to go with the rest of the Tekes in a truck, and it sure was fun, rather wet and cold, but with a whole crowd it was great sport. To cap the climax we had a blue book in Psychology the next day, and after my studying a bare forty minutes before going to Marshall, I got a straight A with the remark, "this is a very good paper."

So you see I'm quite treading on air these days, but am watching for that inevitable fall-but until then—whee! I am already invited to the Teke formal February fifth—I don't know how he happened to crash thru with an invitation so early. It doesn't seem right. Our party is scheduled for March twelfth at the Hotel Hayes in Jackson.

Tonight we had a style show in the recreation room, but I didn't even see anything I wanted—very soon I will become a woman without a desire. (Wouldn't that be terrific.) Nothing seems to down my spirits today, not even everyone else's blues. If this will only hold out till tomorrow—perhaps—well, just perhaps—.

My money came for second semester. My course is nearly worked out. Dr. Carter did me the honor of suggesting I do my practice teaching at Starr Commonwealth next semester. It's a compliment because he feels he must have someone who is responsible and has a good deal of initiative. I don't think I'll do it, however, because it conflicts with part of my schedule, and it would take a good deal more time, and doesn't give much more benefit that any of us can see. It would be teaching under Evelyn and Elta, and I feel that maybe I'd get more out of a more experienced teacher.

Must start in working again, good-night.
Love to you all,
Dorothy

Dearest Mother,

I am a brute, a dunce, and all that sort of thing to keep you waiting so long about the contest and everything. And here you are buying Presses when there is no news in them. No the situation is quite unusual (due to Dorothy's antics). The contest came off Wednesday, and of course, I had spent a little time on it, but not enough. However, I went anyway. There were seven contestants, and when I got up to speak I knew that I didn't know the darned oration very well, (a la Dorothy) but I got thru it. Well, the decision was to come out the next morning, and meanwhile the rumor got around that three of us were tied for first place, all of which was interesting.

I rather gave up the idea of winning, for I knew just how badly I had done. Next morning we went over and sure enough, on the bulletin board was a notice of a new contest in two weeks with the names of D. Hill, E. Watson, and P. Webster as contestants for first, second, and third places. Of course it means that we'll all win some money, but it's really quite ridiculous for knowing that I was the one who was least prepared, they are giving me two weeks in which to improve. It's rather a matter of campus opinion that the judges are sort of staging a new contest for my sole benefit, at least that's the way we have it figured out.

They didn't quite want to give it to me, because they felt I hadn't done it quite well enough, and yet it's evident that they didn't want anyone else to get it. I don't think they thought how it would look to the public or they wouldn't have lain themselves open to a laugh.

Harry says it's my personality (for it couldn't have been the oration!) He is highly indignant, for he thinks it's so simple for me to win anything. I got properly bawled out, and told that he wouldn't speak to me if I didn't win the next one. I am hoping to do it. I still have to finish my term paper and do my seminar over Sunday. Then I'm not worrying about exams, and can work on my oration, and on debate between semesters. I would love to come home, but I don't know yet just how thick it will be around here, and I'd have to get someone to work for me in the kitchen, and with that work to do on debate and oratory, I don't know whether I should or not. That one week will be such a big help because there will be no other studies to interfere.

I'll have to see how things work out. I'm going to be thrown out of debate and oratory both if I don't get going. You can't go forever on personality, although, I did pretty well this morning in registering. I spoke to the man in a nice way and asked him if I could get in and not have to wait for an hour, and as a result, I was all thru registering in twenty minutes. In the bargain, I had another surprise. I had figured that I'd only have about $11 after paying sorority, but when I went to pay my fees I suddenly remembered my scholarship of $50 and don't think it didn't seem like a godsend! So now that I am a rich woman, no telling what will happen.

I'm so very happy now it doesn't seem as if there could be many more nice things to happen. Last night the college allowed us one o'clock permission to go to Jackson to a free show after the games (the other towns are trying to show up our own bum theatre manager) and the Tekes chartered a bus, and we went in great style. It was loads of fun.

Tonight, I will stay home and study. Real event! Harry hasn't even asked me to go out. Maybe he thinks it would be good for my soul to work once in a while. I was all set to work Thursday night, and he called me up and pestered me for nearly an hour, and finally I went out. That energy could sure make a million if rightly applied!

I enjoyed the clippings, thanks so much. My roommate likes the one about the Michigan coeds. I couldn't send my laundry case, because I haven't received a clean smock yet, and I don't dare send my dirty one home till I get another in my case. It's a predicament. Must go to work now.
Love to all of you,
Dorothy

January 31, 1932

Dearest Mother,

The end of semesters, at last, and nothing to work on now, but an oration, and a few letters to answer. It sure seems good! I've cleaned and washed and dusted, dated, and even rested a little. Everything I own is clean except one pair of sox and a blouse. I thought it was just as easy as sending my laundry—there was so much of it. I've mended and am most respectably neat.

Exams week has been most hectic, but I do hope things won't be so heavy next semester. D. Malmborg is back and is rooming in our corridor. Eunice Mary invited me to go home with her this Saturday, but I declined and am glad I stayed here—at least I'm more caught up. This week I'm working fast and furiously on the oration. Here's hoping I can make the grade!

I'm to do my practice teaching under Miss Abbott in English and some play production (coaching) at the high school. I hope I can do it in the morning and conserve my time.

The Western State Debate is February twelfth and I'm to be in it. That's our tough debate of the season and I'm scared! I've paid off my debts and think I'll have my picture taken!

Oh yes, I forgot to tell you the big news. I have a new green corduroy dress—it's keen with a brown suede belt and my suede jacket. Eunice Mary and I sent for dresses just alike from Chicago. Hers is dark red. They have silver buttons on them and are the sensation of the dormitory (we paid $1.95 each, which is our big secret). So I have my new spring outfit.

Tonight I have a date and then I'm coming home and working on my oration.

I had a darling letter from P.E.O. and they nearly died laughing at the things I bought with my $15. They all want me to do their

shopping. They said for me to be sure and wear my sox when I come to see them at Easter time. Will write again soon.
Love,
Dorothy

P.S. Harry wants me to ask you if you know of anyone who would like a job as housemother at a frat house. They want a new matron pretty badly. Do you suppose there would be anyone in our neck of the woods? I think they pay just a small amount $5 a week and room and board and laundry.
I love you a lot—write to me!!

Monday night

Dearest Mother,
I'm still alive and howling—and if you'll forgive me for not writing sooner—I'll be coming home Wednesday afternoon with Dudley. I don't know that he will bring me to Detroit—but if not, I will come in on the bus—expect to leave here about 3:00 p.m. I am so anxious to get home and know I have a family again.
I loved your little lecture note about not dating Harry so much—my roommate and I had many a chuckle as we tried to figure out how you ever got down to the point of really lecturing me! You are a dear—and don't worry about Harry and me, for I never could fall in love with him. He has his good points—and somehow he's so peculiar that I take a psychologist's delight in trying to remedy any given situation. He's never met an animal like me anywhere and I'm sure there isn't his equal in any zoo. Perhaps I'm trying to get him to realize that girls aren't all alike and that the world sometimes hands out a square deal, if a fellow is ready to meet things fairly. One cynic teaching another—a unique paradox, eh?
I had a lovely time at the Teke party—good orchestra— and Harry does manage to give one a nice time. I wore my new blue outfit—or haven't you heard? It was turquoise blue— very long—with short sleeved black velvet jacket and black pumps. Very swanky outfit concocted out of Frannie's old blue dress and Gerry's black jacket.
Marks are coming out so be prepared for the worst! However

there are good features; one A- in Drama from Miss Champ and one straight A from Hance in Argumentation. Incidentally it was the only A in the class, which is full of boys. Do I feel cocky? Even that hardly expresses things.

Later. Just went out for a walk with Harry. We had a disagreement last night, which he tried to fix up this morning. He's going home tomorrow so I won't be seeing him again.

Am planning to study lots while I'm home, but I suppose you'll laugh that off! Oh well, time will tell.
Love—I'll soon be there,
Dorothy

February 12, 1932
My Dear Little Girl:

I am sticking this note into Mother's letter before I mail it, because this is your birthday and I hope that it may be a happy one.

We would like to send you something besides a letter with our love and greetings on your birthday, and I'm hoping that we can before long, as the future looks very good indeed and I am much encouraged.

Business has been very good, but collections are still slow. However, we are very happy and wish we may see you soon.

Permit me to extend congratulations on your success in the recent contest. We are again pleased and very proud of our daughter and I want you to know that. I appreciate the fact that, even with your native ability (which was, no doubt, inherited from your Dad) that you must have worked hard to accomplish what you have during the recent twenty-four years.

I am mighty glad that your dear friend and roommate was also successful in the contest and please extend my congratulations to her.
Heaps of Love and a big hug,
From your old Dad

P.S. We all love you a lot and think about you all the time.

Susanna Wesley Hall

Feb. 16, 1932

Dearest Mother,

I fear I shall have to give you the silhouette after all, for just last night I annexed a huge picture of His Royal Highness—leather frame and all! And my roommate managed to accumulate a large picture of Bill so our dresser is a sight to behold! We have three large pictures, a small one and a silhouette to date! When Eunice Mary got home last night we just sat on the bed and howled. You can't imagine the impressiveness of three stern males lined up! Mrs. Wolfe will probably be cautioning us about the strain on the dresser.

Of course you realize that both my roommate and I have been more than busy acquiring that "picture technique" so that accounts for lack of letters and every other crime committed during the week. Harry went on a debate trip and was gone on my birthday. He sent me a telegram and a Valentine and arrived home Saturday night. Sunday morning I received a heart box of chocolates, and yesterday, the picture. Do think I have been treated fairly. Eunice Mary got a plant and a picture—besides two bouquets the night of the play. Yesterday a friend of her mother's sent a box of chocolates. We are having sorority initiation for twelve girls next Sunday morning. I may be seeing you shortly after you receive this letter. Ha! You'd be surprised, wouldn't you?

I received yours and Daddy's lovely birthday letters. Hope everything comes out all right. I certainly get the lucky breaks. You ought to, too.

My oration is in completed form. I have to give it in freshman chapel the twenty-fourth. The district contest is March third and the state contest is March eleventh.

I rather think I'll make the Wisconsin trip. Have to go listen to Carter now.
Love to you all,
Dorothy

Monday morn

Dearest Mother,

Every time I sit down to write you—either I go to sleep sitting up, or the telephone rings—or I have to go to work.

Last night I led league and that crazy Harry had to come down to hear it. He bothered me all the way thru—just by trying to be very solemn. He says I don't appreciate his efforts in coming to league. I guess I am ungrateful, for he stayed and even washed the dishes!! I haven't recovered from that yet. However, he managed to fight with me later in the evening—about what, I don't know. So I guess I am once more a jilted woman. Am enclosing the flashlight photo they took of us over at the house, the night of the art club party. Tomorrow I give my oration in upper class chapel. And then Friday at Holland, Michigan is the big contest. Please don't expect too much. I may not even get second place—only hoping.

Eunice Mary is still in the infirmary. I sure have been lucky not to get it. The mail is just going out, so will send this.

Love to you all,

Dorothy

Sunday morning

Dear Ones,

Daddy's letter, received, and contents noted with much laughter as well as interest. Write me another, why don't you, it's a real treat from a non-letter writer. I hope Mother isn't working herself to death. Watch that lady, she's apt to put one over on you.

You may be interested to know that I received an invitation to join Theta Alpha Phi, the national dramatic fraternity. But I'm afraid I can't make it. It costs $15, and that's just like $50 as far as I'm concerned. However I shall be the one big shot on campus who can always say—belong to that—why I turned that frat down twenty years ago. I'll be like the speech man O'Neill at the University of Michigan, who has nothing but an A.B. degree, and when asked why he has no Ph.D. says, "Who is there in the field qualified to give me an examination for such a degree!" And there you are. The moral is that in order to really be a big shot, you must be beyond such incidentals as degrees and such. I hope this will be a lesson to all who go out for first places in contests, and who join mere honoraries.

Yesterday and today we are quite alone in the dorm and I had dreaded it, but it really has been grand. It's the first time I've had a minute to relax and be quiet. And this place certainly is quiet now. I was afraid the trip would be the last straw on a busy schedule, but now that I'm beginning to be rested, and I do recuperate fast, I think it will be grand, and a real opportunity.

Harry went home and is going to have his eyes fixed up. They're pretty bad, and he's rather dreading it.

The Senior Prom was lovely; although we were all so dog-tired we could hardly wiggle. The decorations were all in black, with a huge Chinese figure in color at one end of the gym and dragons in color on the sides, with little booths for the different fraternities along the sides, all furnished with their furniture. I was so tired that we didn't dance much, but it was real fun, and quite restful if you could call a dance restful. The orchestra was gorgeous.

Last night I had my dinner sent up from the Green Shoppe (the college pays for it) and was it ever good. It seemed so grand just to lie around and eat, and not have to go anywhere for anything. Then this morning Mildred and I got up and fussed around, cleaned our rooms and went down to the Green Shoppe and ate a huge breakfast, with waffles and everything. At five-thirty tonight we debate Dennison at the Parker Inn. We are having dinner in the Hawthorne Room and the debate around the table. About fifteen of us, quite exclusive!

Tomorrow morning we leave at 9:00 am and debate at Valparaiso at night. Then Tuesday morning we go to Wheaton College, Wheaton, Ill. and debate there that night. Wednesday to Rockford, Ill., and debate there at night. Thursday we set out for Madison, Wis., and the Delta Sigma Rho tournament. I have to be in a discussion contest, and talk about the failure of the Republican Party (imagine my embarrassment). These contests will take place Thursday and Friday, with a banquet Friday night. Then we expect to stay and see the city over Saturday and Sunday, with nothing particular to do. Monday morning we leave for Appleton, Wis. and Lawrence College there. I don't have to debate there, so it will be quite a relief. Finally we get back here Wed. night, March thirtieth. If you want to write me, write to General Delivery, Madison Wis. and I'll get it.
Lovingly,
Dorothy

Valparaiso, Ind.

Tuesday morning

Dearest Mother,

We traveled through the worst weather of the year yester-day—snow, sleet and engine trouble—but we finally arrived last night in time to eat and debate here.

The dorm in which we are staying is some different than ours—old and ramshackle—with iron beds and old oak furniture. The girls have been lovely to us though.

Their dining room arrangement is the funniest ever. The girls all go downstairs and as you come in you see a whole herd of boys jammed back at one end of the room. As soon as the girls begin to sit down—the attack begins—the mob moves suddenly and with one accord scrambles for all the remaining chairs. And how they eat—speed is the thing! Good food served in quantity on blue crockery. Then in the midst of things someone offers a prayer—and the mob of boys immediately after start for the door. Our table hadn't even begun its dessert yet, when that happened. Tell J.M. he'll have to speed up on his eating habits, if he comes here to school.

We finally have our car fixed and plan to leave here around noon. Next stop is a decision debate at Wheaton tonight. It's about seventy miles from here, so that won't be bad at all. I don't feel so peppy, but I guess I'll recover gradually—here's hoping.
Love,
Dorothy

Dear Dorothy,

As you know this was our first Easter without our child and we have missed you, but hope you have had a happy day in beautiful Madison and, more than all, I do hope you have been able to have some rest.

Have been home all day until just now, when Daddy and I went for a walk in the park. It was so lovely—the sky rose color and the sleepy chirping of the birds.

Was downtown a little while yesterday and finally managed to get J.M. a suit. We went to Birds', but before I went, I read the shopping news for Monday and they were offering suits for $15, but we did not see anything we cared for, so I asked them about the suits for Monday and when they found out they were not going to sell, they rustled around and showed us those. There was a gray he liked. And we walked thru Kerns' and Hudsons' and came home. Saw so many things I would so like to have sent you, but probably when you do not need it, I will be able to get you things.

Well, now it is Monday morning and I am washing as soon as the water is hot. I heard about a lady who had some old dishes and I think it will be sort of a thrill just to see them, don't you? I have not told the family, for they might think I would do something wild. They are English people and maybe I will learn something interesting.

Thought perhaps I would get a letter from our child this morning, but didn't. I will be glad to hear from you. I have been afraid you might be sick.

Heaps of love,
Mother

Friday morn

Dearest Mother,

The lost one has returned, and although you may think me dead and gone by this time, I'm fairly lively for an old dog who has the rheumatics from much travel, and who has been trying to ward off such superficial things as colds and flu. As yet they haven't got me, but how long will it last, who knows? We got in Wednesday night, very tired and I had a fever, and was all set to be sick, but aha, we fooled them.

I took a shower and went out with his highness, who incidentally is pretty sick about his eyes. He spent the whole vacation in black glasses, except when he sneaked out and went to a show, and then the doctor met him coming out, and that ended the fun. He has forty per cent defective vision, ten per cent having been lost in the last year. And also the possibility of blindness eventually from cataracts! Interesting outlook? He paid $35 for new glasses, and they still aren't right.

It seemed so good to get back although the trip was a real experience. We met so many lovely people, and saw a great deal of beautiful country. Wisconsin is as lovely as ever. The university is right on a lake, and when spring comes, they say there is absolutely nothing done in the way of studying. We stayed at the Chi Omega House, where I slept in the bed of outstanding woman on campus, and in the same room with the campus beauty, and also the president of the women's self-government association. Imagine my troubled dreams. I awoke in the morning to discover a lemon colored Packard, belonging to my hostess, drawn up in front of the house. So much for my poverty-stricken friends.

It certainly has been a marvelous year, although I haven't had time to sit down and appreciate it all yet. Parties, trips, work, dances and dates, debates, extemp contests, and oratorical ones, it's all grand.

I had a letter from Margaret about a job at Lapeer—in the English dept., and I have written, but haven't had any reply as yet. Also wrote to both Pontiac, and Coldwater, as there may be chances there. Would like to get interviews, but it isn't possible to go right now. I will write you whenever I get a chance. It would seem good to see you all.

All my love,
Dorothy

Sunday afternoon

Dear Dorothy,

It has turned out to be quite a nice bright day. I have not been out. We thought we might get out for a little stroll and perhaps call on the Steeds, but Daddy is pressing his suit, so I do not know whether we will make it or not. J.M. and Patsy went to church this morning. It is rather amusing—she is trying to manage him now. She was over to spend the evening Friday. You would think she was eighteen anyway.

I was glad to get your letter. We had about given up hopes of ever hearing from you again. I did not like the tone of your letter very well, however, if you are not sick yet, I will be surprised and I am worrying, so I think you had better try the infirmary for a day or two until you get rested. I am very sorry you went on the trip, for evidently you were too tired to go and you need not try to laugh this off—I cannot very well come over just now, but if you do not let up a bit, you will be seeing me. A breakdown right now would not be so good. There I am thru for now.

Aunt Minnie was over for dinner last night—first time in ages. Uncle Joe, Daddy and J.M. went down to Ford's to see the new cars. They say they are keen. I guess anyone can be satisfied if they can have a Ford this year.

Harry certainly has worries. I am so sorry for him. I do not see any chance of him studying law. He will do very well if he can even finish next year. It would seem as if he ought to give up all study for a time and let his eyes have complete rest.

I cleaned all the dish cupboards yesterday. It was a big job, but looks so nice you will have to hurry home or it will be all messed up again and you will not know how nice a job I did.

J.M. goes back to school in the morning. The year is nearly over and we have managed to keep him there, so I feel good about it. I have been doing quite a little work for Daddy. We have Mr. Lamb's typewriter here just now. It is a very nice one—hope he leaves it a long time. He may, so they can get the work out faster, for he is working with Daddy.

Alice just took Auntie Steed, Minnie, and me for a long ride. Aunt Minnie and I started out for a walk when Alice came along. It was cold, so the ride had it all over walking. J.M. and Daddy went over to the park and when they came home, found a parcel from Aunt Lottie for my birthday—a pretty little balsam filled pillow with a pillow cover made of woven silk rags. But I do not want a birthday, so I will pretend it is for Christmas.

Daddy wants me to do some work for him, so as long as I have no news to tell you, I might as well get busy for him,

No need to tell you how much we would like to see you. I wonder if you would know us if you met us in a strange place.

If I thought you were really coming home, I would wash the curtains, so you had better let me know.

Lovingly,
Mother

Dear Dorothy,

Have worked on Daddy's old books until I am ready to throw a fit, I guess, so I will throw it at you for a while.

We have not had a license for the car since the first of March. We hope to have it by next week and if you think it wise to come home Daddy said that he would have J.M. take you anywhere around here (like Pontiac) that you would like to go. He would be glad to let you have the car a few days over there, but says it is not safe enough.

You might have trouble with it anytime, but J.M. takes its insides out so much that he would risk it with the two of you and would like to help you any way possible. I thought perhaps Romeo would be a nice place to apply, but I do not know anything about conditions there. We are expecting money in this week, and if you need some to come home, I think we could let you have it by next week.

It was nice to hear your voice, but I am always so surprised, that I cannot think of a thing to tell you. The boys of the family took me to the show in honor of my birthday—our first wild extravagance since the war. It was so cute—*The Lady with the Past*. J.M. got most of the dinner and Daddy washed the dishes.

Sent your laundry case today—am ashamed of your apron, but there was a match in your pocket that stained it. If I had some money, I would send it to you so you would not need to wear it any more this year. However, your family does not seem to rate very much at the helping stunt, although prospects do not look so bad. Daddy is feeling fine and not discouraged, so that helps.

Just talked with Ruth, who was at Vassar. They are having their troubles again—both of the banks are closed and Hope, Bradley and Aunt Lottie all had some money in the one and Doctor also had stock and you know what that means. Fortunately the money she borrowed from the insurance company was in the Saginaw bank, so they have that left. Hope has had a cut for next year and does not know whether they will get paid for the rest of this year. Poor dears, they do not know how to meet it like we do. Wish I could go up to see them. Pete is so queer, he will drive up there with an empty car and not ask anyone else to go along.

Well, as I was tired of typing and it was such a gorgeous day, I put on my bonnet and walked over to cousin Florence's to see her, the baby and the new home. Do not think much of the street, but the rooms are quite pretty and they only pay $20 per, but it is enough considering the way rents have dropped. The baby is so dear with the most beautiful skin and such blue eyes. You will love her.

I had two letters from Uncle Roy and Lola. Hers is so funny, telling about how hard up they are. I told her I was making rag rugs, so she informed me she could not use her rags for that, but had to make clothes from them. I am going to write her right along, so I can get her funny letters.

277

I am terribly busy all of a sudden. I guess it is because spring is coming and I see so much cleaning to do. I never feel sure how long we may be here. We would like to stay here until we know where you will be next year for we want to always keep in your direction as much as possible.

I know Doctor wonders why I do not go to the library and hunt ancestors. Carrie looks for me over there, and there is typing to do, and I want to make rag rugs, and Maude wants me to go over to sew with her and, and, and so on. Anyway, I am glad I am not bored to death. I would rather die running around doing nothing much. Oh mercy, hear me rattle on, and I know you are much too busy to spend your time reading nothing. You will be like Harry, unable to waste so much time. Well I will not do it again.

You can let us know what you think is best about coming home. We know so little about your plans and work that I do not know what is best for you to do. Tell us if you need money and we will try to help you. I would be glad if you would spend a couple of days in the infirmary. It would pay in the long run, I think.

Have you outgrown your family? You write so seldom and tell us so little, I begin to wonder if we rate anymore. Anyway, you still rate with us and we still like to hear either your troubles or joys. I am glad this is being such a happy year, you deserve it all, and I wish we might have made it easier for you.
As ever,
Your big mother

Dear Mother,
I have been a good child today, even you would approve of my cutting classes to go to bed, wouldn't you? I got quite calmed down this afternoon, sort of got my bearings again, and now for about three weeks I will have to plug good and hard.

How would you like to have Harry and me trot in some weekend? There is a possibility of his going to a model League of Nations in Detroit soon. I haven't mentioned his coming home with me. I think he'd rather like to, but perhaps not. Don't say that he may come if you will worry about it, for maybe he wouldn't anyway.

I had a letter from Hope today. Things are pretty bad with her, I guess. The bank closing, teacher's pay cut, and school closing before long, to save expense, no wonder she is worried. She thinks there might be a job at Yale in English. I am applying.

Mid-semesters are over for me, only had two, thank goodness. Practice teaching is getting tiresome. I'm coaching the operetta dialogue now and I'm sick of it already. I can just see D. Hill as a schoolteacher, can't you? Oh well, maybe I wouldn't feel that way if I were rested. The spring is beautiful here as usual. I can hardly wait for it, and yet I dread it, because it's the last lovely one for me here. After dinner at night it's so light out and the birds keep twittering and the sky and trees are wonderful. I have just about an eighth of the time I need to take in deep breaths and enjoy everything that there is. It's a good thing I haven't been here four years, or I would be crazy with outside activities. I'm mad now, literally.
Love,
Dorothy

Dear Dorothy,

I was glad to get your letter saying you were in bed for a day. I do hope you are getting rested. You do not know how I have been worried about you. Of course I know you will think it is foolish, but mothers are made that way, and in the years to come there will be times you will wish there was a little mother worrying. I know from experience.

The money we are expecting has not come in yet. We are expecting some Tuesday. If you want to come home this week and need money you had better wait till you hear from me—we have not been able to get the license for the car yet. If we do not get it this week of course, you could go on the bus to Pontiac.

I do not want you to come home just on our account for we will get along alright and your time is so short there. I know you hate to lose a minute of it. About bringing Harry, do not say anything to him until you have written me first, and if it happens to be a week when collections come in, it will be alright. If not, it might be embarrassing, and that would be too bad.

You know your friends are always welcome if things are so I can make it pleasant for them and probably everything will be alright at the time you might want to bring him.

Do not worry about teaching—time enough to worry when you have a job. Maybe you will be doing office work or something different that you have never dreamed of doing. Who knows—the things we worry about so seldom happen. I wish I could just practice that for I know it is true and when I look around and see nearly all our friends sick or carrying a load much heavier than ours, I wonder why I do it.

Well between J.M. singing and the mouth organ, I do not know what I am doing. I guess one of us will have to stop.

Monday morning

Went to Vassar in the rain, arrived about five and stayed about three hours. It was quite a good day for Uncle Doctor, although he was in bed. Hope looked blue and tired I thought. I did not have a chance to talk with her alone. I imagine the sickness and money problems, which she has never had before, are pretty hard for her. She had such a pretty dress on. She has had such lovely clothes since she has done her own buying.

Hope thinks you will like teaching. She says she has learned more than she did in college and seems to like her work. I imagine the personnel of the school have much to do with one liking it or no.

Do you suppose you could get hold of some old stockings or silk and wool dresses or both? I am making some rugs again and it is surprising how much material one can use in a rug. I do not want you to go to a lot of trouble to get them—just if you see a chance.

Mr. Dunn was just down and wants to have their maid stay here for a while, for they have no extra sleeping room. I guess I will put her in J.M.'s room and that will give us more sleeping room too. She will not have to go through the house all the time—just come in the kitchen way.

If you plan to come this week let us know and we will do our best to have a license—but I am not sure.
Heaps of love from everybody,
Mother

April 9, 1932
Monday night

Dearest Mother,

Have just taken a nice shower and would like to hop into bed, but just remembered board meeting at 10, so I guess I will sleep there instead.

Today I received my invitation to join Delta Sigma Rho. It's all very nice to be invited, but it would certainly take some money to join them all. I think it's rather a gyp to have honoraries and then have them cost so much. Delta Sigma Rho costs $10.

What do you think about my having graduation announcements? Would it be better not to send any, or should I send a few? Let me know what you think real soon.

The proof for the *Albionian* is almost all in now. I'm quite interested to see the book in its entirety.

Tomorrow night I'm going to Marshall to give my oration before a group of superintendents and teachers. Then after that I hope there won't be any more extra activities and I can work on my notebook for a change.

Harry and I have been having some good scraps. Helps liven up the dead atmosphere and then he is most angelic for two days at least. He kids me all the time about not taking him to the show. So the other night I called his bluff—and paid his way. At the end of the evening, after very ceremoniously thanking me, I found a telegram (faked!) awaiting me with the money enclosed, and the message "Thanks for a big evening, here's your change." Imagine my big laugh. I told him I'd take him often at that rate.

Board meeting is over and the world's problems discussed and I just heard a choice bit of scandal about two girls who stayed out all night. Couldn't get yours truly to do that—I'm too sleepy.
Good night
Dorothy

Dear Dorothy,

What a beautiful morning—cannot help wishing you were at home, but of course it is more fun for you where you are. When I wakened the sun was shining and it was so pretty I thought, well, if we cannot go to church we will go for a walk in the park. J.M. is going to church with Patsy—one member of our family is presentable to go out among people and we hope the rest will soon be fixed up.

Aunt Minnie was over for dinner last night. We had a nice visit. She is surely good to me. I am never without a friend as long as she is here. After dinner we walked over to Six Mile Road and

Third to a bakery where you get the best rye bread. It was lovely going over, but turned cold before we were home. Then Daddy and I walked home with her, so that meant considerable fresh air for me.

Your laundry came yesterday—yes I can fix your skirt alright. I will follow directions. How I wish I could send you some money for clothes. Perhaps I can soon—Daddy has to have a suit the first thing. If you were home we could make some clothes so cheap, but you are not.

Friday I went over to see Carrie and to an antique shop to look at a collection of old dolls. I find when I get in the dumps getting out to hunt antiques is a very good thing. I rarely find anything I want, but I meet new people and someday I may stumble on a rare find. You would enjoy seeing the dolls—they are different than any I have ever seen and so quaint.

About graduation announcements—my idea is this. If it costs a cent do not have them for you might better have clothes. The people who care for you most know about it and for the rest it doesn't matter much one way or another. That is my thought and people always feel they should send something and no one has money, but do whatever you wish. I am not there and do not know what it means to you.

The family has decided that they want to give you the cost of the honor societies for your commencement gift. It is $25, isn't it? Will you let me know right away when it has to be paid—you know we would like to do more for you, but as long as we cannot, we felt that would mean more to you than any other little thing we might be able to buy you. Are there any others, if so what and how much? We will at least do the two you have told us about. It makes us very happy to do even a little thing for you.

Our neighbors are moving away and we will miss our little Jeanie. She is so cunning—wish we could move into the flat. It is lovely, but we are very comfortable where we are.

I was pretty blue the last three weeks, but I got out and visited with old ladies about their treasures and troubles and it always puts me on my feet again—they do seem to like me so much, it is really funny.

Daddy has had two good weeks. If the money will just begin coming in for what he has written, we will begin to be comfortable again. Mr. Lamb thinks they are going to do real well—he thinks Daddy is the whole thing. His typewriter is still here and I have more and more work to do. I hope their work will grow so fast that if you do not get a school they can keep you busy too. Daddy is very much encouraged—more than at any other time since we have been here. That helps just to have him happy.

Did I tell you about the old things Mrs. Frank took me to look at? They belonged to a friend's mother. I have had quite a little fun with them. I told them I would pick out the things that I thought I could sell, and took them home with me. I sold two cunning little vases and a wee sampler made with wool to Charlotte, a blue glass bowl to Aunt Lottie for Hope, and a little lacquer bracket to Florence. A dealer who lives near here is coming over to see some other things I found. I think she will want a few glass pieces that are left. Then there are a few things that no one else seems to want. I am sure they will not want me to pay much for these items, when I have done so much for them without charging him. The things left will be two little snuff boxes, a broken luster pitcher, a wee goblet, the quaintest old basket, a darling little sampler, full of holes, made in 1840, dated, and an old bread or dough box and some old frames. Quite a haul for me with no outlay as yet. Do you mind my using the waste typing paper on you? I spoil so much I am ashamed, so I try to use it up in other ways.

Wish I could have the clothes those girls will throw away. I have the rug fever bad. I found such a nice lady who makes the most beautiful rugs and she uses a lot of wool coats, dresses and so forth. I am starting, but it will take me a time to get materials.
Lovingly,
Mother

April 25, 1932
Dear Dorothy,

I talked with Aunt Minnie right after you went. She wanted to know if I was too tired to go downtown again. I said no, hurried and washed the dishes and off we went again, to Frank and Seders, Bedells, Hudsons and bought her a coat at Kerns. We arrived home at seven, but we stopped at the market and Saunders, so we had some eats ready and it did not take long after we got home. J.M. had already eaten three eggs and whatever else he could find.

Then the Langley girl called to say you could ride with her and that made us feel wonderful. Daddy was terribly disappointed at first, but he got over it and realized that it was probably the best thing to do.

Aunt Minnie is sending you the check as we said we would. You can use it as you would like, of course, but I would rather have you pay Prof. Hance than the sorority or if you can get the other honor society cheap we will feel alright about whatever you do. If you cannot get through, of course we will try to help you again, but I feel as if it would be better to let the sorority go until summer as we have so many things to meet.

We were very happy to have you the few hours you were here. I expect we will just have to learn how to get along without you—that is life, isn't it?

Heaps of love, hope you continue to like your dresses. I think they were pretty good buys.
Lovingly,
Mother

Dearest Mother,

I am back in my little room in Albion, all alone tonight. Eunice Mary has gone home. I keep thinking how cheated I am not to be with you tonight and tomorrow, but perhaps we'd only tear around and get tired out (how's that for rationalization?).

I feel right piggish with all my new clothes, but keep consoling myself by saying that you wanted me to have them. It was so good to be home, if only for such a little while. I wish I hadn't had to run off without seeing Daddy again. We got in about a quarter to six and of course I had to wear my new dress to dinner. Everyone stopped and stared! (I guess that will hold them for a minute.)

Harry was waiting for me as per schedule. Said he planned to take me to the Michigan last night. He tried to make me repent not being at home when he called. He was a regular cut-up all the way home. Pestered me to death, but seemed to like my new dress. Tonight we went to the show to see *Beast of the City*. It was quite good. Then I decided to be a gold digger—so we also ate.

Tomorrow I'll be alone and expect to stay home and accomplish heaps. Here's hoping. If I could get my work caught up maybe I could sneak off home again soon.
All my love,
Dorothy

April 26, 1932

Dear Dorothy,

I am enclosing the check promised. We thought that would be the best way to send it. You do not need to write to Aunt Minnie, for we are taking care of it. Hope you are able to swing the things that mean the most to you. Your letter just came—so glad to get it, but cannot answer it just now for Daddy is waiting and I want you to have the check. Aunt Minnie said for you to cash it right away. Everyone feels a little afraid of the banks, so she wants it to come right back—although I guess the bank is alright.

Glad you are so happy about your dress. We are happy about it too, and hope you will not be too unhappy this summer. But you ought to stand what we have all the time, in fact, I think when you are here things will be better, for one of us will probably be able to do something—and collections may be better. Two dollars came in the mail this morning—think of that.

And we love you and just think you have had at least a great part of school that you wanted—no one can ever take these wonderful times from you.
Bye bye till next time, lots of love,
Mother

P.S. Don't spill the inkpot on your new dress.

Dear Dorothy,

Your letter came today—you were good to write so soon. We got the license for the car yesterday. It seems good to be able to use it.

Aunt Lottie helped me with Bradley family history today and it is all ready to copy. She is a live one. Uncle Doctor doesn't want her out of his sight. She is so good to him. He does not seem very well to me.

285

Daddy has been home two evenings, but goes on the rampage again tomorrow—he is tired but feeling fine.

So glad you arrived early enough to avoid trouble with the czar of the dining room. Every little while today I would wonder why you didn't come. It just doesn't seem as if you had really gone again, but the letters will come and that helps.

All I have done today is just visit and get the meals—had such a good dinner—spinach (fresh), asparagus, cabbage salad, strawberry shortcake. It doesn't appeal to you very much, but we liked it.

I have been to bed, couldn't go to sleep, so I'll go back and try again. It has been so warm and lovely today I guess our spring is here. So glad you are all clean and ready for term papers.

Perhaps we had better wish for rain until you get them written. We were so happy to have you home.
Heaps of love,
Mother

Medinah Athletic Club
Chicago

Dear Mother,

It has been a glorious day that I shall never forget! Chicago—I've been shown it in a hundred different aspects—from Jane Addams' Hull House to North Shore Drive, and the imposing chapel and university buildings. Lake Michigan has been beautifully blue all day, and though I have driven at least 250 miles in cars today, I have met just heaps of fascinating people.

I have spoken before the Chicago alumni group, met the President of the first sorosis group (before Kappa Delta went national, it was sorosis). I have been pampered and fairly carried around on a chip, and finally have gone to the College Inn and danced to Ben Burnie's orchestra. I still feel able to wiggle. Imagine your daughter being the belle of the ball! There were a lot of Albion boys there who are going to the professional schools here and I was quite the leading lady. Freddie Hemerick took me out. It certainly was fascinating and besides that, he's adorable looking and a keen dancer.

My room is lovely and such hosts as we have had! They're simply marvelous to us. Dean Whitehouse is going back tonight on the sleeper, but Merrill Walls and I are going tomorrow noon. I think

I'll venture out in the morning and go shopping at Marshall Fields. I already have an invitation to go swimming in their natorium here in the building. They say it is the largest and most beautiful of its kind in the world.

I'm pretty sleepy now, so will try and be very conservative. It's about 2:00 o'clock in the morning so I will go to bed like a good girl.

Love and more news later,

Dorothy

May 3, 1932

Dearest Mother,

A clean room always inspires me—and I have been diligently studying for three hours. All is restful and quiet for a change. So I'm going to take the rare opportunity and write.

I feel as if I had been drawn thru a knothole for some un-known reason, but all I need is a little calm and I shall be function-ing again. Harry and I had another disagreement and I used good sense for the first time in many moons, and told him to go to and stay put—or else come around very suddenly and do a little "apple polishing" with me for a change.

I know you have felt that I was seeing him too much—and would perhaps get so used to him that breaking off would be dif-ficult. However, I've gone ahead and dated him, due partly to liking and also because I know so well how wretched and lonely I have been in the past here. Now, though, I believe I've achieved a pretty good slant on the matter—and from now on, intend to date if it is pleasant, and end things if it isn't. I think too steady dating in college often isn't a benefit, but I do feel that I've had both experiences, and am really trying to evaluate things as I would like them to be.

I like Harry a good deal, and he is the first person who has really made me feel at all desirable. He has his endearing quali-ties, but I hope I have sense enough never to fall in love with him. It would be "hellish!" However, I think I understand feelings, and people, and perhaps have learned some things that have made me more truly mature in having this friendship. Harry is very far from my ideal, but I am beginning to see that none of the men on campus seem to measure up as far as they might.

I hope someday that this experience may help me to fall really in love with someone whom I admire. And after all, experience is a softening, lovely, understanding sort of thing, whether we feel that way about it at the time or not.

Last night the sorority went up the river for a roast at dinnertime. It is lovely here, but not very warm yet. We came home early and then I listened to H.R. apologize for an hour. Finally had board meeting (and incidentally cake and punch!) and decided to give all seniors unlimited late permissions from now on.

I wore my new pink dress today, although we're still wearing coats. I have a real new Theta Alpha Phi pin to show you. It's a dear.

Tonight is Chevron meeting at 10:00 and we'll begin to select for next year's group. Being a senior is somehow a mournful business, just like retiring and handing over all your tasks and joys to someone young and strong. (I'll soon be in the antique class, and be looking for someone to make a home for me!) Ah, me the infirmities of age! But you like antiques, don't you?

Aunt Minnie, the dear, sent me a box of Sanders candy—just when I was deep down in the gloom and Harry hated me. I came upstairs to find a package. She's either a wizard or a mind reader—or I'm the man in the moon.
Love,
Dorothy

Monday afternoon

Dear Mother,

It's the most glorious weather imaginable and I'm just dead tired and sleepy. It's warm enough to go without a coat—and shiny and breezy too. I can't study—my duties won't let me sleep, so here I am at the library getting very little studying done.

I had a lovely surprise Saturday. I did some lit. for Harry while he was gone to Detroit. Saturday afternoon I received a box of Panama chocolates. Talk about shocks! He's getting pretty nice. I saw the first proofs for the artwork on the *Albionian*. I don't know what to think of them. Some of them aren't so hot!

Went over to the Teke house Saturday night and had a real nice time. Sunday afternoon H and I went for a walk, and justified our recreation by doing all our argumentation while en route. Harry is a good influence in one respect. He does see to it that I get my lesson once in a while.

This afternoon is a poor time to write—I'm so near asleep and so down in the dumps, but I'll snap out of it. Good weather is hard on me—I'm not conscientious enough to work in spite of it.

My pink dress looks real good. I'm so glad to have it. You sure are a genius—we're all agreed. Do you need your pen? I'll send it home to you as I have one now.

Harry says he'd like to see my brother—that he sure must have a lot to contend with! (I consider myself properly slammed.) Somehow chocolates temper my judgment in the matter.

Tuesday

I feel more perky today. Went with the rest of the Kappa Deltas to Marshall to the show last night—saw Greta Garbo in *Susan Lenox*. Then home, riding in the rumble seat—then board meeting and finally to bed. I'm fast coming to the point where I enjoy going to bed! Can you stand that shock?
Loads of love to you all,
Dorothy

Saturday night

Dear Dorothy,

Glad to get your letter yesterday. It sure seems good to have you a happy child again. It does not take many clothes to cheer you up—perhaps you would not enjoy them so much if you could have them whenever you need them. However it is fun to hunt for bargains and know that you have made a good buy.

I'm working on my blue georgette dress—will have that ready to wear Monday. It looks quite decent now. I took the sleeves right out and am making caps. It has not much snap, but will be an outfit. The cap and gown are here. I do not want to mail them if you can get home before you need them. I am so afraid the cap may get crushed. Aunt Ada had it at her house so she brought it in with her.

When is Commencement? I would like to know the date, for you know that things will have to be very bad if we do not come. How many invitations will you have? Aunt Nellie thought perhaps

289

she could get a car if we do not have one by that time, so I wonder how many tickets you will be allowed to have.

Do not worry about the check—remember we owe you much more than that—and nothing makes us quite so happy as to be able to do things for you. That has been one of the hard things we have had to bear—that we could not do things for you.

Daddy says if you do not get a school, he very much wants you to go in the business with him. He has had a very good month and is happy—over $20,000 this month in policies. He is going to the company tomorrow to see if they will not handle some of his note, for we have quite a lot of money coming in—so much that it cramps our style to wait so long for it. He thinks they will do it for him—they are treating him very differently and his business is keeping up pretty well. He has not been asking for help, so they are beginning to sit up and take notice. They are starting to turn cases over to him that come in, so he is quite pepped up again. Almost feel so myself. I think his business is about the best thing there is for the next five years. So maybe you could do worse than to go right at it—the way he works of course is very different than going out as a salesman.

I am behind with Daddy's typing and must get at it again. If he keeps up with this month, he will soon have more than I can do with the work. I wish it would and he could keep you busy all summer. It would be so much nicer than working the kind of places one is apt to get. We still have the woman from upstairs here. Wish they would leave her here all the time as it cuts our rent so much.
Heaps of love,
Mother

May 4, 1932

My Dear Dorothy,

I felt highly honored this morning when your mother presented me with your letter at the breakfast table. And as your insurance counselor, I beg to advise that you have $1000 in full force and effect, with one of the best companies in the world, viz. The Michigan Life Insurance Co., of Detroit, Michigan and that I shall be more than pleased to arrange, as your counselor, to have an assignment made to Knights Templar Educational Foundation, covering any unpaid balance of principal and interest should your death occur prior to the liquidation of the loan.

It would be good business for you to write the foundation a snappy business letter stating that you had tried to anticipate any and all contingencies which might arise to prevent the liquidation of their loan according to agreement and that you had purchased life insurance at once to cover that particular hazard and you might congratulate them upon such a splendid plan, but let them know that you beat them to it. Let me know what they suggest, and of course, I shall cooperate to carry out any plan, which seems practicable.
Heaps of Love,
Daddy

P.S. Sending my bill for counselor service later, but will cancel it entirely if you come home again soon and don't run away like you did last time.

May 9, 1932

Dear Dorothy,

Glad to hear from you. Thursday I was downtown with Aunt Nellie and did a little shopping. You may not believe it, but your Dad has some new socks, underwear, shirts and a new suit. Your ma has a new hat, gloves 59 cents, hose 54 cents, shoes, dress $2.98, dress $2.98, and your brother has new socks, shirts and tennis shoes, so we have made a start. Hudson's have patterns for 15 cents and materials are so cheap that I am going to make myself some clothes if I can get any money. Laudry went downtown and bought wool crepe enough for a suit, white material for a blouse, and percale for a house dress. She had $1.50 when she started and had a little change left—can you beat that?

Glad you are not quite satisfied with Harry for your ideal, for while of course I would not oppose it in anyway, I do not feel you have found your mate, although I think it has been very nice for you to have someone to go out with and I am sure the experience has been helpful to you in many ways.

If you do not get a school, I hope you will get right in at Metropolitan Church. There are so many delightful people there. I went to a play called *Patsy*, given by their dramatic group and it was so enjoyable. I think you would enjoy being in the group. We have just got to jump in somewhere and make a place for ourselves and friends. It never has been very difficult and I do not think it will be now.

I am hoping J.M. will go to Vassar for the summer. Aunt Lottie has asked him and if she really needs and wants him, I should have him go, for the crush I have wanted to avoid with Patsy is on, and the family do everything to help it along, so if it works out that he can go to Vassar, I will be very glad. There are always problems, however, he made the honor roll and tries to be awfully good.

Let me know how many of us can come for Commencement, for we are beginning to plan.

It is a wonderful day—all we lack is a car. Hope you can come next weekend. I rather expected you this week, but I know it is hard to get away. J.M. made pancakes and sausage for breakfast, so no one was hungry. It is the middle of the afternoon and we have not had our dinner yet.

Aunt Lucy is coming in June. Isn't that nice? Expect you are busy as can be, happy and yet sorrowful too.
Heaps of love,
Mother

Dearest Mother,

Another rainy day here. We seem to specialize in them for the last week. I was so glad to get your letter, and to hear that things are going pretty well at home. I'm thrilled about the new clothes. Getting pretty ritzy, it seems to me, but don't let it go to your head the way it went to mine. I expect Daddy's terribly stuck up with a new suit and everything.

I'm expecting to come home this weekend, but don't know for sure about a ride yet. I had such a nice time last night, went to the show and saw a crazy picture, serial and everything, all for the price of one dime. Harry had fourteen cents and I had six cents so we went in style. Shows are pretty cheap in this town right now, with two theatres and quite some competition. Harry was feeling grand and we did have such a good time. He was angelic.

I also got properly scolded for staying up to work at night, and received instructions for all day today, and have promised to behave very well. I really do get most amused when I get taken care of so carefully. My size always seems to warrant my apparent helplessness. According to orders, I am to work hard on my notebook today, go to the birthday dinner tonight and then, if I'm very good, have a date.

Well, I have to go to work now, according to schedule. Am feeling so serene and happy today, don't know how long such calm can last.

I haven't found out yet how many people I can have at graduation, but I would guess about four or more.
Love,
Dorothy

Later: Had a letter from Lapeer, saying there is no vacancy there for next year. Pontiac looks as hopeful as any—do wish I had a car for about a week. That's about the only way to apply, and have it amount to anything. Oh well, I can't afford to worry, and I'll do my best and hope that newfound Hill luck lasts. Tra la.

My roommate has been talking a blue streak this morning, and it's been grand, but not very conducive to study. I really am going to buckle down now for about four weeks and get my old practice teaching notebook done, and then I won't have much real work to think about. Spring always does have a disastrous effect on my intelligence anyhow.
All my love—see you soon maybe,
Dorothy

May 20, 1932

Dear Mother,

You certainly are ritzy with your Sunday evening frock. It is adorable and incidentally looks quite well on yours truly. You shouldn't have sent it.

I have had a glorious week. Senior skip day, and Harry was adorable all day, went to Jackson with me in the afternoon while I shopped and bought something very exciting (wait till you see it). Then at night was Delta Sigma Rho banquet and initiation. Then Harry and I went canoeing. I finally got in at one-thirty. Most of the seniors stayed out later, but I was so sleepy.

Would you send me the cap and gown? I'm going to need it for the May breakfast next Thursday. Also my swimming suit if you can.

Tomorrow is the Teke informal at the Marshall Country Club. I'm so thrilled to finally be invited. We go in the afternoon, have dinner and a dance. Today I'm going to try and finish that demon notebook of mine and then life will be a mere song.
Love,
Dorothy

Susie Hall

Dear Mother,

By now you must think me a pill or a piece of baloney, and no doubt I am both. Awfully blue tonight and kind of homesick, but have so much to do that I can't even think, so it's probably just as well.

As you have probably ascertained by now, I couldn't come this last weekend. The sorority president of Gamma Province arrived unexpectedly and we had to put on a tea and also had initiation for her inspection. It was pretty difficult to get out of it, and the only possible ride was just one way to Detroit, so I gave it up because I thought I couldn't afford it.

Oh well, it's all in a lifetime, and I still insist that being poor is the lesser evil when compared with the other discouragements to living. Although it was pretty hard to take tonight when Louise was put up as a candidate for the most outstanding senior, and I knew that the reason she had it over me was because she has been president of the sorority. I could just as well have been president if it hadn't been for being inactive. But I guess maybe I don't care. The more I see of honors and elections, the more I realize how little people know or care about justice. I've done three times the number of outstanding activities in different fields that she has, but what difference does it make? I think I shall quietly crawl into my shell and live in calm, for what does anything or anybody matter?

Tonight we had a fine meeting at the lodge. Mary Barhyte announced her engagement to George Miles from Pontiac, and served Cokes and sandwiches. A silhouette of herself and George done in charcoal was put up on a drawing easel and unveiled at the proper time, then we sang K.D. and Sigma Nu songs, and it was all very nice. There have been so many engagements announced that it's beginning to take on the appearance of an epidemic. Two more are to be brought to light at our informal party. In fact I think I'm going to be the one outstanding unengaged woman, that seems to be as far as I can get in the way of being outstanding, so as Harry says "What ho!"

Tonight after board meeting, when all is still at last, I shall go down to the recreation room with my trusty little typewriter and fulfill all of Dr. Carter's wildest dreams by writing my practice teaching notebook. When that is finally off my mind, I shall be a happy lady, and until then I am completely submerged.

So farewell till then, love to you all, and a big hug. Wish I were home.
Dorothy

May 23, 1932

Dear Dorothy,

I am so sleepy, do not know whether I can write or not. I am mailing cap and gown, etc. in the morning.

Resume: Monday I washed, went to Carrie's, upstairs to Dunns to a surprise party in the evening. Tuesday: ironed. Wednesday: didn't feel good, walked over to Florence's. Thursday: Aunt Nellie and I went to Pontiac—first time she has had a car in months. Aunt Ada was surprised and glad to see me. She has so many new things in her house! We had a nice time.

Aunt Ada said she did not think there was any chance for a job for you in Pontiac. I talked with the superintendent at Hazel Park, who said he had no idea, but you could call on him this summer and see.

Aunt Nellie called up this a.m. and said she was to have the car June sixth, so we will be there with bells on. I would like to go over June fifth too, but probably can't do that.

I was sorry you felt badly about the sorority vote, but as long as we are human I guess we will find injustice. You are having so much more than we have hoped for, that I wouldn't let it spoil my last happy weeks. I am afraid there will be other things too—so many of the girls will be getting lovely gifts and things that we cannot do for you, but we have never brought you disgrace and that is almost unusual these days.

Were you pleased with Aunt Minnie's gift? She is always so thoughtful and she thought you might enjoy it more if you had it right away.

You had better plan to ship your trunk for I do not expect there will be room in the car, you will have so much. Aunt Minnie wanted to come, but I am afraid there will not be room for her.

Daddy has been walking—you should see his girlish figure—but I am putting on weight. Don't imagine my dress looked well on you. I am going to make a coat for it. Would you suggest some material? If you need my pink dress let me know and I will send it to you.

Will know tomorrow whether we stay here or not—Daddy made them an offer. J.M. has worked all week, building a radio—a little crystal set. He finally got results today and we can hear it very well.

Expect you are dreading to come home, but I am hoping you may find something interesting to do after you have had a rest, so that you won't be unhappy. We are so lonely to see you that it seems grand to us to have you at home. I know you will miss Harry and the girls until you make a place for yourself here. If there is anything we can do for you these "finishing" days, let us know.
With all our love,
Mother

May 27, 1932

Dearest Mother,

Had another thrill—Hope sent me $5 for graduation. I guess I'm getting to be fortune's favorite—or something like that. $10 for Dorothy Blanche Hill—I'm overwhelmed. It's going to be a beautiful day today and I'm going to our Kappa Delta party at Battle Creek at 4:00 p.m.

The surprise I bought in Jackson was a new informal dress, which I wore to the Teke party last week, and am wearing again today. It's adorable and you'll never guess what color! It's pure white with a little embroidered organdy jacket and flounce. Harry says I should wear white all the time. It's really quite becoming. I had a wonderful time at the party last week, and am hoping that today will be so grand. I appreciated your last letter so much. It makes me feel just like coming home.

The *Albionian* comes out today, and we're quite proud of it. It's a real thrill to see your own work in it. This is the first time the yearbook came out even financially, they've always had a deficit of about $400 and this year we cleared $500. Don't say Harry isn't a businessman! I think that is quite an achievement besides having an annual as simple and artistic as this one is.

Well, I have raved long enough. Have to work now.
Love,
Dorothy

Dear Dorothy,

I was so glad to get your letter. We went to church this morning. This afternoon Patsy, J.M., Daddy and I went for a long, long walk in the park

Aunt Minnie wants very much to come Monday if she can get away, and if you can get enough tickets. Also if we do not have room enough in the car coming back, what time could she get a bus?

Your dress must be very pretty; evidently you can wear any color you choose. Glad you could have it. Aunt Minnie thought it would be best to send you money and send it early so you could get the good of it now. She is always so practical. The announcements are very attractive. I don't wonder you would like to send them out.

Harry certainly has reason to be proud. It would have been fine if he had just broken even—but to clear $500!

If nothing happens, J.M. will go to Vassar as soon as school is out. He is so pleased, planning what he is going to take and do. I am glad. I think the change will be good for him. He has tried so hard lately to please us and seems so happy. For the first time he said today that he was going to Albion for his college and, of course, that will please us if we can make it. We are counting the days until you will be home. I know you will miss Harry, all the girls, and everything and yet I am hoping you will be happy to be at home.

Daddy is very happy and encouraged about his work and would be delighted if you should decide to work with him. The company is appreciating him.

I do not know what to wear to Albion yet. I only have my blue georgette or my pink dress, I guess it will depend on the weather. Aunt Nellie is so glad she could have the car and that she can go, and so are we.
Lovingly,
Mother

Dear Ma,

Your child is a free woman—only one more blue book and that not until Friday. My practice teaching notebook is all done and at the binders. Pretty snoozy, I'd say. Just got a notice that we are allowed three tickets for commencement, but I think we can arrange to get two more people in to see the exercises, so if Aunt Minnie wants to come, I think it'll be OK. Buses for Detroit leave here about every two hours in the afternoon.

Tonight we have a Chevron dinner with the old and new members present, and finish up with a bang. Saturday and Sunday I won't have anything to do but trot around. Harry is trying to get me to ask him to stay over, but I won't do it. However, I expect he'll stay or get murdered. I can't afford to be bored the last few days of school.

I look forward to seeing you. I'll pack my trunk as much as I can Saturday, and be ready to ship it Monday. Everything is going beautifully and I'm so happy to think you can come and Aunt Nellie too. You see this is the first time I ever graduated from college. It will be fun to go up and collect my prize money, and know you're there.

Harry sent his yearbook home and today he got a letter back from his mother asking if there was any organization that Dorothy Hill didn't belong to? So I judge he has at last intimated to his family that he knows me very slightly!

It'll seem good to be home with the good old sheepskin—I'm looking forward to new adventures and lots of settling.
Love,
Dorothy

A Dream Realized

Dorothy's Yearbook Photo

Dorothy graduated from Albion College on Monday, June 6, 1932, with honors. What a proud and happy moment for the whole family! Their combined efforts had allowed her to achieve her cherished goal of a college education. She was also awarded a lifetime teacher's certificate.

She graduated after spending only three years on campus, partially due to her attendance at Pontiac Junior College and correspondence classes, but also due to taking heavy loads at Albion.

Dorothy was Vice-President of the Senior Class, President of Chevron (Senior Women's Honorary Society), Secretary of the Histrionic Club, Associate Editor of the Albionian (yearbook), and the winner of the Baldwin Oratorical Contest, taking First Place in 1931 and 1932.

In addition, Dorothy won second place in the State Oratorical Contest in 1932 and third place in 1931, and placed second in the Women's State Extempore Speaking Contest in 1931.

She was a member of Kappa Delta sorority, a proctor in Susanna Wesley Hall, a debater, and a member of several honorary societies, including Delta Sigma Rho (forensics) and Theta Alpha Phi (histrionics). She was invited to join Alpha Phi Gamma (journalism), but due to lack of funds, could not accept this honor.

In her first year at Albion she was art editor for the Susanna Wesley Annual. Dorothy also was active in the Women's Self-Government Association and Y.W.C.A.

She truly made the most of her college experience. Her family's sacrifices during the Great Depression helped to make it possible, but her love of learning and enthusiasm for the experience of college life were the deciding factors in her success.

Dorothy on Graduation from Albion College

Life after Albion College

After graduation from Albion College, Dorothy lived in Detroit with her family and searched for work. Teaching jobs were scarce. She found a job as a fundraiser that summer at Starr Commonwealth for Boys and went to work for $50 a month and expenses. She traveled the state trying to raise money to keep Starr afloat. The job was short-lived, since the country was in such a deep depression and money was so hard to come by.

By September she was again looking for work. The family moved four times in Detroit in just a few years, seeking lower rents each time.

In 1933 Dorothy went to work at the A & P Tea Company in Detroit, figuring store inventories and profits for $20 a week.

Harry continued to write her long, detailed letters, but the relationship didn't satisfy her for the long term. A new man, Chuck, came into her life. He was a charming and sociable radio announcer in Grand Rapids. Dorothy had known him at Albion. Chuck was much different than Harry, romantic, but not as practical. Chuck's loving letters and his vision of a rosy future won Dorothy over and she became engaged to him. But working in different parts of the state made for a difficult courtship and eventually Dorothy realized that Chuck did not want children and that their life styles were not a good fit, so they agreed to part ways. She took a break from men.

Dorothy stayed at A & P until June 1935. That summer she took graduate classes in speech at the University of Michigan and there she met a law student named Walter Barningham. He was from the small town of Vermontville, Michigan and had worked his way through Albion College. In spite of Albion's small campus, they had not known each other there: Walter being a quiet country boy and Dorothy an older city girl, involved in sorority life and all her extra-curricular activities.

Walter was smitten by Dorothy's charm and liked her family very much. Though he was usually a man of few words, he began a relentless courtship through letters, which were full of his dry sense of humor. Walter was as dependable as the sunrise, a man with a strict sense of right and wrong, and a work ethic which promised success in any endeavor.

In the fall of 1935, Dorothy landed a teaching position in Royal Oak, which paid $945 for nine months. She taught in an elementary platoon system in grades one through three as well as seventh grade.

Dorothy Hill Barningham on her wedding day

Dorothy found teaching English to seventh grade boys was not her ideal job.

Walter passed his bar exams in September of 1935 and by 1936 had started a solo law practice in Pontiac. He wrote Dorothy and visited her on weekends whenever she invited him. One of his letters from the early days of his practice reports: "I just took in $1—order that mink coat right away!"

After one year of teaching, Dorothy took a better paying job at Fruehauf Trailer in Detroit. Her salary there started at $125 a month. Walter's business was slow to develop, but he was as persistent at that as he was in attempting to persuade Dorothy to marry him.

Dorothy was twenty-nine when he finally talked her into marrying him, and once she agreed, they chose the date: May 22, 1937. Their simple wedding was held at her family's apartment in Detroit. The bride wore a dress she already owned. Her one expense was having new soles put on her shoes. Flowers were white lilacs from the Barningham backyard in Vermontville. Walter wore his best suit and a rare smile for the occasion and Dorothy was a beautiful bride. They had a short honeymoon in Greenbush, at Aunt Lottie's cottage on Lake Huron.

After their marriage, they lived with Dorothy's family in Detroit. Most days, Walter hitchhiked to his law office in Pontiac. They saved their money for a house and later had a modest Cape Cod style home built on West Huron Street in

Walter Lee Barningham, May 22, 1937

Waterford, just three miles from Walter's office in Pontiac. They moved to this home in October 1939.

Dorothy then commuted to Detroit to continue her job at Fruehauf Trailer, where she eventually earned $180 a month. Walter's business was gradually improving and Dorothy left her job just a few months before the arrival of their first child, Sara Lee, who was born October 18, 1941.

During World War II Walter did his part for the war effort by working nights in a Pontiac plant which made warheads. Days were spent in his law office.

Their second child, Mary Ann, was born October 28, 1946. Dorothy stayed home with the girls. Walter had strong ideas about being the sole support for his young family. Dorothy did some writing, as time would allow, and became involved in the PTA at the girls' school. She became known as a willing volunteer and an excellent public speaker.

*Dorothy in front
of new home, 1941*

*Walter, at 2856 West
Huron Street, Pontiac, MI*

The Barningham home

Dorothy, Walter and Sara Lee

Dorothy and Walter

In 1949, Walter began building a cottage just north of Oscoda, on the shores of Lake Huron, only ten miles from the Greenbush cottage, where he and Dorothy had honeymooned. He loved the building process, carefully planning each aspect of construction and doing all the work himself on a snug two bedroom cottage with a kitchen and living room overlooking the lake. Dorothy spent summers there with the children, while Walter worked in his office all week and then headed north each weekend to visit. He often rode a Greyhound bus for his trip and Dorothy and the children would stand by the road with an old lantern to flag down the bus so the driver could let him off at the cottage.

*Dorothy reading The Antiques
Journal at the lake*

*Dorothy, Walter and Mary Ann
during construction*

*Dorothy, Walter
and Mary Ann*

*Barningham cottage
in Oscoda, Michigan,
1951*

Blanche—the Final Years

Blanche and John Hill were still struggling to make ends meet, as they had their entire married life, when Blanche was diagnosed with tuberculosis. The whole family was devastated when she had to enter the local TB sanitarium for more than a year. During this time, John, whose memory had been failing, passed away. Blanche was not even allowed to attend his funeral, which made his loss even harder for her.

But, in characteristic fashion, Blanche made the best of her time at the san, participating eagerly in all the craft making opportunities offered there. She learned to make leather goods, hammered copper pictures, chenille animals, jewelry, and other things she used as gifts for the family.

When she was finally released from the sanitarium, Blanche lived with Walter and Dorothy and her granddaughters for some time. Eventually she had her own apartment in Pontiac, a short distance away. She still spent a lot of time with her grandchildren. Blanche was an avid genealogist and had her plants, antiques and crafts to occupy her. She shared these hobbies with the children, who visited her often.

High blood pressure had been a problem for Blanche for many years, and in November 1957 she had a stroke and died a few weeks later, having only regained consciousness for a few brief intervals.

Dorothy in photo taken by John Merritt

Sara Lee and Mary Ann Barningham

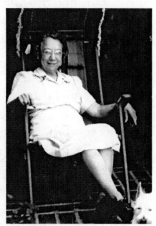

Blanche at rest, enjoying the outdoors

Dorothy wrote this account of her mother's final days:

Mother was in her apartment alone on November twelfth. She chatted with the neighbor across the hall and appeared to be in high spirits that morning. She left the neighbor's apartment with the remark, "Hill, you'd better get to work," and confided, "I feel in the mood to scrub today." During the morning I had a long telephone visit with her, outlining the latest of Sara's antics and dating problems. Then at, or near noon, she called me back to offer a hand at the office, if needed, as I was filling in for Walter that morning. At 12:30 she was downstairs talking to another neighborhood acquaintance.

Blanche

Between that time and 3:15 p.m., when I reached the apartment, we surmise from the appearance of the house that she came back from visiting downstairs, had her lunch, did her dishes and had spread out the family history on which she was working, on a table just a few feet from the phone. She cannot have had any warning of more than a few seconds when the attack came on, as she was unable to dial, but had reached for the phone, and had fallen along with it, to the floor. The only way we can guess at the interval before help came, is that the other party on her line said that she herself was using the line, hung up, and in less than thirty minutes tried to make another call and heard Mother's difficult breathing. She reported it to the phone company, and their repairman located the apartment and brought the caretaker in to open the door. He called the ambulance before he found my number. She had oxygen within three minutes, and the fireman remarked at the strength of her heartbeat.

I reached the apartment before they had her in the ambulance. Since the hospital is practically across the street, it was no time at all until she was getting care. She was paralyzed on the left

306

side, and that always affects the speech of right-handed persons. So it was amazing that she managed to speak my name after she reached the hospital. The doctor was amazed. She put forth such an effort, I think to let me know that she could hear me and knew I was there. She was not conscious long, but knew we were all there with her.

The coma, the tube feeding, the long nights in which we stayed but could do nothing, are all a sort of nightmare of activity and fatigue. We finally spent daytime hours cleaning out the apartment, as we knew she could never return, even if she lived. The Doctor held out no hope from the beginning, due to the severity of the stroke, and felt that the coma was in the nature of a blessing, as she felt no pain.

The day after Thanksgiving Mother regained a degree of consciousness, although she was unable to speak. We moved her from the hospital to a nursing home a short distance from both our homes, where she had kind and excellent care.

On Sunday Mother was quite alert, and seemed to enjoy having us there. We are positive from her eyes that she recognized everyone. At one point the four of us had decided to go next door for a cup of coffee, but as we turned to go, Mother coughed, and the nurse, who had been watching her, called to us. It was plain that she was not having anyone leave, if she could prevent it. So we stayed on until she dropped into a sleep and wouldn't miss us. Monday she was much worse, and the nurse and all of us felt that she was weakening. Her daughter-in-law, Norma, and I were with her most of the day, and then the four of us spent the evening with her, though by that time she was sleeping heavily again, and did not know we were there.

At 2:00 a.m. the nurse called to tell us that Mother had slept quietly away without waking. And as we recalled the pitiful paralysis cases in the room with her, some in that condition for four to ten years, we could not be sorry that she was at rest, and free of the pains and ailments of her tired body.

Her service was very lovely, we thought, with a note of inspiration, which is not always present at such a time. I had shown Dr. Bank, our pastor, Mother's crowded, but colorful bulletin board which she always kept over her sink. It typified Mother's living;

warm, cheerful, busy, with bits of philosophy, notes of admonition to herself, and lists of things to do, that would have tired a more robust soul. He used it as a part of his talk.

Her flowers were beautiful. More than one person remarked. "Wouldn't Blanche have loved this one." And she herself, who never wanted to be old, looked much younger than her seventy-five years in her favorite soft blue knit dress. The flowers closest to her were of soft pinks and pale orchid. Though the funeral was not large, it was amazing even to me, the number of people to whom her passing was a real heartache. She had felt that she no longer had many contacts, and that her circle was very small.

But as I find myself typing, writing, addressing envelopes to British Columbia, and points West and South, I have to chuckle a little at Mother's small circle, which of course was as far as her sympathies and her pen could reach. Now I know why she said she never could seem to keep any stamps.

Dorothy—the Creative Writer

Dorothy wrote as time allowed, and submitted stories to several magazines. Her only published work after her college oration, Our Finishing Schools, was the story of Annabel, the antique walking doll, which was published in an antiques magazine.

This story shows how her inner muse drove her to writing:

Why Do I Want to Write?

I don't want to write. My life is as full as the purple satin gown of an opulent but imprudent matron at the end of a long holiday dinner. It bursts at the seams with activities for which there is never quite time or space enough. There are the demands of two children, not yet in their teens, the care and responsibility of my parents, both ill right now. And there is a husband who strangely enough wants a share of companionship and attention. Then there's the dog. He's only an idea now, but the shine in the little one's eyes and her pleading tones assure me that he will arrive any day now.

As if that were not enough there's that woman upstairs. You

see my life is sort of a duplex. I live on the ground floor. She rents the upper story. She has all the things I sigh for—solitude, the time to ponder a thought, the independence to go her way without hindrance. Yet what does she do? She hovers, she nags, she interrupts. I have never yet stolen an hour to read a good book or a stimulating article that she hasn't been at my side, whispering at me. "You could write like that if you'd only try. Have you noticed how that plot is put together?"

"Don't be silly," I reply, "it takes years to become really good, and I'm too old to start. Besides you have to have some native talent." But my opposition fades as I pull the story apart. I become absorbed, she shakes me rudely. "Your roast is burning!" She yells. I fly to the kitchen, rescue what remains of the meat. But have I shaken her off? No, she's there peering over my shoulder, a gloating evil gleam in her eye. "You'll never make a cook," she grins mockingly, "you aren't interested enough."

In a fury I turn on her, point an accusing finger and cry, "Have you ever tasted my lemon pie? Or apple or mince for that matter. The crusts are flaky, they melt in your mouth." She nods, but the grin remains, "They melt all right, just disappear." She shrugs, "What have you got to show for them?" She stands unmoved, examining the perfect pink oval of her nails. I wish desperately that I had her time for grooming. I lash out once more. Somehow I must be important in her eyes.

"You think I'm a failure, that I have no domestic skills. Remember that party dress I made for Sara last week? Can you ever forget how she twirled in it and said, "See mommy, my skirt dances."

"Yes" she replies, grudgingly, "but don't forget how it looked two hours later, after she fell in that mud hole coming home from the party. You never did quite get those mud stains out, did you?" Her gaze is cold and hard.

Then as if trying to get back in my good graces, she adds, "Those puppets you were making, what ever became of them?" Then with lifted hand, "Don't tell me, I know. The children didn't like the faces and painted them over. Gruesome weren't they? They couldn't appreciate the elegance of that queen's costume either, could they? Too simple, too beautiful for their taste." She turns to go as I stand mute before her. Then with a change of mood, a sparkle in her glance, she says, "By the way, there's a terrific play on TV tonight. Going to watch it?"

"Oh, that would be fun," but I check myself in time. "No, I'm painting stained glass windows tonight. I've got the nativity scene yet to do."

"Better hurry, or you won't be through for Christmas. That one angel is really quite something. Too bad you'll have to wash them all off by New Year's. Well, it keeps your hands busy, if not your head." On this devastating note, the creature departs.

If only I could rent to someone else up there. She must have insomnia; she walks the floor at night. It keeps me awake, and I fight her mentally till two in the morning. Such a tenant!

I made a speech at the club today and I came in just glowing with the pleasure of doing a rather good job, and what's more, having someone else's admiring comments. I spent a good deal of time organizing and writing that speech too. But it's all in ruins now. I only said in the warmth of the moment that Mrs.Doolittle, president of the club, thought it the best speech of the year. This only set the vixen howling with glee.

"Why don't you tell it all? You know that the whole group came gushing up to you and said, "What a remarkable gift. My, it must be wonderful to speak like that with no preparation at all!" Then she doubled over with laughter, wiped the tears from her eyes, and said, "How long was it you spent? How many hours? For a thirty minute speech?"

Sobering at last, she leaned toward me, "Is that the kind of audience you want? If you have to have one, try writing. Create something that doesn't blow away over the heads of a bunch like that."

So here I sit at a cold, empty typewriter. Eventually something will come out. Not the simplicity or clarity of fine writing, but perhaps the excitement of a story will warm the cold hard keys. I hope so. At any rate, I have one satisfaction; the woman upstairs is still at last.

For my mother, writing did quiet the "woman upstairs" and satisfied some of her creative urges. It was also good therapy for her following Gram's death. The two were so close that her passing left a huge hole in Dorothy's world, as it did for all of us.

310

Mother took in many of Gram's treasured antiques and preserved all the letters, diaries, family history, photos, memorabilia, and scrapbooks she left behind. I am grateful to have these tools to tell the stories of their lives. These two exceptional women live on in my heart.

Their written legacy preserves their talents and personalities so that all of their descendants may know them by reading their stories in their own words.

Mary: the Writing Tradition Continues

I am Dorothy's daughter, and like my mother, I also have the "woman upstairs" nagging me to write. For years I was intimidated by my mother's writing talents, and thought I could only do journalistic writing. I was afraid to follow in the steps of someone so articulate and gifted in descriptive writing.

With maturity, I have gained confidence, and now write regularly about things close to my heart. Mother would love the Oscoda Writing Group, which keeps me writing every week. The support of this group has helped me develop my skills and encouraged me with this project.

Here are a few of my stories, which will show that the writing tradition, as well as the powerful love between mother and daughter, continues through generations:

Mothers: Belly Buttons and Beyond

Mothers are like belly buttons, everyone has one; some people are pleased with theirs and others would like to trade theirs in for a better one. Personally, I am satisfied with my lot in life, thanks in large part to my good fortune in drawing Dorothy Hill Barningham for my mother.

While our sturdy, pulsing umbilical cords are essential for our survival and growth in the womb, they seem to be unnecessary after birth. But even when the cut cord withers and falls away, revealing our belly buttons, mother and child are still bound by imperceptible tethers whose flexibility and strength are unparalleled; neither time nor distance breaks their hold. At times, we struggle against this linkage, striving to break free and become our own independent selves, but we still need nourishment, guidance, and love from our mothers to help us along the way. This powerful connection runs both ways. We take from them when we are weak and they are strong, and at some stage, a tipping point is reached and places may be exchanged. It is an ingenious system, with an odd visual reminder, the navel.

As a child, I was tenderly cared for, but never smothered. In my teen years, Mother showed her faith in my good judgment. She gave

me independence when I was ready for it. During trips home in my college years, Mother and I would sit up half the night chatting and catching up on our experiences. I loved our visits and I also loved the way she never made me feel guilty when I left again. Our connection was strong and very elastic. Even far from home, I always felt the security of our bond.

Dorothy, Mary Ann Althaver and baby Emily

When I became a mother, Dorothy became a proud grandmother. My daughters adored her and were thrilled when she came to visit. Her interaction with the girls was beautiful to see. She understood their very unique personalities. Having her stay with us for a week or so made all of us happy. Mother was amiable, interested in everything, full of appreciation for life, and supportive of all our interests and endeavors. Life was nearly ideal.

But far too soon, things started to change. At age seventy Mother began showing signs of minor confusion. Later, she became lost while driving and forgetful about life's many details. As Alzheimer's Disease staked its

Sara Thurman, Dorothy, baby Beth and Laura

early claim on her, both of us were terrified by the changes and devastated by the gradual dulling of her keen mind. Her frustration and pain were agonizing to watch.

When she could no longer live alone, we tried several options before finally placing her in a nursing home. This was one of the hardest things I have ever done, but in typical fashion, Mother had given me a powerful gift when her mind was still strong. As a social worker with a nursing home caseload, she had told us that she never wanted to live with us or be a burden. She had seen families crumble under the burden of caring for someone with dementia.

I visited her daily at the nursing home. In the beginning, Mother thought she was there to serve as a social worker to the patients. She roamed the halls and chatted with everyone, looking deceptively normal. But steadily and relentlessly the disease took its toll. More of her faculties deserted her over the next several years, breaking my heart along the way. The last full sentence I heard from her was memorable. A nurse asked her if I was her daughter, to which she replied, "No, my daughter is much better looking than that!" We had to laugh, or cry. I chose to laugh and still smile when I think of it. How I missed her conversation and humor as she gradually lost her once impressive power of speech.

It was a long, painful trial to watch her steady decline into complete helplessness. Eventually she could not speak a word, nor roll over in bed, nor signal her needs. Feeding her lunch was part of my daily routine. I took extra desserts to her. I knew she enjoyed these delicacies only because she swallowed them eagerly. She showed no sign of recognizing anyone.

Her nurse once misspoke and introduced me as Dorothy's mother. In truth, at that point in her life, I was serving as such. It was my turn to figure out her needs, exactly as she did for me as a baby. With roles reversed, I was glad to help make her more comfortable in her last years. Unfortunately there were no clues from her eyes in that sad time, only a blankness that left me wondering if I was doing a good job understanding her requirements. Eight difficult years passed. At her death, she left me a precious gift, which comforts me still. Just before she crossed over, her face changed and comprehension returned to her eyes for a brief moment, as if she glimpsed something beautiful, something which suddenly made sense to her. Holding her hand, I told her it was okay to step into the light. That brief look of peace and understanding blossoming on her face meant the world to me.

I did not realize then that the relationship between us would continue to be such a strong force in my life. I still had a lot to learn about the power of our mother–child tie—that bond that started with the umbilical cord and grew into a force which can transcend even death.

Mother has been gone now for over twenty years, but I still feel the pliable, silvery threads of connection between us. They tug at my heart when I remember her at her best, back when she

Dorothy at 70

knew me so well and loved me, and even when I remember her as she was much later, when she no longer seemed to know me. These invisible ties pull at me, reminding me of the joy she took from the beauty of nature, and from her love of family and friends. I am grateful for these reminders, as they make Mother a part of my everyday life. Our bond is indestructible, eternal. I thank God for this.

My Heart's Home

Summers were endless then, back in the fifties, when I was young. They began the last day of school when I received my report card, saying I had been promoted to the next grade. Full of excitement, I would race home and start packing. Surely the luckiest child alive, I spent every summer at our cottage on Lake Huron. Vacation stretched ahead full of promise and the next day of school seemed years away. I was free, free to be the real me—the up north creature with wind in her hair and sand between her bare toes. I belonged there and was never happier than when we moved up for the summer.

Our days were full of swimming and boating. My sister, our friends, and I stayed in the water for hours. It never felt cold to us! We spent a lot of time diving to the sandy rippled lake bottom for shells, doing underwater handstands and other tricks of our own devising. Riding our heavily patched inner tubes in every conceivable way, as well as just floating peacefully, watching the incredibly blue sky and the always fascinating display of cloud forms overhead made the days melt away. Our tiny white rowboat, built by our dad, gave endless hours of pleasure. The waves carried us, sometimes gently, but often hurling us rapidly to the shore.

Days were spent designing cities on the beach, landscaping them with sand structures, shallow ponds, weeds, pieces of wood, feathers, and anything else interesting we could find. Then we went hunting in the lawn for grasshoppers and crickets, the reluctant residents of our towns, who soon hopped away. Before long, in a burst of boyish destructiveness, the neighbors would come crashing through our carefully constructed creations, proclaiming themselves tornadoes, or the dog would race through, bringing that entertainment to an end for the day. A sand bakery, a beach store, or tents fashioned from blankets and poles could be our next fun. Hikes along the water's edge might yield gull feathers and suddenly we would decide to make Indian headdresses from them. We didn't know we were creative or that exercise was good for us, it just came naturally. On rainy days we happily played games such as Sorry, Monopoly, Pirate and the Traveler, and various card games.

Always an avid reader, one of my fantasies was to have a small lending library right on the beach, in our boathouse. That never became reality, but I also dreamed of writing, and one year started a newspaper for the neighborhood. I would write all the news my friends and I could unearth from the local residents. My red cocker spaniel, Penny, was the delivery service, going to each neighbor with a copy rolled up and pushed through her collar. Hand typed at a slow speed, it was labor intensive. I charged a dime for this paper, and the circulation figures were pretty low, so it wasn't a big moneymaker.

The days and weeks slipped by, but they all seemed very long and were so full of fun. Our neighborhood friends came and went, since not all of them stayed for the whole summer. There were big tribes of kids a short way down the beach, Catholic families with six, seven, even thirteen children, so it was pretty well guaranteed we wouldn't run out of playmates.

Even after a long summer crammed full of fun, I was never ready to go home. Mother took us to town, where we shopped for scratchy plaid school dresses and stiff brown leather shoes that pinched our summer spread bare feet. Saying good-bye to our friends was painful. We packed to leave reluctantly.

I cried as we left then and yes, even as an adult, I have shed tears upon leaving this place even for a few months. Now my parents are gone and my name is on the official deed, but I am well aware that I am owned more than the place itself could ever be.

Lauren, Andrew, Lexi and Ellis on the beach, 2010

To my great delight this tiny cottage, built lovingly from the ground up by my parents, home to my heart since 1950, is now our one and only home. The place has doubled in size, thanks to my husband's building skills. The nucleus of our home is the old summer cottage, with additions front and back to make it comfortable for the visits of our whole family of ten, which includes four lively grandchildren, our two daughters, their husbands, Daryl and me. We cherish the vacation time the children spend with us.

Daryl and Mary Ann Althaver's Family, 2013
Back: Andrew, Andy, Lexi, Ellis, Bill   Front: Amy, Daryl, Mary, Emily, Lauren

It is no surprise to me that the youngest generation is captivated by the same simple joys I grew to love in my childhood. The world has changed drastically in countless ways, but when the children are here they go back to the basic elements which make this place timeless and treasured.

Swimming, building sand castles, catching tadpoles, patiently watching them turn into frogs, walking the beach, gathering feathers, shells, stones, and bones still bring joy. Having campfires with s'mores, watching fireworks and shooting stars, playing board games, feeding willing adults an array of sand cakes, cookies, and pies, drizzled with wet sand for dramatic effect—all these simple things enthrall the youngest generation of our family, just as they did my generation.

This place, which I love as much as my parents did, is an intergenerational bridge. It now ties four generations together. The timeless beauty—the ever changing blues of the sky and the water, the warmth of the sun, the lure of the shifting sands, the endless movement of the water—brings us back time after time and restores our spirits.

I am confident that this treasured place will own generations I may not live to see. I hope my spirit will be able to look down and see these future children fall under an ageless spell. My greatest desire is for this place to become home to their hearts as well.

Shaky Apron Strings

I was alone one day and picked up a scrapbook I made several years ago, which was dedicated to the cottage and the changes in it that have taken place over the years. While slowly perusing it, I paused when I saw pictures of my mother. My fingers caressed her photos as I spoke to her about the book I am putting together, the story of her life and her mother's, told through their letters.

Dorothy and her friend, Christine Wilcox, pictured in the local newspaper for a fall story

I asked her for help in creating a title for the book. After enjoying the moments feeling connected to her, I returned the scrapbook to the shelf and went to the kitchen to prepare our daily salads for lunch. Out of the corner of my eye, I noticed the string on my apron was rotating slowly. I was not wearing it; it was hanging on its hook between the bedroom doors. I thought at first I had disturbed the air currents in the room and that was making it turn, but it continued even when I was motionless.

I gazed at it for some time and started talking to Mother again about her book and about what a clever way she had chosen to let me know she is with me in this process of telling her story.

When I was a child, one of my rare pranks was to sneak up behind her in the kitchen and pull the strings on her apron playfully, then dash off laughing. She never seemed very mad about it, just amused. So now Mother is shaking my apron strings and I take that as a sign that she approves of the book and has suggested the perfect title for it.

The apron string message was very welcome, and I smiled at her choice of ways to communicate. What a perfect symbol. We are, after all, tied to each other forever, bonds of love between mother and daughter, which clearly transcend death.

Losing our Voices

We are losing our voices in today's world. It isn't laryngitis or someone taking away our freedom of speech. We have become so addicted to telephones, texting and emails that we no longer write letters. We are in serious danger of disappearing after death, and leaving no comforting words of wisdom, no humor, no messages of love to those who survive us. And while we may leave behind our recorded voice in a home movie, or on an answering machine, our written voice may be gone forever when we are gone.

Those of us who write are fortunate; we will leave our unique voices for those who mourn us and those who are born after we are gone. Our descendants will have a way of knowing us by our paper legacy. But for the vast numbers of people who do not write anything more than a to-do or a grocery list, their voices will disappear with them when they die.

If we could make journal writing, creative writing, and letters to friends and family popular again, start a new trend, perhaps we could help people preserve their voices for posterity.

I have no recordings of my mother or my grandma speaking, but I do have a treasure worth far more. I have their written voices. Mother wrote short stories, powerful and amusing letters, and her author's voice is balm to my soul. Like every writer, her voice was distinctive. Her positive outlook, humor, and wisdom shine through everything she wrote. She is with me in a very intense way when I read her words and look at her handwriting. I can travel back in time to when she was young, and follow her journey through life via her letters and diaries.

Grandma's letters and diaries tell her story equally well, keeping me close to the feelings I had for her in childhood. Their letters distill their lives into clear snapshots of life in their own eras, at work, at school, in their social lives, and in their own homes. Their descriptions of everyday events, as well as love, loss, illness, and hardships speak loudly. I feel so blessed to have this precious link to those who left this world so long ago, but who are still so much a part of my own voice.

For those who do have letters, diaries, and scrapbooks—preserve them. If you don't, buy a blank book, start writing on a regular basis now. There may be a day when someone wants to know your story, wants to hear your voice in their head. Leave those you love a gift that lives on after you are gone.

Dorothy's Descendants

Mary Ann's Family

Emily Althaver Mason and Amy Althaver Hill

Emily's sons,
Ellis and Andrew Mason

Amy's daughters,
Lexi and Lauren Hill

Sara Lee's Family

Laura Thurman McLean and her son, Preston

Beth Thurman Herbert and her sons, Nathaniel and Noah Canales and the newest member of the family Aaron James Herbert

Acknowledgments

Some say it takes a village to raise a child, but bringing this book to publication took the support and encouragement of family and friends from all around the state of Michigan and beyond. My husband, Daryl, and my daughters, Emily and Amy, have been endlessly patient during the twenty-three years of my obsession with this project. I am sure they are happy that I have finally, in my grandma's words, "born this child."

Special thanks to Christine Wilcox, neighbor and dear friend of our family since before I was born. Christine surprised me by remembering me in her will when she passed at age 101. She and my mother were very good friends and both aspiring writers. I think Christine would be pleased to know that her bequest funded this book. Her photo is included in the *Shaky Apron Strings* story.

I am so grateful to Anissa Emery for her fine editing and for her enthusiasm for this project. Her vision as well as her love of letters and bygone eras made her the perfect editor.

Thanks to Lyn Behnke for leading me to Anissa, as well as suggesting (during one of our conversations as she performed acupuncture on me) that Shaky Apron Strings could be the perfect title.

Thanks to my friend from college days, Joan Ramseyer, a talented writer and photographer, for her cover photo and to her cousin, Susie LeaTrea, for providing the setting for the cover shot.

Kris VanThomme, graphic designer, has done a phenomenal job turning my manuscript into a book. She did all the interior layout, photo insertion and final cover design. I am so grateful for her excellent work. Thank you, Kris, for bringing this project to fruition.

While working at Albion College, the focus of much of this book, I met Sarah Briggs, Albion's Associate Vice President of Communications. Sarah's interest in my book and my mother's letters led to an excellent article in the Albion alumni magazine, *Io Triumphe!* Her article, *A Glorious Time*, in the Fall 2005 issue, contained several of my favorite letters. Seeing them in print made me begin to seriously consider publishing this book. I am grateful to Sarah for her quality work and for encouraging me along the way.

Though I never knew Patricia Sherman, I am indebted to her and her daughter, Lucy Fazely, for the Patricia Sherman Memorial Writing Contest, which gave me encouragement and confidence in my writing. Lucy created The Oscoda Writing Group after the first year's contest. I thank the members of this group for years of fun and laughter, as well as support for my project.

Thanks to Jane Stagner, dear friend and fellow writer, for her help as I wrestled with the issues involved in creating this book. Near or far, Jane has always been there for me and I appreciate her so much.

I thank Cindy Cooke, friend and neighbor for most of my life, for helping me prioritize tasks when I was overwhelmed, and for her early cover layout work. She is especially appreciated for sharing her dad, Clem Cooke, who is like a father to me. Both Clem and Cindy have been supportive and loving, encouraging my efforts for decades. They were also early readers of my first journalistic efforts, the newspaper, The Polar Bear News, which I created at a very early age.

"Team Dorothy" friends, Katherine Head and Carol Hojnacki, have given me a lifetime of friendship and shared families. Their input has been very helpful, in life, and in the creation of my book. Because they knew my parents so well, they give me precious perspective.

Special thanks to Teresa Irish for sharing her knowledge about the process of creating a book of letters. Her book, *A Thousand Letters Home*, has been very helpful and her kindness greatly appreciated.

Thank you to Nicole Garrett, for providing early photos of Albion College landmarks from the college archives.

And a special thanks to all my early readers, who read the first binder edition of my book many years ago. Your interest, comments and enthusiasm contributed to making this book better.

My heart is full as I write this. I could not have done this without all of you.

CPSIA information can be obtained at www.ICGtesting.com
Printed in the USA
BVOW04*0601230415

396963BV00004B/9/P